PRAISE FOR *ENDPOINT SECURITY*

*"By the time I finished Mark's book, he'd complete
things. Most important, I realized closed-loop endpoint security is not such the complex nightmare it seems. For embedded devices, where closed loop is not achievable
at this time, he identifies what you can do to start closing the loop on these devices,
identifies which controls are missing, and makes plausible conjectures about how
the missing controls will fall into place."*

—Deb Radcliff, award-winning industry writer, computer crime and security

"Just what's needed to cut through the hype surrounding NAC and its cousins."

—Joe Knape, Security Engineer, a leading telecommunications provider

*"This book moves beyond monitoring the network for security events and provides a
thorough guide both the novice and experienced information security specialist can
use to improve the security posture of a wide variety of endpoint devices."*

—Kirby Kuehl, IPS Developer, Cisco Systems, Inc.

*"Network perimeter is no longer a solid demarcation line at the company's firewalls.
The perimeter appears to have disappeared, and the question is, 'How can a manager secure the disappearing perimeter?' Mark Kadrich has approached the subject
of securing the network perimeter using a new paradigm. His revolutionary, yet
simple approach will cause experienced security managers to wonder, 'Why has this
method not been discussed before?' Mark provides a scientific methodology that any
system administrator or security professional can quickly adopt and put into practice to secure their networks and endpoints."*

—Curtis Coleman, CISSP, CISM, MSIA

"*Kadrich has successfully delivered an insightful and engaging perspective about the real world of information security and why effectively addressing endpoint security is so critical. Delivered with wit, humor, and candor, this book also serves as a wake-up call to those who provide information security products and as a viable roadmap for security professionals to better address both strategic security initiatives and the attendant issues du jour. Bottom line: This book should be considered essential reading for the layperson and the security professional.*"

—Harry Bing-You, President, Anasazi Group Inc.

Endpoint Security

Endpoint Security

Mark S. Kadrich, CISSP

✦ Addison-Wesley

Upper Saddle River, NJ · Boston · Indianapolis · San Francisco
New York · Toronto · Montreal · London · Munich · Paris · Madrid
Cape Town · Sydney · Tokyo · Singapore · Mexico City

Many of the designations used by manufacturers and sellers to distinguish their products are claimed as trademarks. Where those designations appear in this book, and the publisher was aware of a trademark claim, the designations have been printed with initial capital letters or in all capitals.

The author and publisher have taken care in the preparation of this book, but make no expressed or implied warranty of any kind and assume no responsibility for errors or omissions. No liability is assumed for incidental or consequential damages in connection with or arising out of the use of the information or programs contained herein.

The publisher offers excellent discounts on this book when ordered in quantity for bulk purchases or special sales, which may include electronic versions and/or custom covers and content particular to your business, training goals, marketing focus, and branding interests. For more information, please contact:

U.S. Corporate and Government Sales
(800) 382-3419
corpsales@pearsontechgroup.com

For sales outside the United States please contact:

International Sales
international@pearsoned.com

 This Book Is Safari Enabled

The Safari® Enabled icon on the cover of your favorite technology book means the book is available through Safari Bookshelf. When you buy this book, you get free access to the online edition for 45 days.

Safari Bookshelf is an electronic reference library that lets you easily search thousands of technical books, find code samples, download chapters, and access technical information whenever and wherever you need it.

To gain 45-day Safari Enabled access to this book:

- Go to http://www.awprofessional.com/safarienabled
- Complete the brief registration form
- Enter the coupon code XZFL-PURG-UHW5-AMGZ-KTF5

If you have difficulty registering on Safari Bookshelf or accessing the online edition, please e-mail customer-service@safaribooksonline.com.

Visit us on the Web: www.awprofessional.com

Library of Congress Cataloging-in-Publication Data:

Kadrich, Mark.
 Endpoint security / Mark Kadrich. — 1st ed.
  p. cm.
 ISBN 0-321-43695-4 (pbk. : alk. paper) 1. Computer security. 2. Computer networks—Security measures. I. Title.
 QA76.9.A25K325 2007
 005.8—dc22

                        2006102875

ISBN 10: 0-32-143695-4
ISBN 13: 978-0-32-143695-5
This product is printed digitally on demand.

This book is dedicated to my father, John Richard Kadrich. He taught me how to take things apart, to ask questions when I didn't know what the parts did, and put them back together with no leftover parts.

Contents

Foreword

Moving forward. This is the direction that information security needs to move today to have an even more secure cyberspace tomorrow. Moving forward means that we need to continue to innovate and be creative. In the past, people have innovated when they believed that they had a better way of doing something and they thought that they could make a difference. This book is about security innovation—it's about doing something new and making a difference.

We need new tools if we are to continue to secure our critical infrastructure from those who would do us harm. Today's security world isn't just about hackers and thieves. We have to add to that list organized criminals, spies, and even "hactivists." A day doesn't go by when some part of our critical cyber infrastructure isn't under attack. Nation states are trying to steal trade secrets and military secrets. Organized criminals are constantly chipping away at our cyber security with the hope of breaking through to a system that will afford them the opportunity to do some real damage. Organized crime is also turning the personal information of everyone into a commodity that can be traded, exploited, and hedged.

How we innovate is going to be the key to success in this battle, and part of that innovation is going to involve looking at things a little differently than how we have in the past. We need to be more than one step ahead of our enemies.

We need to move forward and quickly.

Information security has often been considered something between dark magic and art for quite some time, whereas the underlying technology has been considered an engineering discipline. The circuits and chips are all part of the world of electrical engineering; the software is generally considered the domain of software engineers.

Encarta[1] says that an engineer is

1. Somebody who is trained in a branch of professional engineering
2. A member of a unit of the armed forces that specializes in building and sometimes destroying bridges, fortifications, and other large structures
3. Somebody who plans, oversees, or brings about something, especially something that is achieved with ingenuity or secretiveness

I like these definitions because we are truly professionals. But, besides being professionals, we are also engineers. We don't guess at what an answer might be. We analyze, we test, and when we believe that we have an answer, we act. We are the ones who are building the fortifications that protect our networks. We are the ones who work to destroy the logical fortifications that hackers create and hide behind while they attack our endpoints. We are the overseers and protectors of everyone's privacy.

The fact that information security is a science and discipline in its own right is clear. We are beginning to see this reflected in the curriculums at colleges. Institutes of learning are providing master's degrees and doctorate programs in information security. More people are learning our engineering discipline, and they are learning about the processes and tools that we use to secure cyberspace.

This book adds to that by explaining why things are presently not completely working, and it provides an engineering framework that explains how things could work better and with more predictable results. This book serves as another tile in the mosaic foundation of our engineering discipline. We have another powerful tool in our battle to secure cyberspace so that we can continue to enjoy it and benefit from all it brings us all.

—Howard A. Schmidt, CISSP, CISM
   President & CEO
   R&H Security Consulting, LLC

---

[1] Encarta World English Dictionary © 1999 Microsoft Corporation. All rights reserved. Developed for Microsoft by Bloomsbury Publishing Plc.

Preface

That was some of the best flying I've seen to date—right up to the part where you got killed.

—Jester to Maverick in the movie *Top Gun*

INTRODUCTION

I suppose the thing that bothers me the most is this: We think that we're doing great right up to the moment that the network melts down. Over the years, we've seen the number of security tools deployed on our networks increase to the point where we are completely surprised when our computing environments are devastated by some new worm. We then ask, "But how can this happen?" How can we be spending so much money to increase our security and still be feeling the pain of the worm du jour? And not just feeling this pain once or twice a year, *we're feeling it all the time.*

To begin to answer this question, all you have to do is pop the word *vulnerability* into Google and sit back and wait. My wait took a mere .18 seconds and returned more than 69 million hits. Adding the word *hacker* added an additional .42 seconds but did have the benefit of reducing the pool of hits to a tad more than 4.2 million. More than 4 million pieces of information in less than half a second, and for free! Now that's value.

So, getting back to our problem and looking at the results pretty much sums up our present situation. We're buried under all sorts of vulnerabilities, and we're constantly struggling to get on top of things. The problem of patching vulnerabilities is so big that an entire industry has sprung up just to address the problem. The problem of analyzing and generating patches is so big that Microsoft changed its release policy from an "as needed" to a "patch Tuesdays."

What are they really trying to address with the patches? You might think that it's about protecting the endpoint, what we're going to call endpoint security. This is a big topic of discussion. If we go back to Google and enter *endpoint security,* we get a little more than 2.5 million hits. We can reduce that stratospheric result by entering the word *solution.* Now we're down to a much more manageable 1,480,000 hits.

So, what's the point? The point is that a lot of folks are talking about the problem, but they're doing so from the perspective of a vendor-customer relationship: a relationship that is predicated on them selling you something, a solution, and you paying them for it. The sheer motive of profit motivates vendors to produce products that they can sell. Marketing departments are geared toward understanding what people need and how to shape their product in a way that convinces you that they can fill your need. How many times have you gone back to visit a vendor Web page only to be surprised that they now address your problem? Look at how many vendors moved from PKI (Public Key Infrastructure) to SSI (Single Sign On) and finally to IM (Identity Management). Why? Because nobody was buying PKI because of the enormous expense; so, the marketing departments decided to switch names or "repurpose" their product. Now it was about "leveraging their synergies" with the multiple sets of user credentials and promises of vastly simplified user experiences. When that tanked, the marketing people invented IM. Yep, that's what I said, they invented IM so they could once again distance themselves from a failed marking ploy and get more people to give them more money. Profit.

Ask any CEO what his or her mission is. If the CEO doesn't reply, "To maximize shareholder value," I'll show you a CEO soon to be looking for a new job. It's all about making sales numbers and generating profit. The more profit, the happier vendors and their shareholders are.

Now don't get me wrong. Profit is a good thing. It keeps our system working and our people motivated. However, when the system of generating profit still refuses to produce a good solution, we must ask, "What is the real problem that we're trying to solve here?" I don't want to be part of the solution that says that the problem is how to maximize shareholder value; I want to be part of a solution that says that the problem was understanding a well-defined set of criteria that ensured that my enterprise and the information that it produced were safe, trustworthy, and secure.

But, for some strange vendor-driven reason, we can't seem to do that.

This book makes the assumption that if we've been doing the same thing for years and we continue to fail, we must be doing something wrong. Some basic assumption about what we're doing and why we're doing it is incorrect. Yes, *incorrect.* However, we continue to behave as if nothing is wrong. The pain is there, but now the problem is that it's so ubiquitous that we've become desensitized to it. Like the buzzing that fluorescent lights make (yes, they do make an annoying sound) or the violence on TV, we've just gotten so used to having it around that we've come up with coping mechanisms to deal with it. Why hasn't anyone asked why the pain is there in the first place?

This book does.

This book is different because it uses a basic tenant of science to understand what the problem is and how to manage it. This book uses a process control model to explain why securing the endpoint is the smartest thing you can do to manage the problem of network contamination and infestation. You'll learn the differences between endpoints and how to secure them at various levels. We start with the basic tools and settings that come with each endpoint, move to those required tools such as antivirus, and progress to endpoints that have been upgraded with additional security protocols and tools, such as 802.1x and the supplicant, that enable a closed-loop process control (CLPC) model that enforces a minimum level of security.

INTENDED AUDIENCE

If you're a security manager, security administrator, desktop support person, or someone who will be or is managing, responding to, or responsible for the security issues of the network, this book is for you. If your job depends on ensuring that the network is not just "up" but functional as a tool for generating, sharing, and storing information, you'll want to read this book. If you've ever been fired because some script kiddie managed to gain access to the CEO's laptop, you'll want this book on your shelf. If you're worried about Barney in the cube next to yours downloading the latest "free" video clip or the latest cool chat client, you want to buy this book and give it to your desktop administrator.

INTENDED PURPOSE

Many books describe how systems can be exploited or how vulnerabilities can be discovered and leveraged to the dismay of the system owner. If you're looking for a book on hacking, this isn't it. If that's what you want to do, this is the wrong book for you. Give it to your admin friend; I'm sure he'll need it after you go get your book on hacking. So, instead of the "hacker's eye" view, this book gives you something a bit more useful: the practitioner's eye view.

This book not only shows you what to look for, it also tells you why you should be looking for it. Yes, in some places it is somewhat of a step-by-step guide, but this book follows the axiom "give a man a fish and he eats for a day, but teach a man to fish and he eats for the rest of his life." It's a corny saying, but it gets the message across pretty well.

This book teaches you how to configure your network to be secure by addressing the issue at its root: the endpoint.

This book also takes a look at how we got here in the hopes that we won't make the same mistakes again. Some of my reviewers took offense at Chapter 2 because I placed a portion of the blame for much of our situation squarely on the shoulders of the vendors that have been crafting our solutions. Yes, there are open source security tools, but they don't drive our security market.

My hope is that when you have finished with this book you will understand why I believe a CLPC model works and how to apply it in your day-to-day security solutions.

On Ignoring Editors: "We" and "Them"

Editors are wonderful people. Many writers hate editors because they change the magnificent prose that the author has spent hours generating and refining. They reinterpret what the author has said and change the way the ideas are presented to the reader by changing the order of words or the use of tone. Some authors hate that. Not me. I'm a rooky, and I'm lazy. This is a bad combination for a writer, so I don't mind some constructive criticism. Usually.

We is a simple word that when used by an author is supposed to imply that an intimacy exists between the author and the reader when the reader is engaged in the pages of the book. When an author says "we," it's supposed to mean that small group of people who the reader is tied to by the story line of the book—that is, unless the author isn't using the second person as a construct. For instance, the writer could mean the "we" of the group exclusive of the reader (as in, "We hacked into this computer to find evidence of kiddy porn"). The reader is clearly not included in that group of "we."

So, why have I brought this up at the beginning of a book about endpoint security? Because I made the mistake of using the word *we* throughout the book without explaining who "we" are each and every time. I thought it was obvious who "we" are.

My editor hated that. Politely, concisely, but nonetheless, she hated it.

Every time I got a chapter back, the word *we* was highlighted, and a polite note was attached asking who "we" referred to. "Mark, who is we? Please tell us who 'we' is." Yep. Each and every time I used the word *we*, I got a highlight and a note. I was quite annoyed because I thought that it was clear. So, in an effort to find the final answer, I asked an authority—my girlfriend, Michelle—to read some of the magnificent prose that I'd generated with the hope that she would agree with me. I should have known better. She asked, "Who is 'we?'" Because this was not the response I was expecting, all I could do was look at her blankly and stammer, "Well, um, we is us!"

I felt like an idiot. Her look confirmed it. I was an idiot.

But "we" is us. We are the security people of the world trying to solve a huge problem. So, when I talk about "we" in this book, I'm referring to all of us who have tried, are trying, to create secure and reliable networks.

Now, I'm sure that "they" is going to come up next, so let me attack that here. "They" is them, those who are not us. Vendors are great "thems," and it's usually who I'm referring to when I say "them."

So, we and us are the good guys, and they and them, well, aren't.

WHY ARE WE DOING THIS?

As I said earlier, if you're doing something and it doesn't work no matter how many times you try it, you must be doing something wrong, and it's time to take a step back and make an attempt at understanding why. The old stuff isn't working, and it's time to try something new. Now, securing the endpoint isn't a new idea. The methods to accomplish endpoint security are well known. However, we have done a great deal of research that seems to indicate that without considering the endpoint as a key component in your security program, as a point of enforcement, that you are doomed—yes, doomed—to failure.

Okay, doomed might be a bit harsh; but if you get fired because some weasel changes two bytes of code in a virus and it rips through your network, what's the difference? You're hosed, and hosed is just the past tense of doomed.

ACKNOWLEDGMENTS

I want to start by thanking Jessica Goldstein for listening to someone who probably sounded quite crazy when he talked about information security and security theory. Her wisdom, help, and guidance have been absolutely invaluable to the production of this book.

My friends on the reviewing team deserve an immense thank you for taking time out of their overcommitted schedules to review the drafts and to add comments and corrections. I had a great team that consisted of Dan Geer, Curtis Coleman, Rodney Thayer, Debra Radcliff, Joe Knape, Kirby Kuehl, Jean Pawluc, Kevin Kenan, and Harry Bing-You. When I started to rant, Dan and Rodney called me on it. Kirby and Joe pulled duty as my technical editors, making sure that my facts (and my references to NetBIOS) were correct. Curtis and Deb provided the view from the business side, asking questions that the executives would want to know the answers to. Jean, Kevin, and Harry got to review the fruits of their labors and provide the final comments.

I also want to thank my editors at Addison Wesley, starting with Sheri Cain (who did a great deal of the original editing), Jana Jones, Kristen Weinberger, Romny French, Karen Gettman, Andrew Beaster, and Gina Kanouse. Kristen and Romny are largely responsible for managing me and the project and making sure that I didn't blow past my deadlines too far. Not to be left out, Keith Cline has to be the best copy editor on the planet. Thanks to him, it sounds like I actually passed my grammar classes.

I especially want to thank Howard Schmidt for his foreword to this book. Coming home to find the power to his house gone for the duration due to winter storms, Howard proved that a handheld device can do more than connect calls and play music.

Finally, I want like to thank my beloved girlfriend, Michelle Reid. She tolerated me while I cursed and worked and cheered me on when I was ready to quit. Michelle was also invaluable as my sounding board when I needed to explain something technical in plain English.

I owe each and every one of these people a debt of gratitude. They made this book immensely better through their contributions and insight. I couldn't have done it without them.

About the Author

For the past 20 years, **Mark Kadrich** has been a contributing member of the security community. His strengths are in systems-level design, policy generation, endpoint security, and risk management. Mr. Kadrich has been published numerous times and is an avid presenter.

Mr. Kadrich is presently president and CEO of The Security Consortium (TSC), a privately held company whose mission is to provide better security product knowledge to their customers. TSC performs in-depth testing and evaluation of security products and the vendors that provide them. As CEO and chief evangelist, Mr. Kadrich is responsible for ensuring that the company continues to grow successfully.

After the Symantec acquisition of Sygate Technologies, Mr. Kadrich took a position as senior manager of network and endpoint security with Symantec. His role was to ensure that the Symantec business units correctly interpreted security policy during their pursuit of innovative technology solutions.

Mr. Kadrich was senior scientist with Sygate Technologies prior to the Symantec acquisition. In his role as senior scientist, Mr. Kadrich was responsible for developing corporate policies, understanding future security trends, managing government certification programs, and evangelizing on demand. Mr. Kadrich joined Sygate through the acquisition of a start-up company (AltView) of which he was a founding member.

As a founding member of AltView, Mr. Kadrich was the principal architect of a system that scanned and contextualized the network, the endpoints on it, and built a detailed knowledge base. Eventually known as Magellan, the system could determine what endpoints were on a network, how the network was changing, what endpoints were manageable, and if they were being managed.

As CTO/CSO for LDT Systems, Mr. Kadrich assisted with the development and support of a Web-based system used to securely capture and track organ-donor information.

Mr. Kadrich was director of technical services for Counterpane Internet Security. He was responsible for the generation of processes that supported and improved Counterpane's ability to deploy and support customer-related security activities

Mr. Kadrich was director of security for Conxion Corporation. As the director of security, his role was to plot the strategic course of Conxion's information security solutions.

Prior to Conxion, he was a principal consultant for International Network Services (INS), for which he created a methodology for performing security assessments and interfaced with industry executives to explain the benefits of a well-implemented security program.

Mr. Kadrich is a CISSP, holds a Bachelor of Science degree in Management Information Systems from the University of Phoenix, and has degrees in Computer Engineering and Electrical Engineering (Memphis, 1979). Publications contributed to include *TCP Unleashed, Publish Magazine, Planet IT, RSA, CSI,* and *The Black Hat Briefings.*

Defining Endpoints

As with any process, to understand it, you first must define the elements that comprise the process. Consider, for example, the temperature-control system in your house or office. The system is composed of the building, doors, windows, insulation, heater, cooler, thermostat, fans, and ducting (see Figure 1-1). The thermostat is used as the control point; the building, doors, and windows define the perimeter. The thermostat controls the heater, cooler, ducting, and fans, and, you hope, the building (assuming that the windows and doors are closed) stays at a constant temperature.

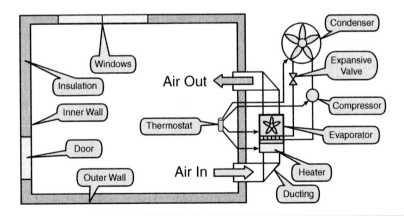

Figure 1-1   A basic heating, ventilation, and air-conditioning (HVAC) system takes air in, heats it, cools it, and then pumps it back into the room. The thermostat controls the entire process. Room components such as walls, doors, windows, and insulation control how efficient the process is.

Unfortunately, defining the *process* for the purposes of endpoint security is not as clear-cut as this air-conditioning example. Folks in the building industry have a few advantages over us. First, they have a fairly well-defined set of nomenclature that allows them to capture and express their ideas in a universally accepted manner. Second, they have a fairly well-defined set of requirements and success criteria: to keep the room at a constant temperature. The result is easy to see; you just have to look at the thermometer.

The diverse nature of our industry leads to disparate definitions of what an endpoint is. Therefore, this chapter defines what *we* mean by an endpoint. We increase our spectrum of defined endpoints because to do otherwise would do us a disservice by ignoring those endpoints that could cause the most harm.

PRÉCIS

Whatever we decide an endpoint is, we have to come to grips with the fact that because of technology and how our applications deal with data as a programming language, our security perimeter is constantly changing. For instance, PostScript is really a language for defining how a printer is supposed to render a document on paper. Many applications, such as databases and Web browsers, allow programming commands to be embedded in the data to format or manipulate data.

As devices connect to or leave the network, the perimeter changes, and so our security policy must adapt. There has been talk about the death of the security perimeter, and some have even given it a cool name: deperimeterization.[1] However, the arguments that they use to make their case also prove my point that the endpoint is the new perimeter.

If we make a first attempt at a traditional definition, an endpoint seems to be those systems that people sit in front of: the desktops and laptops that we use to create, store, manipulate, and destroy data. These are endpoints. But, a simple look around a busy Starbucks will show you that folks are really doing those tasks on all sorts of systems. Laptops, Personal Digital Assistants (PDAs), smartphones, and Blackberrys—all are part of the latté scene. Furthermore, ubiquitous purpose-built systems, many of which we might not even be aware of, also generate, process, and share data. All these systems have one thing in common: They are at the end of a network connection. The connection might be a wire, or it might be wireless. It might be fast EVDO[2] or the older and slower General Packet Radio Service (GPRS), but it is still a network connection.

---

[1] www.opengroup.org/projects/jericho/

[2] Evolution Data Optimized, a wireless radio broadband protocol used over CDMA (Code Division Multiple Access) cellular phone networks

And, by implication, if it is sitting on a network, someone is going to try to hack into it, infect it, or otherwise use it as a spam launching point. The only way to prevent this is to ensure that the target system configuration has some capability to prevent a successful attack. Some systems we might be able to control; others perhaps not. Those systems that we control will obviously be easier to deal with; those that we do not control will have to use other corrective or protective means (such as firewalls).

So now the problem becomes determining which systems we can influence and which ones we must accept as less secure. Clearly, the ubiquitous system, Windows, is an endpoint and one that we can control. Usually. Entire industries have sprung up to meet the needs of Windows users over the past 20 years. I say "usually" because, unfortunately none of these industries has been able to deal with what is often referred to as the "hidden problem"—the elephant in the room, the one system that always seems to elude any and all efforts to secure it, the one system that ends up in the news as "a single computer containing critical information." Yes, I'm referring to the CEO's notebook.

Other systems, such as the printers and network-enabled power strips, are another story all together. That's right, network-enabled power strips are used in data centers so that help desk workers can recycle the power on a single computer (and thus not risk contracting pneumonia in the giant freezer that is most data centers). They have a basic operating system and usually have a Web server on them for easy access. I once did an assessment of a data center only to discover that the entire population of network-controlled power strips lived outside of the network firewall, meaning that any 14-year-old script kiddie with a basic understanding of Web server vulnerabilities could gain access to them. I like scaring CEOs, and it was fun demonstrating the "feature set" of that configuration.

Speaking of pneumonia, how about the systems embedded in medical respirators and integrated circuit (IC) manufacturing plants? Network connections are being used at an ever-increasing rate to provide data for management purposes or control. The medical systems can't be changed without violating their certification, and the folks in the IC plants are loath to turn off any functioning systems lest profits fall. These are examples of endpoints that can't be directly secured, so some other method has to be used to protect them.

SPECIAL POINTS OF INTEREST

Network configurations are changing at a frenetic pace. Every day, new devices are added to our networks that extend the notion of what an endpoint is and where the perimeter is. As more of the user community becomes mobile, we're going to rely more heavily on wireless technology and smaller, easier-to-lose handheld devices. Add to that more "smart" devices that don't look like computers, and what is actually on your network begins to get fuzzy. It's not just Windows or UNIX anymore.

So, now we face these important questions: What is an endpoint, and where is my perimeter? How can you protect something that you can't see? Keep these questions in mind as you read this chapter.

WINDOWS ENDPOINTS

A Windows endpoint is any system that is running any version of the Microsoft Windows operating system, from Windows 95 on up. Why not an earlier system? Because before Windows 95, Windows was essentially a Disk Operating System (DOS) with a Windows manager that acted as an interface to the operating system. Granted, some native 16-bit applications existed, but when the Windows manager became integrated into the operating system, things changed.

We can debate whether this change was for the better, but what can't be debated is that the ease of use and the large number of applications made Windows the de facto standard for businesses and home users. (By all accounts, the Microsoft operating system represents more than 90 percent of all installed operating systems.[3]) Consequentially, Windows is also the biggest target for hackers, crackers, and malware.

That's a pretty big target. Scott Granneman[4] reported that in late 2003 there were more than 60,000 viruses for Windows compared to about 40 for the Mac and Linux, and a grand total of 5 for commercial UNIX versions. Total virus counts for late November 2006 seem to have leveled off at almost 73,000 according to Symantec.[5] I did a search for Macintosh and Linux viruses and didn't find anything contemporary. We can be sure, however, that there are folks working on them. SANS reported on proof-of-concept code that loads spyware on a Mac.[6] Discovered by F-Secure, the malware loads as a system library and doesn't require root access to do so.

In the early days of computing, the Mac was the target. As a young security engineer for Lockheed, the first thing I did in my daily security assessments was to make sure that the antivirus software was loaded on the Macintoshes. Time and market share can be the enemy.

---

[3] Mary Jo Foley, Microsoft Watch, 4/27/2004

[4] Linux vs. Windows Viruses, *The Register,* 10/6/2003

[5] www.symantec.com/avcenter/defs.download.html

[6] SANS NewsBites Vol. 8 Num. 94

Another change to Windows was the integration of a usable IP stack. Even as late as Windows 3.1, the IP stack was an add-in that could easily be changed. I remember more than a few discussions that revolved around the efficacy of the Microsoft stack, and many opted to replace it with another stack.

On a positive note, the nice thing about Windows—well, most versions of Windows— is that it does have a great deal of things that you can do to harden it without spending any money. To that end, we will be looking at the following:

- Is there a firewall?
- Is the firewall up and configured properly?
- Are unknown or unnecessary services running?
- Are patches up-to-date?
- Have basic security settings been made?

I've spent some time looking into the third question, and you would be surprised at what is running under the hood! A number of Web sites are dedicated to identifying services and helping you understand whether they can safely be removed. We cover those resources in the section "Initial Health Check" in Chapter 8, "Microsoft Windows."

We can add to the basic strength by adding some third-party programs that look for viruses and spyware, and thereby significantly increase the endpoint's resilience to attack.

NON-WINDOWS ENDPOINTS

Anything not a Windows machine is a non-Windows endpoint. I know what you're thinking: "This covers a lot of territory." However, we're going to narrow this somewhat broad expanse of territory by saying that we're talking about human-driven computers in the traditional sense (such as desktops, notebooks, and servers). We're going to exclude other systems because they can be classified in other ways, as discussed in this section.

So, for the purposes of our discussion, non-Windows endpoints include all variants of UNIX: BSD, XENIX, IRIX, HP-UX, AIX, Solaris, and Linux. Granted, not all of these are direct decedents of AT&T, but many, if not all, of these operating systems have been used in nearly every environment. Remember the network-enabled power strip? It was running Linux and a Web server called Apache.

Like Windows, these types of endpoints do have a great deal of resilience if configured properly. They have built-in firewalls and plenty of tools that enable them to substantially increase their security posture.

EMBEDDED ENDPOINTS

Embedded systems aren't really all that well known to most IT people because the whole purpose is to bury the operating system functionality in such a way that it is non-apparent to the end user. As mentioned previously, things as innocuous as power strips[7] can have a stripped-down version of an operating system, and possibly a Web server, helping with the network interface via a graphical user interface (GUI). Just for fun, pop the IP address of one of your big printers into your browser and see what happens. Most printers now have a network interface that enables you to gather status information or set configuration parameters. As you can see in Figure 1-2, embedded systems are common office/home network appliances.

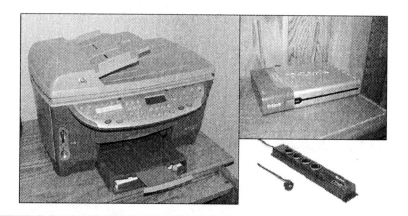

Figure 1-2   An embedded system is designed to be operated remotely (anything from a printer, to a wireless access point, to a remotely managed power strip).

One of the biggest sources of embedded pain besides printers is access points (APs). APs are the devices that provide wireless network connections over the 802.11 specification, thus allowing wireless-equipped endpoints to connect to your network. APs have two sides to them: the wireless radio-based side and the hardwired side. Some APs have a switch or hub on the wired side that allows multiple devices to connect via Ethernet cables. Most APs have a setting that only allows the Web server to be accessed from one of those internal hardwired connections.

An emerging use for embedded systems is supporting Voice over IP (VoIP). Many of you have seen the applications that turn your computer into a telephone, but few of us

---

[7]   www.leunig.de/_en/_news/prs/2002_02_eps/eps_mfot.htm

have seen the handsets that use the network to connect voice sessions. These handsets differ from the old telephone handsets in that they have an embedded operating system in them. The digital phones have analog-to-digital converters and support electronics that manage the digital signals. These systems use a private branch exchange (PBX) to route calls in much the same way that the old-style analog phones did. The use of digital data just makes them more efficient. IP-based phones replace the analog switching technology and the PBX with an IP stack, switches, and routers. Figure 1-3 contrasts a large, manned, old-style PBX with a modern automated version.

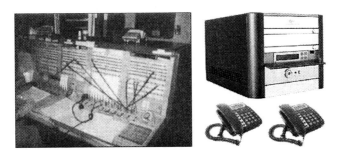

Figure 1-3   Old-style manual PBX (on the left) contrasted with a modern PBX and VoIP handsets. Many PBXs now support VoIP. Modern PBX photo courtesy of PBXpress.

One of the most common yet hidden applications of embedded Windows is in a system that most of us come in contact with often: automated teller machines (ATMs). ATMs use a version of Windows to drive the motors and widgets that take your card, process your request, and drop money into your hands. You'll be pleased to know that the makers of these machines realize the critical nature of their business, so they've taken many steps toward ensuring that their embedded applications are as secure as possible.

Popular versions of embedded operating systems include the following:

- Windows NT (older systems)
- Windows XP
- Windows CE
- Linux
- Purpose-built operating systems

Consider the last one the catchall, because some systems are just too small to be able to utilize even the small footprint of Windows CE.

As you can see, embedded endpoints have the interesting trait of being operating system agnostic—in that Windows, Linux, and Cisco have been used as the base operating system. Add to that the fact that some embedded operating systems are proprietary, and you begin to get a sense of the problem. Because of their somewhat closed environment and lack of vendor-supported patches, these systems represent an interesting, but not insurmountable, challenge.

We explore classes of embedded systems, which systems can be upgraded and patched, and how to protect systems in Chapter 12, "Embedded Devices."

MOBILE PHONES AND PDAs

Now the endpoint is starting to get interesting because it's mobile. As you can see in Figure 1-4, mobile phones and PDAs come in all sizes and configurations—not the kind of mobile that says, "Unpack your notebook at the local Starbucks and do your email," but the "I just got a text message read to me over my wireless headset from my auto-answering voice-recognizing smartphone while I was in the restroom" kind of mobile. This has created all kinds of problems in our society, not from the phone itself, but from the extra features that have been tacked on to them. Who would have thought five years ago that while you were having your email read to you while in the restroom that you would have to be watchful for camera phones or, worse yet, Bluetooth packet snarfing! Bluetooth is a short-range radio connection that enables wireless headsets and synchronization. Packet snarfing is the process of capturing packets. This is potentially a bad combination of capabilities if you can't keep track of how they're being used.

Figure 1-4   Mobile phones and PDAs have evolved in a way that enables a PDA to be a phone and a phone to be a PDA. Cameras, voice recorders, Bluetooth, and network connectivity are standard features.

I regularly attend an annual security convention called the Black Hat Briefings, and in 2004, one demonstration showed how to identify and track people from their

Bluetooth-enabled cell phones and PDAs.[8] How could they do this? Don't the vendors claim that the signal only works for 3 or 4 yards? Yes, they do. And, for most of us, that's where it ends. I've been more than annoyed when I've walked 15 feet away from my phone only to discover that my Bluetooth headset has lost the signal and terminated the call. These things only use very low-powered transceivers that put out on the order of about a tenth of a watt. Remember, however, that NASA uses transmitters on deep space probes that only use a few watts of power. The strength is in the receivers and their capability to separate a good signal from the noise. Hacking isn't just about breaking into computers; it's about understanding and coercing the protocols and technology to suit your own, sometimes evil, means.

PALM

Although not as popular as it once was, the Palm operating system is still fairly prevalent and will continue to be for the near future.[9] A large number of sites offer downloaded applications, and thus lots of opportunity for compromise. A quick search of two popular Web sites, www.freewarepalm.com and www.palmgear.com, demonstrates that this is just as viable a software platform as anything you'll find in your cube. Everything from astrology to adult applications is at your stylus tip.

A huge amount of productivity is packed into a very small place. The downside to this productivity-enhancing tool is that the Palm's security is inextricably linked to the security of the endpoint to which it is bound. Through a tool called HotSync Exchange, email and files are synchronized with those on the desktop (whether it's a Windows machine or a Macintosh). If the endpoint is compromised, so is the data going to the Palm. This link has been used as an attack vector in the past. The Palm/MTX_II.A virus dropped a fairly harmless but annoying application onto the Palm by compromising the host desktop.

A number of third-party suppliers of software allow Palm owners to directly access Post Office Protocol (POP) or Internet Message Access Protocol (IMAP) servers. This access is great, but only as long as you understand that you can be connecting to a server and passing your password in the clear to anyone listening to your wireless traffic.

Research into recent attacks came up with little other than the fact that intellectual property can be removed from the device and that it can be used as a jumping-off point for an attack on the endpoint.

---

[8] www.blackhat.com/html/bh-usa-04/bh-usa-04-speakers.html, "Tracking Prey in the Cyberforest," Potter and Wotring

[9] Blackberry pips Palm to top spot, Vnunet, May 5, 2005

WINDOWS CE—WINDOWS MOBILE

Once relegated to PDAs only, as you can see in Figure 1-5, the Windows CE operating system is being used more and more in smartphones. Typically taking the form of a PDA with phone capabilities, this operating system can support general-purpose programs such as Word, Excel, and PowerPoint, thus making it look more like a portable desktop than a smartphone. Can you say macro attack?

Like Palm, Windows CE devices can bind through a trust mechanism to the endpoint to synchronize files and email. With a network connection, you can also sync with a mail server via the Internet. Some viruses and worms have worked their way into the wild recently. An example of this is Backdoor.Brador.A, a nasty little back door that gives the attacker the ability to do the following:

- List the directory contents
- Upload a file
- Display a message box
- Download a file
- Execute specified commands

With wireless connectivity via 802.11, various cell phone networks, and Bluetooth, it's clear that the future looks bright for Windows Mobile malware.

Figure 1-5   Windows Mobile, or Windows CE, is a small Windows computer in your hand. Some, like this example, come complete with a QWERTY keyboard.

SYMBIAN OPERATING SYSTEM

Part of the fun of writing a book is the endless hours of research required to confirm the accuracy of facts. I'm getting old, and my memory is starting to fail; therefore, I rely on the greatest collective memory device ever built: the Internet. With Internet research, every once in a while you have what I call a great moment. I had a great moment while working on this section. I went to the Symbian Web site and immediately found on its home page a list of quick links. At the top of this list was Security! I thought, "Wow, this is going to be easy!" So, I clicked the link to learn about Symbian security. This is what I got:[10]

Keeping mobile phones safe and secure is increasingly important for everyone involved in using or making a mobile phone. Symbian takes its responsibilities on security very seriously and works to ensure that Symbian OS continues to be the most secure operating system available to mobile phone makers.

Symbian OS is only one of the software components that mobile phone makers use to build mobile phones. For this reason, Symbian is unable to respond to security issues that individual users may have with phones that use Symbian OS. Should you experience any sort of problem with your phone you should contact your handset manufacturer or network operator/carrier to receive appropriate support and advice for your specific handset.

I guess this means that security, or the lack of it, is the problem of the handset manufacturers and the application providers. Now, to its credit, Symbian provides links to the handset vendors, application providers, and other third-party vendors that supply security-enhancing tools. However, they didn't provide a link to information on EPOC.Cabir, also known as Symbian/Cabir.a.[11] EPOC.Cabir, first detected in 2004, is a proof-of-concept (POC) worm that tries to infect other phones via their Bluetooth connection. Proof of concept is just that: proving that you can make something work. From this POC work, we learned that our phones could be successfully attacked more than two years ago. Fortunately, the Symbian operating system requires the user to authorize the attack; unfortunately, however, there are users who will.

---

[10] www.symbian.com/security/index.html

[11] www.f-secure.com/v-descs/cabir.shtml

BLACKBERRY

Blackberry owners have made it clear that they would rather lose an arm than their Blackberry. I'm not sure how they would type with only one thumb, but it's clear that Research In Motion (RIM) is pleased that this fearsome loyalty has put them in the top spot of the PDA world.

A quick search of US-CERT[12] turned up 31 vulnerabilities that ranged from denial of service (DoS) attacks to execution of arbitrary code—not many, if you consider how long they've been around, but enough to require careful consideration of just how secure the Blackberry is. RIM was worried enough about it that they had @Stake perform a vulnerability test against the server and the handheld.[13] @Stake gave both the BB Enterprise Server (BES) and the handheld a clean bill of health, saying that they weren't able to break into either. (Data from the BES is encrypted in transit.)

During my research, I came across a presentation for the National Security Agency (NSA) on the Blackberry.[14] The presentation concluded that although the Blackberry was a good platform, NSA-level security would require adding S/MIME and restricting modes of operation. Both @Stake and the NSA mentioned that Java-based handsets execute only digitally signed applications. That's good, because it raises the bar on what a hacker has to do, but it seems that the bar has been lowered a few different ways. As recently as 2006, vulnerabilities that crash the handset and the BES were posted.[15] One attacks the heap memory inside the handset; another attacks the BES, causing it to crash.

There is also the issue of email and data that don't originate from inside the enterprise. If you send an email from your Blackberry at Foo.com to a friend at Bla.org, as the message traverses the Internet, it's not encrypted. It makes sense why it works, but it's still not optimal.

DISAPPEARING PERIMETER—HUMBUG!

A movement is afoot to eliminate the security perimeter and classify it as dead. Deperimeterization arguments focus on the idea that the notion of a network perimeter is old and should be jettisoned and replaced with new technology. The Jericho Forum

---

[12] www.us-cert.gov

[13] @Stake was a security consulting group that was acquired by Symantec in 2004.

[14] www.fwuf.gov/slides/may02slides/havighurst.pdf

[15] www.kb.cert.org/vuls/id/570768

claims that different technology—such as Identity Management and Intellectual Property Management—will replace the perimeter.[16]

This is not the first time a group of pundits decided that something was dead or obsolete. A Patent Office bureaucrat made the same declaration about the need for the Patent Office in the early 1900s. A more recent example of this is the Gartner announcement in 2003 that intrusion detection systems (IDSs) were useless and a waste of money.[17] Thankfully, cooler heads prevailed, and the jet engine was patented, as was the computer, the television, and IDSs.

Being somewhat suspicious of claims of obsolescence, especially from competing vendors, I decided to chat with some folks who really understand security perimeters: the military. It would seem that the first thing you do when you secure an area is establish a perimeter. After you have established a security perimeter, you can begin the sordid task of ensuring that everything present within the perimeter is allowed (or, in our network vernacular, compliant with policy). Those that aren't allowed within the perimeter are, as the military puts it, "prosecuted" or "neutralized" (interesting euphemisms for kill, remove, and arrest).

Establishing and maintaining a security perimeter is not an easy task for us (or for the military). However, the tragic security failures of the past few years don't have the military claiming that the procedure of establishing a security perimeter is dead (and so they're not going to bother establishing one). Far from it![18] The military admits that it's difficult to establish a security perimeter that also allows day-to-day business activities to be carried out safely and securely. It takes constant vigilance, trained personnel, an adaptive policy, and attention to the smallest detail.

For a more personal view of the military model, all you have to do is look at any international airport. You go through a security checkpoint, and a determination is made as to your level of compliance with the policies that control access to the secure area. You must comply with search requests; otherwise, you're not allowed to pass. Yes, they look in areas that you'd rather share only with your doctor, but it is for the safety of all those others, and yourself, while in the secure area. In that respect, the checkpoints are like firewalls, letting only permitted protocols through, and the gates are like routers and switches, guiding folks to their aircraft that in this model represent the network.

Looking at the military model and comparing it to our network model, we see a number of blatant similarities. First, by establishing a perimeter, they are attempting to

---

[16] www.opengroup.org/jericho/

[17] Hype Cycle for Information Security, 2003, 5/30/2003, Wheatman et al

[18] Fort Irwin National Training Center Trip Report, Commanding Officer, Marine Wing Communications Squadron 38, November 9, 2003

provide a demarcation line where a method for discerning who is trusted and who is not trusted can be used. We call that the perimeter. Inside the perimeter is trusted; outside the perimeter is not. Second, they also have those individuals who are hell-bent on breaking through the perimeter to disrupt activity. So far, our network disruptions have created only productivity and financial losses, but more disastrous consequences may lurk in the future. Finally, we both have methods for identifying violations in policy and "prosecuting" the perpetrators. The military calls them guns and soldiers; we call them antivirus programs and IDSs.

The Perimeter Is Adapting

A nice thing about our present technology and the businesses that use it is businesses' ability to adapt to the changing demands placed on them by adapting technology. We see an opportunity, and if the technology doesn't exist, we create it or modify something we have to meet our needs. Over the years, our applications have adapted to leverage the network to make us faster and smarter, and our security tools have adapted to address these new additions of functionality and, in some cases, new technology altogether.

What this tells us is that as our application base adapts, our security must adapt with it. I have never been in a meeting in which someone said, "We have a multimillion-dollar deal, but we won't be able to execute because of our security policy." Someone who did say such a thing would be met with laughter. Business will always trump security, and businesses—successful businesses—will always adapt as required to meet the challenges they face. So, our security must continue to adapt. If not, security will be the first casualty in the search for increased profit.

Fast-Moving Isn't Gone

Imagine something that is fast-moving and difficult to see. As a youngster back in the cold Midwest, I used to ride my bike back and forth to the nearest airport to beg rides from the local pilots. Pilots, being who they are, didn't work to my schedule, so I spent a great many hours sitting around the terminal and fidgeting with my trusty ride, sometimes turning my bike upside down to adjust some aspect of it that I believed wasn't performing properly. Adjust the brake, spin the wheel. Adjust the derailleur and give the tire a good yank and watch the spokes disappear while I adjusted some tension spring. It only takes slipping with the wrench one time to know that *not visible* doesn't equate to *not there*.

I also hear people talk about getting a "snapshot" of the network. Good luck. If you're still thinking of the network as something that you can take an effective snapshot of, you should consider new work. The network is more like a movie or TV program, with each still frame changing a little bit to the next. You need to perceive these changes in a way that allows you to see not just the big picture, but also the subtle nuances of the plot.

Therein lies my point: Just because we can't see the changing picture doesn't mean that it isn't there.

As with virtually every other security subject, there is an opposing opinion. In an article in *CSO Magazine*,[19] Simpson Garfinkle discusses the issues with the deperimeterization debate and makes some convincing arguments. First, perimeters perform a basic blocking function in acute situations. When something new is discovered, often the quickest way to stop the pain is to block it at the perimeter. Second, defense in depth is critical to dealing with the large, fast, and diverse security issues that we see every day.

The deperimeterization idea has some compelling arguments regarding the addition of new technology and how it will be applied eventually, but I don't agree with the notion that the perimeter has disappeared. It's just moving too fast to see.

ENDPOINTS ARE THE NEW PERIMETER

As discussed previously, as devices join, change, and leave our networks, our networks take on the characteristics of a movie rather than of a still photo. And, just like the difference between the tools that one uses to edit a photo versus a movie, our attitudes (and our tools) must adjust. We need to think of our network, and the network perimeter in particular, as a fast-moving, fluid entity that needs constant attention. Tools that only give us snapshots no longer suffice. We need an approach that embraces the fact that the perimeter is dynamic and fast. The way we're going to approach that is by ensuring that all endpoints that connect to us are trustworthy.

Because so many of our devices can attach to our networks in so many different ways, it only stands to reason that the endpoint is now the perimeter that we need to protect. This isn't a turn back to the hard, crunchy shell, soft gooey interior paradigm, but it is an admission that the endpoint is where all the damage is introduced. We have network firewalls that filter network protocols and control large-scale access to our networks, but it's the small-scale access violations that are killing us. It's the 5KB virus that comes into the network from a user and uses his or her endpoint as the launching point.

---

[19] *CSO Magazine*, "The Perimeter Problem," Simpson Garfinkle, 11/2005

Protecting Data

A brief note on the present and a look into the not-so-distant future.

What we're trying to do is provide a secure platform for people to get their work done. Period. I would like to talk about some esoteric philosophy about making the Internet a better place, but it would be garbage, because it's really about the money. We're trying to ensure that the data that people generate doesn't get stolen, modified, or otherwise compromised in any way.

We're trying to do that by validating and ensuring that an intruder cannot hijack the underlying operating system and applications. At the end of the day, however, it will be the authorized user doing unauthorized things that will compromise the data. What we're talking about is providing a reliable platform for people to launch their ideas and to communicate those ideas with colleagues.

After the system is secure, we need to provide some protection for the data. We discuss this very point when we discuss some of the additional tools that are available from—dare I say it—the vendors.

Key Points

Endpoints can be defined in a number of different ways, but we have chosen to break them into Windows, non-Windows, embedded systems such as printers and ATMs, and mobile devices such as smartphones and PDAs. These devices represent the first point of attack for many different and virulent forms of malware. Without some form of protection, the data that these devices store and manage is at great risk of compromise. Because they are the subjects of attack, whatever kind of endpoint you're looking at, it is now part of a quickly changing security perimeter.

Endpoints Are the New Battleground

We know that the network is about connecting endpoints, and if we don't secure them, we're going to lose the battle. The endpoint is the single most important aspect of the perimeter, and we need to ensure that it's protected to the best of our ability.

New devices are going to be added to our networks, and chances are that if they're not an infrastructure device, they're going to be some kind of endpoint that will need to be managed.

THINGS ARE MOVING TOO FAST FOR HUMANS

Because so many people seem to think that the perimeter has disappeared, one can only conclude that things are moving way too fast for human comprehension. What this means is that we need to look at our processes and tools to understand how they are helping or failing us.

Why Security Fails

Human nature is a funny thing. Take smoking, for instance. We know that it's bad for us, but millions of people continue to smoke. Even in light of the facts that were uncovered during the lawsuits against "Big Tobacco" in the late 1990s, including the findings that they conspired against the public to hide the dangers of smoking, people still smoke. Yes, the number of smokers is down in the United States, but the rest of the world sees the profit in lighting up. Big Tobacco is even taking their message, and their marketing, to the rest of the world (specifically, China).[1] Why? Because cigarettes make money—lots of it![2]

So, that brings me to the discussion presented in this chapter. If cigarette companies can produce and *successfully* market a product that *kills people,* because of the potential for profit, why can't we make the assumption that other vendors would operate in a similar vein? I'm not ascribing anything to the security vendors so venal as knowingly killing people; I'm just trying to point out that security vendors exist as a business. Making money and generating dividends is a powerful motivation to sell a product, even a flawed one.

For many, security is about business.

However, like the reasons that people smoke, our security failures are part of a complex situation, with many subtleties and subtexts at work to keep the solution obscure.

---

[1] http://en.wikipedia.org/wiki/Philip_Morris_International

[2] http://en.wikipedia.org/wiki/Altria_Group

In the following pages, I suggest that vendors play a role in our failures and that some basic human nature is at work that continues to perpetuate those failures.

I also suggest that security isn't all about business.

PRÉCIS

This chapter covers vendors and their role in getting us buried under our own problems. Dealing with network security is a multi-billion-dollar a year business, and this chapter examines how vendors have driven the process and why this is part of our problem.

The discussion then turns to the growing list of malware, including viruses, Trojan horses, worms, and bots. We cover some of the big failures and how bots present a huge potential threat. Yes, this is a bit of fear, uncertainty, and doubt (FUD), but it's important to understand how these failures have affected us in the past.

This chapter then examines why we have poor results and how much money we're spending to get them. We continue to use the same tools, expecting different results, and we're surprised when things go sideways. We can't predict results, and this chapter discusses why. Something must be missing; we must be overlooking something pretty basic.

The chapter wraps up with a discussion of the key points regarding malware, vendors, and what may be missing from our solutions.

SPECIAL POINTS OF INTEREST

In the Preface, I defined the difference between *we* (us) and *they* (them). I was trying to hammer home a point (but in a nonthreatening way). Well, this chapter is as much about the basic problem of us and them as it is about the threat. As you read through this chapter, keep in mind that basic engineering processes aren't at work in the security industry. I also want you to understand that I think that the basic business processes that make successful vendors also mask our potential for failure. We continue to suffer failures, and we have no way of knowing when our security solutions are successful. Clearly, we are doing something wrong, and we need to take a step back, reevaluate our present solution, and make some decisions.

As engineers, when we approach a problem, one of the first things we do is explore the limits or set the boundaries. I've taken a stance, a somewhat harsh stance, at one end of the spectrum to help illustrate what the worst-case scenario is.

As you read through this chapter, keep the separate notions of business and engineering in the forefront of your thoughts. Also, keep in mind some questions that we should be asking, but aren't.

SETTING THE STAGE

Some people aren't going to like this section because they believe that it implies that I think that people are stupid. So, let me clarify that I do not think that people are stupid. I think that we are sharp, smart, motivated, and driven—just like the folks in the marketing departments of our security vendors.

Marketing departments spend a great deal of time trying to figure out how to make their message compelling enough for you to spend your money on their product. The marketing people have strategy sessions to discuss how to get you to divert money that you have earmarked for other security technologies to the purchase of their product. I can't even remember how many times I've heard marketing people mention "getting the IDS dollars" or consider "what argument would it take to get the customer to shift their spending patterns to include our products." Marketing isn't bad, it's just a pragmatic approach endemic in any business. You *have to* compete for your customer's money!

So, crafting a message is just good business practice. After all, vendors know that you only have so much money to spend, and they want you to spend it with them. Send a message that resonates with your customers. Help them understand how your product works. Help them with testing and evaluation and proof-of-concept deployments. Get them to trust you and your message. It might be good business, but it's a terrible security practice. Why? Well, one reason is that it eliminates objectivity from the engineering process.

So, knowing this, what can we do?

Our lawmakers seem to think that they can legislate a solution. Let's tell the consumer when their information becomes compromised and maybe, just maybe, they'll get mad enough to do something. A lot of people think that HIPAA[3] is supposed to make medical information more secure; its real intention, however, is to ensure that patients can take their medical information from one doctor to another without having to pay fees or redo tests. It was designed to help patients get out of a bad medical relationship without paying through the nose for more tests. Oh, and there were some security things added because some insightful legislator understood that the world was really digital.

Another interesting legislative "solution" was the Sarbanes-Oxley Act of 2002 (SOx), or as it's known in the security world, the Financial Auditor Entitlement Act. SOx was intended to address the weaknesses in the financial accounting system that enabled some executives to game the system to their financial benefit. Through various accounting tricks, billions of dollars were funneled into a few unscrupulous executives' pockets.

---

[3] http://aspe.hhs.gov/admnsimp/pl104191.htm

The reason it worked so well was that the financial auditors and the financial consultants understood the concept of "closing the loop." The consultants advised their customers on how to move accounts, cash, and debt, and the auditors only looked for things that demonstrated compliance with financial "best practices."

The term *collusion* comes to mind when examining how this arrangement worked. The first thing that happened after SOx was passed was that companies that provided financial advice could no longer provide audit services. A good first step. Break the chain of collusion and insert a new monitoring process to again close the loop, only this time the loop would be closed by the government through regulation. A bad second step. It did, however, do what it was intended to do: give the public the impression that something was being done to restore the trust in corporate America. People went to jail for their crimes, and those not complying with SOx would join them. You see, SOx made the CEO and CFO responsible and criminally liable for noncompliance. They could go to jail if they didn't pass a SOx audit twice in a row. Both the CEO and CFO had to sign their name on a legal document that went to the Securities and Exchange Commission (SEC) attesting (remember this word) that their systems and process were SOx compliant.

This is a gross oversimplification, but this is not a book on SOx.

The attestation is where the security part of it crept in. SOx said that you had to demonstrate that only those requiring access to your financial systems could gain access. You also had to keep records of that access and be able to produce them. I'm not aware of any financial systems that aren't handled by computers, so it stands to reason that whatever solution you put in place must address your enterprise network and the financial systems on them.

The security marketing people exploded. Now everything was about SOx. Instead of focusing on the real security issues, security vendors provided SOx templates for their products. Once again, an opportunity to look at why our security was failing was passed up. I'm not aware of any SOx template that ever stopped a worm. Granted, it was a great example of "find a need and fill it" mentality, but it also gave many people the false impression that being SOx compliant meant being secure.

The point I'm making here is that even with all this legislation and vendor support, we still have security failures. Security vendors used the opportunity to remarket their products in a way that characterized legislation as part of the security solution, even when it wasn't. Viruses still rip through networks, worms still turn, and endpoints still get compromised. It's clear that a new approach to understanding why we're failing is needed.

A year doesn't go by without a hundred new security products being introduced into the mix, all claiming to be the silver bullet, the one product that will increase security and make our lives easier. Their salespeople give you the line that says no one product can solve your security problems, while their marketing message says that if you buy their product, your security problems will magically disappear. I've seen this happen with firewalls, antivirus, intrusion detection systems (IDSs), and virtually every other security product over the past 25 years.

And it's getting worse.

Hundreds of security products earn millions of dollars a year, all claiming that they add security. However, I can take a traffic dump from any point on the Internet and see any version of every worm introduced over the past five years. Add to that the fact that new threats are being introduced all the time and you have the state of our networked world: We live in a constant state of cyberterror. At any time, a new threat can destroy all that we've worked for, and we won't see it coming until after it has hit us.

How can this be? We have antivirus! We have firewalls! We have IDSs! We have authentication systems! We have HIPAA,[4] SOx,[5] and let's not forget GLBA![6] With all this heavy artillery, how can the evil worms of war still manage to break through our defenses? Why do we have systems infected with bots? How can we have all this security and still have a polluted network? What the hell is going on here? Or, better yet, what the hell isn't going on here?

Basic science.

That's right, basic science. Before we get into that, however, let's examine in detail how we got to our present situation. When we understand how we got here and what the real problem is, we can begin to craft a solution based on science.

VENDORS DRIVE PROCESS

In light of the previous rant at the beginning of this chapter, I want say that we need vendors. Without them, we don't get the new tools that we need to do our jobs. Yes, there are open source tools, but if there weren't a commercial market for vendors, vendors wouldn't exist. Just like a natural environment requires predators, prey, and scavengers, our work environment requires vendors. They are necessary to the balance of our environment. (I leave it up to you to decide where vendors, and we as users, fit into that analogy.)

---

[4] Health Insurance Portability and Accountability Act of 1996 (HIPAA, Title II)

[5] Sarbanes-Oxley Act of 2002, or Public Company Accounting Reform and Investor Protection Act of 2002

[6] Gramm-Leach-Bliley Act, or the Financial Modernization Act of 1999

Having said all that, we've been letting the wolf guard the henhouse. The very people who benefit most from this mayhem are the ones we've been expecting to provide an answer: the vendors. Let me ask you a simple question: If they did in fact have the one security product to solve our problems, how many would they sell over time? Not enough to support their revenue growth objectives quarter after quarter!

I'm not saying that it's bad; I'm just saying that it's business. Each vendor has their chart that shows how their product is about "best practices" and how you can't accomplish the security cycle without their product. We've all seen the circular wheel of arrows pointing to each other: assess, report, prioritize, mitigate. This is the cycle that they use to push their business. For us, however, it's still the business of pain when a point product inevitably fails. Andrew Jaquith calls this "the hamster wheel of pain." We spin on the wheel like a plucky little hamster in a cage. Not because we're stupid, but because we're busy and we're trying to solve a complex problem with a partner that's not interested in solving the Big Problem. Besides, we're not in a position *not* to trust the vendors. We just need to change some of the questions that we ask them.

Look at the present model that security companies use: They identify a pain point and create a product to address it, like SOx templates, and then explain how it fits into the wheel of best practices. Firewalls did that in the beginning. Evil people were getting onto our computers and that had to stop. How? We prevented access to the network by evil protocols such as TELNET and FTP.

Antivirus is another great example of a point solution to a problem. When on the network, computers could become infected, so a product was created to address that problem. If you look at all the products today, that's the model that was used. Even the Security Information Manager (SIM) market started that way. The problem was too much information, so we created a SIM to manage it. The end result is that we've let the vendors treat our pain as a series of independent problems with no apparent intersection points.

So, how will science provide the answer if business hasn't? We have to look at what hasn't worked first.

SOLUTIONS ADDRESS THE PAST

Allow me to briefly recap: One vendor supplies the "problem," and another vendor supplies the "solution." It reminds me of a *Saturday Night Live* skit in which a man in a white suit convinces two rubes that he'll jump into their septic pond for a mere dollar. He jumps in and then gets out of the septic pond smelling pretty bad. The rubes, who are anxious for the now very soiled salesman to move on, are informed that seeing him jump in only costs $1, but seeing him move on down the road will cost them $10.

The real criminal part of this whole process is that it's all about addressing problems that have occurred in the past. Discover a class of vulnerabilities and generate a new product classification to cover it. We are in total reactive mode here, with the vendors on both sides of the problem. The problem of managing vulnerabilities and resulting patches has gotten so big that there are a number of companies whose business model is based on providing a solution to the complex problem of patch management in large enterprises. The same can be said for firewall, antispyware, antivirus, IDS, and worm-prevention vendors. You have to go out and purchase a third-party application from another vendor to address the underlying weakness or just careless programming techniques of our software vendors.

But, like any war zone, if you stick your head up, you will get noticed. I would like to point out that security vendors are the new targets for hackers, and vulnerabilities are being discovered in the very products designed to protect us. ZDNet reported in June 2005 that Symantec, F-Secure, and CheckPoint Software Technologies were among a list of vendors that had seen increases in discovered vulnerabilities.[7]

WE'RE NOT ASKING VENDORS HARD QUESTIONS

I think that we may believe that because we're paying for a solution that it has an intrinsically better quality associated with it. The open source world disagrees. And, based on my knowledge of how things work in security companies, I disagree, too. We can no longer take the products at face value. The organization that produces the product has to have some clue about why security flaws exist and how they can be effectively eliminated early in the product development cycle. There has to be some quality in the development environment if there is to be quality in the final product.

So, to judge the quality of their solutions, I started asking two questions:

1. What type of systems development life cycle (SDLC) do you use?
2. What software analysis tools do you use to discover coding flaws in your software?

I bet you'll be surprised at the answers you get to these questions. I was. I have been told by product vendors that their customers aren't interested in their products' capability to protect itself or the host operating system. As recently as early 2006, a vendor that was providing a database replication product in a large production environment made that very claim. However, when faced with these questions, and the prospect that we were going to discontinue the use of their product in favor of a clued-in vendor, they started

---

[7] http://news.zdnet.com/2100-1009_22-5754773.html

taking the time to learn more about what an SDLC was, what a software assurance program was, and why they should be worried about their product being abused.

VIRUSES, WORMS, TROJANS, AND BOTS

In the first few years of the twenty-first century, we saw a steady increase in the global losses suffered by businesses from virus and worm attacks. In 2001, we lost $13 billion.[8] In 2002, that loss amount jumped to $25 billion. The astounding estimated loss in 2003 was $55 billion.

ICSA Labs, a provider of security product certifications, sponsors an annual survey to track trends, and the results aren't promising.[9] In a report released in April 2005, ICSA concludes that all indicators are on the rise.[10] According to its report, 2004 saw the trend continue with a 50 percent increase in incidents, implying that we're looking at nearly $75 billion in losses. The FBI estimates that losses for 2005 topped $67 billion just in the United States.[11] These numbers track pretty well.

On a more interesting note, of the ICSA respondents, more than 30 percent said that they suffered a virus disaster, where a disaster is defined as more than 25 PCs and servers infected at the same time, causing significant damage or monetary loss. The number of respondents saying that they suffered through such a disaster was up by 12 percent over the previous year.

The most interesting fact is that of all the respondents, none said that they thought things were getting better.

Then came the eleventh annual CSI/FBI report.[12] In a surprising reversal of trend, the 2006 CSI/FBI survey reports that although we're still suffering attacks, the average loss from attacks is down from $203,606 to $167,713 per incident. However, a more disturbing trend is that companies are less likely to discuss financial losses. Fewer than half the respondents in the CSI/FBI survey were willing to discuss financial figures. I'm sure that this masks the real numbers.

Another interesting fact is that the CSI/FBI survey and ICSA survey agree that virus attacks constitute the biggest financial drain. Unauthorized access placed second.

---

[8] Reuters 1/19/04, www.silicon.com/software/security/0,39024655,39117842,00.htm

[9] www.icsalabs.com

[10] www.cybertrust.com/pr_events/2005/20050405.shtml

[11] http://news.com.com/Computer+crime+costs+67+billion,+FBI+says/2100-7349_3-6028946.html

[12] www.gocsi.com/forms/fbi/csi_fbi_survey.jhtml (You must register to get the report.)

TODAY'S MALWARE: BIG, FAST, AND DANGEROUS

MessageLabs, a provider of messaging security services, reported that W32/Mydoom.A was propagating at a rate of almost 60,000 copies per hour.[13] It was estimated that 1 in every 12 emails contained a copy of this prolific little devil. If you do the math, you come up with about 16 new infections per second. That's an amazing rate, and not one that we can even think about trying to keep up with.

Being the anal-retentive engineer that I am, I decided to figure out just how much time I would have if something fairly virulent hit my network. I started by making some basic assumptions:

- I had a 10,000 node network.
- I had fairly good security, and only 20 percent of my systems were "vulnerable."
- I was operating on a 100Mbps full-duplex network.
- The virus or worm had a rate of infection of 2 devices per second.
- The viral payload was 5KB.
- Time to repair (TTR) each node was 2 seconds.

Figure 2-1 shows the results. The graph in Figure 2-1 plots the percentage of network throughput as a function of the percentage of infected computers against time. As you can see from the graph, even at a modest two systems per second, your network has less than a minute to live. Mydoom was eight times more virulent.

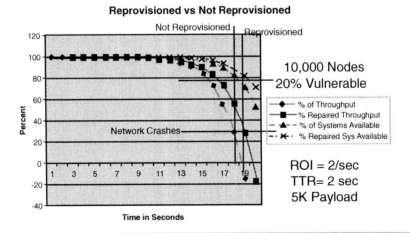

Figure 2-1   As more systems are infected, the available network bandwidth drops even if you can fix systems. In this chart, ROI is rate of infection; TTR is time to repair.

---

[13] www.messagelabs.com

Another interesting thing shown by this graph is that the network melts down long before all the available systems are infected. If you're relying on your network to push out your remediation solution, you're in serious trouble. And, while we're on the subject of remediation, you'll also notice that remediation gives you less than a 2-second increase in longevity. The lesson? It's better to prevent than to try to repair.

HIGH-PROFILE FAILURES

In June 2005, it was discovered that 13.9 million credit card accounts were compromised at CardSystems Solutions in Tucson, Arizona. The breach affected customers of MasterCard, Visa, and Discover, and is thought to be the single largest credit card theft so far.

In December 2000, 3.7 million credit card numbers were stolen from Egghead. After an investigation, CEO Jeff Sheahan sent a letter to customers explaining that fewer than two tenths of 1 percent, less than 7,500 cards, had displayed fraudulent activity. I suppose that it was good news for the other 99.8 percent who didn't have fraudulent charges on their bills. But what about those who did? Have you ever had to deal with a fraudulent charge on your credit card bill? A casual poll of my friends indicates that all of them have had to deal with credit card fraud, and 100 percent of them said it was a pain.

These two incidents, although years apart, have one similarity: Both companies went out of business due to the breach. Egghead was gone within six months of their breach, and as of October 2005, CardSystems was acquired by Pay By Touch. In both cases, their customers had a significant role in their respective demises. As a retail outlet, Egghead had let their customers down, and nobody wanted to take a chance buying there again. With the substantial news coverage, you would have to have lived in a cave not to know about the breach. As for CardSystems, Visa dealt the first blow by revoking their certification to process transactions. MasterCard and Discover followed suit. Although CardSystems did pass a Payment Card Industry (PCI) data security audit in August, and they did supply a Report on Compliance to Visa, MasterCard, American Express, and Discover, the damage had already been done.

WHAT IS BEING EXPLOITED?

With few exceptions—the Bank of America (BoA) tapes come to mind—all successful attacks have been against the endpoint. In the BoA incident, a number of tapes with confidential customer information on them "disappeared." The reality of that situation was that you need the right machine to read them and the right software to extract the data. Neither is likely found in your typical hacker environment.

CardSystems was an attack against an endpoint. Egghead was the same thing.

BOTS

Botnets are the ultimate expression of the exploited endpoint. Botnets are networks composed of compromised computers that have some variant of a Trojan horse program loaded on them. There are various type of Trojan horses. Some are designed to give their owner remote access to your system, and some are designed to be tattletales reporting various bits of information back to their master. Some are just remotely triggered attack drones. All are dangerous.

Trojans get loaded in numerous ways, but most rely on the user to do something (such as clicking Yes when asked). For example, W32/Bropia arrived via Microsoft Instant Messenger. The promise was that the user was downloading a sexy image, but in fact he was actually downloading a variant of the W32.spybot.worm.

Instead of a sexy image, the user got the picture shown in Figure 2-2, a suntanned chicken with a nasty payload. Clearly, the focus of this attack was the male user and his endpoint.

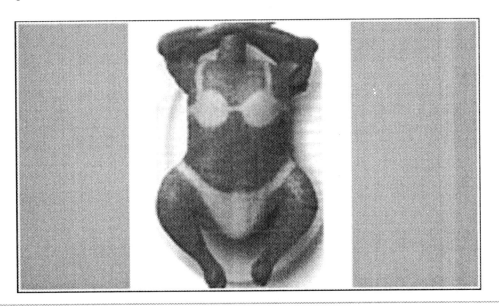

Figure 2-2 Chat users thought that they were getting a sexy bikini-clad beauty but instead got this image and a spybot Trojan.

A study by Earthlink came up with some grim statistics.[14] The worst of which is that they estimate that up to 90 percent of all Internet-connected computers have some form of unwanted program (sypware, worm, Trojan) loaded and running on them. Another interesting statistic is that on average each machine has about 25 installations of some sort of spyware on it.

Not all spyware is completely evil. Some of it is just partially evil. I had an interesting experience recently that I think is relevant to the discussion, because it proves that there are many ways that the endpoint can become infected. I will once again pick on the marketing folks; after all, they seem such easy targets.

On a sunny day, a marketing droid and I were trapped in a conference room going over a presentation that should have been done days before. It hadn't been, however. The marketing people didn't like the lack of specificity that security people like to hide behind. We don't like to say that our product will prevent breaches,[15] but we're willing to say that we can greatly reduce the possibility that a breach will occur. "Greatly reduce" doesn't sound as sexy as "prevent," so the marketing folks were trying to wear me down to admit that we prevent evil stuff. While we were having this discussion, we were asked to move from our bright and sunny conference room to an internal conference room with all the accoutrements of a dungeon. For some reason, the buzzing of the florescent lights seemed especially annoying, so my attention wandered to the fact that the notebook we were using to work on the presentation was now painfully slow. Specifically, it was slow running the presentation. Hmm. The only difference between this venue and the other conference room was that in the other room we'd been connected to the network. So, I suggested that we reconnect and try again. Zip—a fast presentation.

My steel-trap mind realized that something in the presentation was being held up by a lack of connectivity to the network. Many Microsoft programs are network aware, but I suspected something more nefarious was at work. I suggested that we disconnect from the network and test again. With the network disconnected, the computer was dirt slow at slide 10.

A hub- and sniffer-equipped notebook later and we had an answer: a graphic object that the marketing person had downloaded from the Internet was phoning home. The offending object was a cool-looking spinning checkmark that was placed in front of each bullet on our Claims of Security slide. When the notebook was connected to the Internet, the checkmark scraped the IP address of the notebook and sent it back to the mothership. The "owners" of the checkmark could then track who was downloading their code and where they were presenting it. I'm sure that this is information that many

---

[14] www.earthlink.net/spyaudit/press/

[15] Yes, I was part of the machine that I blasted earlier.

competitors would love to have. Where is your competition making presentations, and are they successful in the sale? With a little bit of correlation, this information is easy to determine.

Our security software missed the checkmark, and the marketing person was now convinced that "greatly reduce" was really pretty good wording.

Let's get back to the endpoints and the bots loaded on them. Specifically, let's do some math on endpoints and connections. If you have a typical home connection to the Internet, you can probably manage at least 128Kbps upload speed. Let's also assume that your business has a T1 line giving you a 1.544MBps connection to the Internet. That means that 12 infected home computers equipped with evil bots aimed at your corporate network could cause a denial-of-service attack. Only 12!

Now, according to Pewinternet.org, 24 percent (or almost 50 million) of Americans have a high-speed connection such as Digital Subscriber Line (DSL) or cable.[16] Add in the Earthlink statistics regarding spyware and bots, and the math says that there is a hugely powerful machine sitting out there waiting to get switched on.

PREDICTABLY POOR RESULTS

When you are looking at results, the bottom line is actually the bottom line. We know that we're spending more money on security because we can see it. We're trying to determine ways to convince the bean counters that we know what we're talking about by using convoluted return on investment calculators because we keep asking for ever more money and can't seem to slow the tide. ROI (in this case, return on investment) calculators are a valuable tool; in the security world, however, they still rely on a bit of squinting, some smoke, and a dash of faith.

SPENDING MORE THAN EVER

There are a number of ways to calculate how much money is spent, but the most popular seems to be the survey of security professionals, such as CSOs and CISOs. The numbers are then anonymized, normalized, and presented as fact in an "official" report, such as those produced by the CSI/FBI and the ICSA.

I have a problem with a process that relies on subjective answers converted into facts and presented as information, especially when that information is used to convince people that they're not spending enough money. (And yes, I do realize that I used these very reports to make my point previously, but I did more research to verify my facts.)

---

[16] John B. Horrigan, Ph.D., Senior Research Specialist (202-296-0019), April 2004

So, how do we find out how much money is being spent on security? We follow the money. Most of the security products are supplied by a few industry heavyweights. When folks want to find out how many computers are sold, a simple first attempt at the answer is to count how many Windows installations were sold over a given time. I propose that we use that same process to determine how much "security" we're buying. We look at the major security vendors and see how much money they made last year!

So, who are the major security vendors, and how much did they make? Infonetics Research reported that the 2005 market leaders are the following:[17,18]

- **Cisco:** 35%
- **CheckPoint:** 10%
- **Juniper:** 8%

Between the three of them, they represent 53 percent of the total $3.6 billion hardware and software security market. According to Infonetics, the rest of the market is split between Enterasys, ISS, McAfee, Nokia, Nortel, SonicWALL, and Symantec, each of which claims between 1 percent and 6 percent of the market.

Our financials haven't even factored into the result the impact of security services on our spending habits. A few years ago, the term *managed security services* (MSS) snuck into our lexicon, and another industry was born. According to the Reseller Channel,[19] the MSS market drew $1.5 billion in 2002 and is expected grow to almost $4 billion in 2006. In 2004, the MSS folks rang the bell at the $2.3 billion mark, bringing the global security market forecast as of November 2004 to $12.9 billion.[20]

Infonetics also reports that as of the end of the third quarter[21] of 2006, network security sales are up and are projected to top $5.48 billion by 2009. Add content security devices to the mix, and the total goes up to $7.57 billion just for those two security markets.

WE HAVE NO WAY TO PREDICT SUCCESS

No matter how much we spend, security people have a simple question to answer: How do you know when you're done? How do we know when we're as secure as we can be and

---

[17] www.enterprisenetworkingplanet.com/nethub/article.php/3532031

[18] www.infonetics.com/resources/purple.shtml?ms05.sec.3q.nr.shtml

[19] 9/2004, by Tara Seals (Data source Yankee Group 12/03)

[20] www.techweb.com/wire/networking/53701345

[21] www.infonetics.com/resources/purple.shtml?ms06.cs.sec.3q06.nr.shtml

still be able to do business? The answer is that we're never completely done, but we can be "done enough" so that we can manage to keep our heads above water long enough to not get fired. The problem is that we spend our days in firefighting mode because as much as we think we understand the problem, we really don't. Sure, we have documents that claim to be representative of best practices, but they're based on different levels of what is considered secure. The bad news is that when something new is introduced, "best practices" can't help us sort out the problem.

I have a simple premise: If you can describe it and you can measure it, you can understand it.

As proof of this claim, I can point to numerous working groups that are putting together various descriptions of metrics designed to tell us how secure our networks are. Okay, so what is secure? Secure as compared to what? As you can see, a basic element of the problem is at its heart very subjective in nature. What may be secure to me may not be secure to you.

So, we've failed the first test because we can't describe *secure*. Setting aside our inability to describe secure, let's take a crack at measuring it. Many people say that you should measure risk. The word *risk*, as defined by the dictionary, is the possibility of suffering harm or loss; danger.

Security people describe risk as the probability that your network could be exploited to your detriment. They take into account the number and types of vulnerabilities, the availability of an exploit that exercises the vulnerabilities, and the types of protections that surround the vulnerable system that prevent the successful use of the exploit. But, just looking at risk in such simple terms doesn't even begin to get at the heart of the matter. Isn't risk a little higher if the system we're talking about is your finance server?

The bottom line in this discussion is that because we don't understand the problem well enough, we don't have a way to predict success; the converse of that is that we can't predict failure.

WE'RE STILL BEING SURPRISED

The news media would have you believe that the security of our computing systems is a new problem—that only recently have hackers and thieves been working to steal information from computers. Not so. Even in the old days of the mainframe, nefarious individuals found ways to break through security. That's the reason applications such as Resource Access Control Facility (RACF) and Access Control Facility (ACF2) were developed. But the problem, and the surprise that security failed, still persists.

We can be thankful, however, that many security people aren't surprised. They've lived for years with the reality that our processes are broken and our tools aren't sufficient.

Their problem is that they're spending most of their time treading water in an attempt to keep the evil out of their networks.

Why do viruses get through if we have antivirus? If it's not working, why buy it?

Newspaper editors have a saying: "If it bleeds, it leads." Things make the front page because they are spectacular, they affect a lot of people, or they profoundly affect us as a society. For some reason, it seems that war, murder, rape, and political scandal garner the most attention. Lately, however, we can add identity theft to that list of banner headlines. Why? Because millions of people are affected, and there was no warning. One day, you woke up and read in your local rag that your private information is probably the topic of discussion at hacker parties and is getting a better rate of return than your savings account.

IS SOMETHING MISSING?

The scientific method says that when you want to learn about something, you study it, make an attempt to understand it, postulate the outcome of a test, perform that test, and compare your answer to your postulate. If your answer is correct, you move on. If you're like most of us, however, there will be some difference between your postulated solution and the actual answer you get from your test. That difference is due in part to the fact that there are some things that you didn't know about, and they affected the outcome of the test.

A classic example of this process took place more than 100 years ago at Kittyhawk, North Carolina. The Wright brothers were using a set of tables provided by Otto Lilienthal, and they based the size and shape of their wing on the information in Lilienthal's tables.[22] When the wing didn't perform as well as the tables said it would, the Wrights did what any good engineer would do: They questioned the accuracy of the information provided to them! They made a wind tunnel and through the scientific method refined the equations so that they could accurately predict how a wing would perform. It was hard, and it took a lot of time, but in the end, that single decision to use the scientific process made all the difference in the world.

WHAT ARE WE DOING WRONG?

As much as I hate to say it, we, the security industry, are not using sound engineering or the scientific method to figure out what is wrong. Worse yet, we continue to make the

---

[22] The First to Fly, Sherwood Harris, Tab Aero (1991)

same mistakes year after year. We rely on the vendors to tell us what the solution should be instead of turning the formulation of a solution into a science.

For some strange reason, we continue to use the same failing methods to draw our conclusions. Some people say that if we eliminate the vulnerabilities, we will be secure. But, eliminating the vulnerabilities only reduces the number of attack vectors, and it still relies on someone finding security flaws in our software. In short, it's a reactive method that has proven that it doesn't work. Besides, any good security person will tell you that although having vulnerabilities implies that you are less secure, not having vulnerabilities does not imply that you are secure.

HAVE WE MISSED SOME CLUES?

In my opinion, yes, we've missed a clue every time there's been a successful attack against the Internet community. I'm not just talking about single hacks against specific targets, but rather those failures that seem to indicate an endemic and ubiquitous situation.

The clues we're missing aren't ones that point to vulnerabilities, but they're the clues that point to the fact that we're continuing to do the same wrong things. We've also failed to gain insight from other IT solutions that have turned what they do into a science. Take the network management folks, for instance. When networks began to spread, only a few talented individuals understood how they worked. So, they were the consultants called in when the network needed tuning. They came with their tools and sniffers and watched the traffic to see what was wrong. Then, after what always seemed like an eternity, the network wizard tweaked some parameter and the network started humming again. When networks started to get big, the tools were commoditized and sold to the network engineers who were responsible for keeping the network going. It wasn't long before someone realized that a network sniffer was a powerful tool but not one that was easily scalable, so fledgling network management systems were born.

What this points to is that someone said, "Hey, this old stuff isn't working, and our reliability has gone to hell. Maybe we should try something different."

What's happened over the years is that our networks have gotten, and continue to get, more complex. But, that complexity has been hidden behind management systems and cool GUIs so it can no longer be seen. More complex architectures, more complex operating systems, and more complex applications have predictably reduced overall reliability. To illustrate my point, take a look at Figure 2-3, while keeping in mind that there is no real data in the chart. Why no data? Because the data differs for each type of solution. As parts counts go up, the failure rates multiply, thus reducing the overall reliability of the entire system. As relationships multiply, the possibility that one failure will affect multiple systems multiplies.

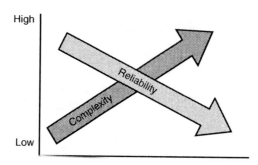

Figure 2-3 As complexity increases, the trend is for reliability to decrease. Systems that demonstrate excessive complexity, such as software and networks, tend to have lower reliability.

It's difficult to see in our networking system, but we do feel the trends, and we do see the results every day. More cars mean more roads, and more roads mean more choices, and more choices mean more accidents when people can't manage the complexity of traffic decisions well enough or fast enough. We know that complexity affects the reliability of systems because we have redundancy solutions to deal with the eventual failures. There is math to support this in numerous places, but the trend is simple: More complexity means less reliability. To address this, we add more complexity in parallel with the knowledge that both systems failing at the same time is a remote possibility.

A note to contemplate: Complexity does not mean large. Small things can be complex because of the relationships that exist within them.

KEY POINTS

We—and when I say "we," I'm indicting all of us in the security world—know that we've had a fairly systemic failure in our security solutions that has us constantly throwing money at the problem in the hope that something will work. We fail, yet we continue to use the same method of selecting our solution: We turn to the vendors.

MALWARE CONTINUES

Despite the efforts to contain and remove malware, we still see it on our networks and on the Internet. We add products and technology, and although we might stop some immediate pain, we are never sure when the next "big one" is going to hit us. We're still losing a huge amount of money through loss of productivity, fraud, and theft, and the bleeding just goes on and on.

Vendors Aren't Helping

Vendors continue to produce products that enable hackers, spies, and thieves to take advantage of our networks for their own purposes. Operating systems have holes large enough to drive entire databases through them with little or no warning. Vendors are pumping out products, but they continue to use the "I have a hammer, so each problem must be a nail" approach to security. Security vendor marketing departments spend more time retooling the Web site to make sure that it addresses the issue of the day instead of doing real research that may help identify what products really need to be made.

We Need to Ask Harder Questions

Simply supplying a solution is no longer adequate. Vendors need to prove that they understand what the problem is by leading by example, and we, as buyers, need to push the point. We need to ask vendors what type of SDLC they're using. We need to ask vendors what type of source code security testing tools they're using. We need to ask vendors how they incorporate flaw detection and remediation into their product development cycle.

Are We Missing Something?

All the evidence points to the fact that we don't fully understand the problem. Yes, networks are complex, but they're not so complex that we mere human beings can't understand them if we take the time. Each time we apply the scientific method to solving a problem, we begin to make progress. Perhaps it's time to ask this question: What can we do differently?

Something 3 Is Missing

I'm going to start this chapter by saying that a toilet has a better control system built in to it than our networks do. We understand how toilets work, what happens when they don't, and most important, why they fail. I know it sounds strange, but there is a similarity here that can be exploited—we just need to understand the science behind it.

So, from the preceding two chapters, we know that something is clearly missing. We're spending like mad, have no way to predict success (much less failure), and we still have the day-to-day problem of being attacked constantly.

I think part of the problem has to do with the fact that many people honestly believe that the network is too complex to understand and that "security" is the purview of hackers and vendors. I've actually had security people tell me in meetings that their network is too large, too distributed, and too complex to identify all the endpoints on it! On another note, I've actually had a hacker sit across from me in meetings, pound the table, and scream—yes, scream at me—"I can own your network!" I told him, "Great, I'll need a weekly status report." He didn't seem to be a bit amused with my sarcasm, but using fear, uncertainty, and doubt to sell a service has never been a big hit with me.

I touched on the idea that we should use science to help solve our problems, and I really think that's where the answer lies. We need to understand not just how, but why our networks operate the way they do. We're being driven by the fire of the day, and we're letting it drive our solution space. This is not how engineers do things, and for all practical purposes, no matter how we got here, we are engineers.

In this chapter, we explore the notion that the network and the endpoints that populate it is a problem that can be expressed as a closed-loop process control problem.

Like the system that controls the heat and power in your building, a closed-loop process control system establishes a "set-point," such as the temperature, and works the system's compressors, coolers, and heating elements to maintain the temperature within a few degrees of the set-point. I submit that our networks have no such control and that's why we're having the problems we have now.

The network folks have known about this kind of a solution for years. All critical systems, such as switches, routers, Uninterruptible Power Supplies (UPSs), file servers, and even things like network-enabled power strips, all talk to a central system called a network management system (NMS). Properly instrumented systems talk with the NMS using a standard protocol called the Simple Network Management Protocol (SNMP). Using SNMP, systems report on their status, throughput, and general health. Details such as the number of packets passed, packets dropped, types of packets, temperature of the system, voltage level, battery life, routing protocols in use ... well, you get the idea. All that information at their fingertips enables the good folks in the network operations center (NOC) to keep the network up and functional.

As things change, the information is reported to the NOC, where decisions can be made to set things right. Using the capability of an NMS-equipped network, administrators can make tactical decisions to address acute situations, or they can use the trending information for strategic purposes.

It wasn't all that easy, but after many years of development, the network management people have successfully closed the loop, and our networks have become a commodity resource because of it.

We have no such solution in the security world.

PRÉCIS

I start our journey through this chapter by discussing a new way to look at our network and the security systems that inhabit it. As discussed in the previous chapters, our present methods aren't working, so I discuss a new process that will help us understand how our network technology interacts with our security technology. Each system has a distinct role and a unique mode of operation. When we understand these control modes, we can begin to understand how they talk and who they talk to. Like the NMS systems, we need a way to leverage communications protocols in a way that gets us information quickly and reliably.

Now the hard part: We're going to have to map our business processes to our security model. I say "hard" because when I've seen security fail, a good many times the reason it happened was because the security process didn't mesh properly with the goals and objectives of the business. We already know that if it's a choice between better security and higher profits, security gets the axe.

At the end of the chapter, I cover one other issue: nomenclature and iconology. Every engineering discipline has its own language and way of expressing things pictorially. Security people have resorted to drawing pictures of walls to represent firewalls, and I think that it's time we begin to standardize on some schematic representations that enable us to convey the complexity of our environments in a concise manner.

When these really easy things are complete, we can begin to understand what is missing in our present network, build a better model of our network, and understand how we can use the endpoints to control the amount of risk introduced into the enterprise.

SPECIAL POINTS OF INTEREST

Any time you use a toilet to explain something, especially something as serious as the flaws in network security, you should expect the occasional snicker or guffaw. Many people have used "toilet humor" through the years to highlight elements of our society that we don't like to discuss in public forums. From Frank Zappa to *South Park,* toilet humor has been used as a way of getting a message out. So it is with this chapter. So, I ask you to open your mind up a bit as you read this chapter, because I'm going to apply process control as a method to understand our present security problem, and I'm going to use a toilet to explain why it works.

As you might suspect, this isn't a traditional application, and some people will question the notion that the network can be controlled in such a way. However, I believe that I make a good case for it and provide a solid foundation for my claims.

So, this chapter is about looking at things in a different way. By deconstructing why we're failing, we can gain some insight into a method of understanding that will enable us to apply some "new to us" technology to our solution. I say that it's "new to us" because lots of other folks have been successfully using control processes for quite a few years. As a matter of fact, we will examine one group of dedicated control computers in Chapter 12, "Embedded Devices." (Remember when you read Chapter 12 that I said "successfully" here, not "securely.")

I also suggest that you pay special attention to the section that maps process control modes to existing security; that section reveals some interesting traits regarding our security technology selections to date.

At the end of this chapter, you'll find some proposed icons and symbology that allow us to reduce a large and complex network environment to a simple drawing. I believe that this type of schematic representation of the network and its security functions is crucial to helping us understand how to build better security systems.

PRESENT ATTEMPTS HAVE FAILED (PRESENT MODELING)

Many security-modeling tools are on the market, and it would be easy to spend a week listening to salespeople tell you how well their products work. These tools talk about "risk" and measure it as a product of endpoint vulnerability and the availability of a suitable exploit. If you have a vulnerability, and you have a way to exploit it, you have a risk that someone will use the exploit on your system. The message here is that if you eliminate the vulnerabilities on your network, you will be secure.

If you think about it, that's not a bad way of attacking the problem if all you're interested in is removing the known vulnerabilities from your network. Many networks can operate this way because they're essentially "open" in the sense that no private data is being loaded on them and anyone can use their resources. The main concern is to keep them up and functional. Public libraries and universities operate in this mode, with the main difference being that a library owns the endpoints and a university hosts its students' endpoints.

In the library, the users browse the Internet or do research. Some systems allow the use of office tools such as word processors and spreadsheets, but you use them at your own risk (because you'll be leaving a copy of your data somewhere on the system). I wouldn't be comfortable working on my diary at the local public library. To ensure that they're as available as possible, libraries lock down their systems to the point where the user is unable to make any changes to the system at all. Users are not allowed to install software, remove software, and in some jurisdictions, browse to some sites on the Internet. I see this same type of installation at airports that have made computers available to pilots for flight planning.

At the other end of the spectrum, universities are not concerned with the security of the endpoint per se. Their concern comes from their charter regarding the network and their service level agreement with the students. The university's mission is to provide a reliable network service to their users, and because the university doesn't control the endpoint, they need a different way of managing the connections. They register users and the machine address that they're working from. When they detect that a specific machine address is abusing the system, they cut it off.

The problem with this kind of an approach in a corporate environment is that it's not practical to rely solely on vulnerability management. There are other threats to your network, such as trusted systems doing untrustworthy things.

We Don't Understand Why

I say that "we"[1] don't understand why security continues to fail because there are so many people saying that they have the answer. To me this means that

- We have many things wrong with our networks.
- We don't understand what's really wrong.
- Both.

I'm one of those people who believe that the answer is really closer to the last bullet than either of the first two. The fact is that there are so many things that are broken we haven't taken the time to figure out what the real problem is. We spend our days trying to keep the barbarians from the gates, so we don't have the time to really craft a reliable model of our security.

Various enclaves of thought bring up good reasons for our failure, such as we don't measure enough things, but it boils down to the fact that there are lots of broken bits and no way to replicate a successful model.

In many ways, our world is like the world of the theoretical physicist—they're trying to make sense out of a science that they can't see. There are many theories, but little empirical evidence to back them up. The most fleeting of these is the unification of the three forces into a grand definition of the universe. They keep hammering away at it by devising experiments to prove some minute aspect of their theories. Each time, they get one more tiny piece of evidence that brings them closer to the truth. I'm sure that one day they will succeed in completing the grand model of the universe, but we don't have that kind of time to wait for a security solution.

We Continue to Use Old Thinking

Present systems use vulnerability management models to understand what will happen when the network is attacked. You take your vulnerability information and pop it into the model, and out comes a result that tells you how much "risk" you have of suffering an attack.

Consider a simple model where all you want to do is control the temperature in your house. Using vulnerability management as the basis for your design philosophy, you would start by getting an idea of how much heat your house leaks. The simple way to do this is to have somebody point an infrared sensor at your house and take a picture of the hot spots. This is analogous to having your network scanned for vulnerabilities.

---

[1] I covered what *we* refers to in the Preface; in case you're confused about who *we* are, however, *we* refers collectively to all the security world.

Now that you have an idea of where the heat is leaking out, you can plug the holes using better insulation, or, if you're cheap like me, clear plastic and duct tape.

According to the vulnerability management dogma, all you have to do to keep your temperature constant is to take periodic infrared snapshots of your house and fix the discovered leaks that might have popped up. The thinking is that there could have been a storm that tore the plastic over the windows, or worse, somebody could have opened a window and left it open. Therefore, this recurring analysis of your house is needed.

Before we move on, this is in no way intended to be a complete dissertation on the many ways one can model a network, but I believe that a brief description of the most popular methods will help lay the foundation for what we're going to talk about later.

Threat modeling is a way to understand how an attacker would attempt to breach your security. You start by assessing your network and applications the way an attacker would. The first thing you do is scan your network using something like nmap to find out what endpoints are on your network and what applications are running.[2] You then drill down into those applications using other tools to look for weaknesses. For example, your scan might have discovered a Web server that hosts a custom application that is supporting the HR benefits service. These types of applications are typically Web-based user interfaces with a database back end. The next step is to use a Web scanning tool such as nikto[3] to find out whether the Web server and database are vulnerable to things such as cross-site scripting or Structured Query Language (SQL) attacks.

After you have a list of potential attack methods, you prioritize them based on the value of the target endpoint and the probability that an attack will succeed. Web servers buried deep in your enterprise behind firewalls and layers of networks are obviously less susceptible to external SQL hacking attempts than the systems in your DMZ.[4] However, as you can see in Figure 3-1, anything in your DMZ is only one hop away from both sides of the security perimeter.

Conversely, application servers on your DMZ would be the first systems that you fix because they are the most exposed.

Now that you have this list, you can better understand how a hacker might penetrate your network.

If you've been in the security business for more than a week, you've heard the term *risk analysis* mentioned more than once. Risk analysis is another way of looking at your vulnerabilities and determining how they can be leveraged against your enterprise.

---

[2]   www.insecure.org/nmap/

[3]   www.cirt.net/code/nikto.shtml

[4]   Demilitarized zone. A special part of the network that provides limited access to specific applications to Internet users.

The difference is that the result is expressed as a probability, or, as we say, risk. Now, you're probably saying that risk is a pretty subjective thing, and you are right. There are those who say if you have a vulnerability, it's only a matter of time before it's exploited, and they are right, too.

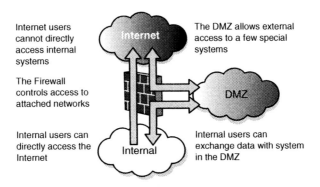

Figure 3-1   A simple pictogram that depicts how close the DMZ is to the Internet and how it can act as a bridge to the internal network.

> **WARNING**
>
> You must protect this information in the strongest possible manner. It is a complete roadmap for an attacker; and if you lose it, you and your enterprise are in serious trouble. Think seriously about changing careers, because you'll never get a job in technology again. On the other hand, you will be famous ... for a short time.

There are other, more esoteric modeling techniques, but they all pretty much use the same vulnerability assessment methodology as their baseline foundation.[5] The problem with this approach is that it is a *reactive* way of addressing the problem. Now before everyone starts filling up my inbox, the reason I say that it's reactive is because from the time that the endpoint is deployed to the time that you do the scan, you have a vulnerability on your network.

If you start with a vulnerability-based approach, you need to ensure that every single endpoint hasn't been compromised before you're sure you're more secure than when you

---

[5]   I had the word *dogma* here, but some found it too harsh.

started. Who's to say that some evil person hasn't already used one of your vulnerabilities to make a nice nest in your network somewhere? Not all hacks are apparent or obvious. As you will recall from Chapter 1, "Defining Endpoints," some hacks are placed on a system for later usage.

Now please don't run off and say, "Kadrich says that threat modeling and risk analysis are useless." Far from it. What I am saying is that although they are indeed useful tools for helping you understand the security posture of your network, they are not the models that are going to solve our endpoint security problem.

However, I am saying that there might be another, more effective way to model the network. It might be a bit unconventional, however.

DEFINE NETWORK AS CONTROL PROBLEM

Security is about control. If we can't control our environment, we can't give any assurances that we are secure. One day it hit me: Out security problem is really a process control problem.

Allow me to digress for a moment and explain how I reached this conclusion. I had the unique experience of being an electrical engineer while I was also responsible for securing the network. It wasn't uncommon for me to be designing a flight termination system for a missile while I was writing the security procedures for a classified network. (By the way, if you have a sleep-deprivation problem, I highly recommend either "Standard Practices and Procedures for the Classified Network Supporting the Theater High Altitude Area Defense System" or "Range Ordinance Safety Specifications for the White Sands Missile Test Range." The last one is a little hard to get because they're mimeographed copies,[6] but if you can get it, it's cheaper than Ambian!)

One of my other tasks was designing and installing a system that was designed to control the world's second largest cryo-vacuum chamber. A special type of computer called a programmable logic controller (PLC) is used to interface with the valves, pumps, switches, and sensors that are needed to simulate a deep space environment in the cryovac chamber. The computer knows what the set-points are for atmospheric pressure and temperature and manages the devices to achieve that goal. Whereas the thermostat in your house is really a bimodal control (it turns the heater on and off), my cryovac system used a proportional process control methodology. The difference is that the only feedback to your home system is via the thermostat, whereas in a process control system numerous feedback paths help to achieve and maintain a specific set-point.

---

[6] An ancient method of reproducing documents that used an ink drum and special typewriter-generated stencils to create many copies of the original document.

Why do we need these numerous feedback paths? Because there are time constants associated with each control action. For example, when your home thermostat detects that the air temperature is too low, it turns on the heater. The heater does its job of pumping hot air back into the house through the various paths provided by the air ducts. The temperature isn't changed instantly, so the thermostat has to wait for the warm air to reach it. What that means is that by the time the thermostat reaches the correct temperature, the temperature by the heating ducts is actually higher. The rate of change, all things being equal, is fairly constant.

The net result of this bang-bang type of control is that the temperature in the house actually varies around the set-point by a couple of degrees. If you set the thermostat to 68 degrees, the temperature in the rooms typically oscillates around the set-point, as depicted in Figure 3-2. I know that this is going to sound a bit anal, but I have a recording thermometer in my bedroom that records the minimum and maximum temperatures (along with the humidity). With the temperature set in the hallway to 68 degrees, the temperature in the master bedroom, way down the hall, records a minimum of 66 and a maximum of 70 degrees, as shown in Figure 3-2.

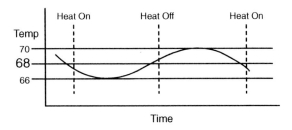

Figure 3-2 Typical room temperature variance around the set-point as verified in the author's master bedroom. Notice the time difference between when the heater turns on and when the room temperature begins to rise.

Now let's look at something also close to you—your car. If you're fortunate enough to have a car with an environmental control system, you'll notice that the fan is running *all the time*. If you look closely, you'll also notice that the air conditioner is running. The reason is that your car uses a proportional sensor that tells the computer what the temperature is and how much difference there is between it and the desired temperature or set-point. Your car actually mixes heat and cold to produce an output air temperature designed to keep the temperature inside the car where you set it. When the sun beats down on the windows, the system mixes in more cold air. When you're scraping snow off the windshield, it mixes in more hot air.

This how they can sell cars with dual-zone environmental controls.

I brought this up at the beginning of the chapter, and I want to discuss one more device in your life that is a great example of proportional control: the toilet in your house. Yes, the toilet in your house has a proportional control mechanism in it. As you can see in Figure 3-3, the proportional control in your toilet is a combination of two valves and a float. One valve, the refill valve, allows water to refill the system at a rate based on the position of the float. The other valve, the control valve, or as it's known at the hardware store, the flapper valve, allows the system to be "activated" and reset.

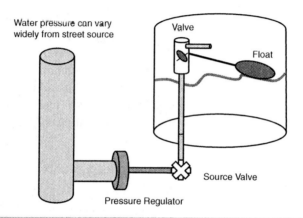

Figure 3-3   A toilet is a basic proportional control at work. The float controls the level of water in the system within a narrow band. The pressure regulator ensures that the float and valve fill the tank to the same level every time.

When the system has completed its designed task, the reset process kicks in, and this is where the proportional control takes over. This is a fairly critical process. If not enough water is put back into the system, it fails when we try to use it. If there's too much water put into the system, we have another, arguably less desirable, failure mode to deal with. We need the same amount of water each and every time no matter how much water pressure there is. The float connected to the refill valve provides this type of proportional control. As the float rises in the tank, it gradually closes off the opening in the valve, thereby slowing down the rate at which the tank fills until the valve is shut off completely and the tank is full. The system has been successfully reset.

When you activate the system, the water rushes out cleaning the bowl, the flapper valve closes, the float drops, and the water is allowed to refill the tank. The metric for success is simple: You look into the bowl and either know success or hit the lever again. If the system fails, the failure is obvious … on many levels.

MAP CONTROL MODES TO TECHNOLOGY

Because we're looking to proportional control technology to help us solve our problem, let's look at the basic components of that solution.

As mentioned in the preceding section, the main component in this process is the proportional control, the central process that acts as the foundation for the system. In our previous examples, we found that this process was a combination of a sensor, such as the thermostat or the float, working in conjunction with an energy source, such as the heater or the water pressure. However, we know that in those systems there is always variation. Sometimes, the doors are open a bit longer, and the heater has to run longer to catch up. The result is that the temperature in the room doesn't stay a constant 72 degrees. It varies around the set-point by a few degrees because there is nothing to tell it how fast the room is cooling down or how fast it's heating up.

To address the basic shortcomings of a proportional-only control, two other "helper" processes make it easier for the proportional control to do its job. These control modes are derivative and integral.

The derivative process controls the rate of change. Using our toilet process in Figure 3-3, let's say that the water pressure doubles in the system. Because the float and valve are designed to work within a fairly narrow band of water pressure, doubling the pressure causes the tank to fill up much faster and to a slightly higher level. This is because the float and valve can't work fast enough to prevent the overflow. So, to control the pressure, we add a pressure regulator to the system to keep the water pressure that the intake valve sees at a normal level or slightly below it. What this means is that it will take a little bit more time to fill the bowl. What this also means is derivative controls lower the response frequency of the system. Instead of 60 flushes per minute, we might only get 50 flushes.

Unfortunately, using proportional and derivative controls means that it's possible to have a stable system that still doesn't hit the set-point, because the resolution on the sensors is not capable of seeing the potential error. Enter integration. The integral process adds the small errors over time to create an accumulated error that forces the system to once again correct itself.

Although a toilet is a great example of a proportional control, being a simple mechanical device it's not a great example of either a derivative or integral control. (After all, I don't know of anyone with a regulator on his or her incoming toilet water.) So, we'll have to go back to our climate control example to explain integration.

Our system can sample the air temperature once every 20 seconds and in doing so discovers that the temperature is 71 degrees rather than 72 degrees. Because our thermostat has only a 2-degree resolution, we need a way to tell the system that we're not really at our set-point if we want to exactly hit 72 degrees. Integration enables us to do this by accumulating our error each time we collect a sample. We add the 1-degree difference to our feedback signal each time we take a sample. Eventually, our feedback signal exceeds our 2-degree threshold, the heater is forced back on, and the process starts all over again.

We can see that it takes all three control modes—proportional, integral, and derivative—to make a functioning PID control system. Derivative and integral functions are there to ensure that the set-point the proportional control works around is accurately achieved and maintained.

IDENTIFY FEEDBACK PATHS

The reason closed-loop control processes work is because they have identified what kind of feedback they need to close the loop. In the heating example, it's the thermometer in the various rooms. In the toilet example, the feedback path is the float. As the water rises, it pushes the float and slowly closes off the valve.

The lesson here is that feedback can be either electronic or mechanical. We just need to identify what kind of feedback we need in our system. The good news is that an examination of our network reveals that it's just one big potential feedback loop!

Each system that lives on the network produces logs and alerts, and most can exchange management messages. Authentication protocols are designed to provide a feedback loop such that failed attempts are reported as alerts and accounts can be locked out. This is a great example of an integration function because it takes a number of them over time to generate a change in the system.

Another good example of a basic feedback loop can be observed in 802.1x,[7] an authentication protocol designed initially for wireless networks. 802.1x works in conjunction with a Remote Authentication Dial In User Service (RADIUS) server and can act as the backbone in a proportional control process because it can act as the valve that meters the amount of risk introduced onto the network.

An 802.1x-enabled network could query each endpoint that makes an attempt to join the network based on the following:

- Endpoint security state
- User authentication
- Resources accessed

A decision can be made to allow privileged access, decline all access, initiate a remediation plan, or allow restricted access. This is a bit more than present 802.1x authentication does, so we discuss how this works a bit later.

---

[7] www.faqs.org/rfcs/rfc3580.html 802.1x RFC reference

IDENTIFY METRICS THAT INFLUENCE OTHER METRICS

You can find some good books on metrics,[8] but by using our process control model, we can more accurately identify metrics that have a greater impact on our security. As you might recall from the previous discussion, time constants are associated with the control process. By adding controls, we're essentially adding delay lines. These delay lines can help us by slowing down the spread of fast-moving worms, or they can hurt us by slowing down the remediation process. Without understanding where and what these metrics are, we have no way of planning for their usage or implementation.

If we make the assumption that no endpoint is going to join our network unless it meets a minimum level of trust, and part of that trust is based on the security posture of the endpoint, it stands to reason that one element that we must consider is patch level.

A good metric to examine at this point is as follows:

- How many endpoints need patches?
- How many patch levels are required per endpoint?
- How long does it take to deploy new patches to the enterprise?
- How has this changed since the last time we looked at it?

An answer to these questions would look something like this:

- 546 of 785, or 70% of endpoints require patches[9]
- 50% require the latest patch (one level down)
- 5% require the latest two patches (two levels down)
- 2 days to approve a deployment
- 45 minutes to deploy to the enterprise
- 6% improvement over last week

Many people would measure the time it takes to load the patch file into the server and push it out to the endpoints, saying that anything else is out of their control. This would only be the tip of the iceberg, however.

Automated patch management systems do help a bit, but how many of the endpoints are truly being updated? Other, "long" time constant questions must be asked:

---

[8]   An especially good one is Andrew Jaquith's book *Security Metrics: Replacing Fear, Uncertainty, and Doubt*, Addison-Wesley (2007).

[9]   Actually, it's 69.554%, but I rounded up for ease of comprehension.

- How long does the approval process take for the deployment?
- How long does it take to determine just how many endpoints are on the network?
- What percentage of the endpoints meets the requirements for the patch?
- What is the difference in deployment time between desktop endpoints and critical resources?

The difference here is that these questions usually generate long-time constant-based responses because a human has to get into the loop to provide an accurate answer.

MAP BUSINESS AND TECHNOLOGY PATHS

This might sound like a no-brainer, but it's a bit more complicated when you dig into it. We've learned to think of technology as complex mechanisms and sophisticated software. However, if you talk to an archeologist, the stone axe is also an example of technology. Ancient technology, yes, but technology nonetheless.

I think this opinion of what "technology" is, is the reason that we ignore a major type of technology that glues our present solutions together: people. When an organization engages in process reengineering, the first thing that they do is look at the relationship of people and how efficiently they exchange information in the quest to accomplish their mission. They ask how well they use the tools that have been afforded them and how many workarounds are in place to "fix" poorly engineered processes. All too often, we're given new technology, but instead of reexamining how we can put this new technology to good use, we just use it to take the place of an older process without understanding how it can make the overall process better.

We do this with our security technology by trying to make it completely transparent. We overlay it on top of our existing processes in the hope that we can get some level of increased protection without disturbing the user community. The problem with that is that it obscures the human element of the security problem to both the practitioners and the users.

To counter this, we must examine our business processes with respect to security so that we can understand where the human paths are with respect to the technology paths. We must also be willing to push for change where needed. Our technology paths, both human and technological, need to be understood if we're going to create a closed-loop process.

We need to be able to identify them and measure them to understand how much of an impact any delay is going to have on our security process. For example, your organization might have an automated patch management system that pushes patches and updates out to thousands of endpoints in a few minutes. Because of this technology, you can stand up in front of the board of directors and tell them that your solution pushes updates to vulnerabilities in minutes! The problem is that in many organizations there's a manual process of evaluating the patch, called *regression testing,* that can take as long as three months!

I'm not saying that you should eliminate regression testing. What I am saying is that for a process control solution to work, you must embrace the idea that you do have human feedback paths that can dramatically degrade your ability to respond to an attack. Regression testing is a business process that has a huge effect on security.

Another example of business and security intersecting is during the incident response cycle. Many people think of incident response as responding to an intrusion detection system (IDS) alert. What if I call the help desk and claim that I'm the CFO and I want my password changed? This is clearly an indicator that my network may be under attack and that something should be done, but how long will it take for this information to move through the business process of the help desk?

This means that we, as security people, need to understand our company's business processes and instead of saying "no," we need to find ways to say "yes" that encourage the business plan to grow and adapt to the changing business objectives. When new technologies appear, we need to understand how those technologies will impact our security and our ability to compete effectively in the marketplace. How many organizations, because the security group is afraid of it, haven't deployed wireless technology regardless of its demonstrated ability to simplify deployment and reduce associated costs?

Who do you think is going to win in the marketplace when the market gets tough and margins get small? The organization afraid to use technology because their security process can't handle it, or the agile group that understands that security and business processes can work together?

CAN WE BUILD A BETTER MODEL?

I believe the answer to this question is a resounding yes. I think that most of what we need is already here; we just need to connect it a little better than we have in the past.

The answer lies in identifying how we allow risk to be introduced into our networks and setting a low limit that prevents endpoints that don't meet our criteria from joining. That instantly begs the question of how to define risk. Well, I think that's the wrong question to ask. I think we need to ask this: What is an acceptable risk? When I go car shopping, I know what I don't want. I don't want a car that's so old that it doesn't have air bags and antilock brakes. I don't want a car that has broken windows and bald tires. I don't want a car that has a torn-up interior or rusty fenders.

I know that I can have a mechanic go over the car with a fine-tooth comb, but that won't eliminate the possibility of a flat tire or an exploding engine later on. I've reduced my risk by examining the car prior to buying it, but I still run the risk that something could happen later.

What I have done by taking the effort to examine the car is begin the process of engendering trust. By setting a minimum level of capability, I have enabled myself to trust the system—in this case, my car—to behave in a manner acceptable to me. I believe that this is also possible on our networks. By setting a minimum level of capability, we can set a minimum level of trust in the systems that join our network.

IDENTIFYING CONTROL NODES

Now that we have a new way of approaching the problem using closed-loop process control, all we have to do is identify those parts of our network that can assist with the basic control modes associated with proportional, integral, and derivative controls.

MAP TECHNOLOGY TO CONTROL NODES

A control node is a place where we can enforce a condition or extract data for the purposes of managing the process. In our networks, we have multiple devices that we can easily consider control nodes, including the following:

- Switches
- Routers
- VPN gateways
- DHCP servers

These are great examples of control nodes because they all have the capability to decide what happens to the traffic that passes through them. In addition, they all can report data that enables us to make other decisions in support of either derivative or integral control functions.

From a basic security perspective, we also have the following:

- Firewalls
- IDSs (intrusion detection systems)
- IPSs (intrusion prevention systems)
- AV systems (antivirus systems)

MAP CONTROL NODES TO CONTROL MODES

When we consider their roles in our PID-based solution, we can see that most of these systems, with a few exceptions, fall under the category of derivative controls. Their purpose is to help us understand just how fast things are changing and to give us notice that we might have to deal with an overshoot of our expected status quo. I say "overshoot" because it's not often that our systems notify us that nothing is happening.

As mentioned previously, we can use some log information to provide an integration function. Three failed login attempts and the endpoint is locked out for a period of ten minutes is a good example of this function.

The exceptions I was referring to earlier are firewalls and VPN concentrators. Firewalls and VPN concentrators can also function as proportional controls if their operation is tied to some action such as limiting traffic loads rather than the simple bimodal yes or no. However, some people are not comfortable with the idea that an automated system can change the configuration of the network. Failures have occurred, and money has been lost, so now there is usually a human in the loop.

In Table 3-1, you can see how the different types of technology map to the four control modes. Devices can be classified as proportional, derivative, or integral. Some devices are simple bimodal on or off and are called *bang-bang controls*.

Table 3-1   Devices Mapped to Control Modes

Device	Function	Proportional	Integral	Derivative	Bang-Bang
Firewall	Perimeter control	Not alone	No	No	Yes
HIDS	Intrusion trigger	No	No	Yes	Yes
NIDS	IRP trigger	No	No	Yes	Yes
HIPS	Attack prevention	No	No	No	Yes
NIPS	Network protection	No	No	No	Yes
SAV	Server AV	No	No	No	Yes
EAV	Endpoint AV	No	No	No	Yes
Router	Traffic control	No	No	No	Yes
Switch	Traffic control	No	No	No	Yes
VPN	Privacy enforcement	Not alone	No	No	Yes
DHCP	Network provisioning	No	No	No	Yes

continues

Table 3-1   Devices Mapped to Control Modes (Continued)

Device	Function	Proportional	Integral	Derivative	Bang-Bang
Probes	Vulnerability assessment	No	Yes	No	No
Logs	Due diligence	No	Yes	Yes	Yes
Alerts	IRP trigger	No	No	Yes	Yes
Correlation (SIM)	Policy management	No	Yes	Yes	No

Now, just to confuse things a little, all these systems also function as bang-bang controls, because they make binary decisions about what to do with traffic. Either it passes traffic or it doesn't. I think it's this dual-mode operation has masked their possible contribution as control systems.

QUANTIFY TIME CONSTANTS

A time constant is just the amount of time it takes to complete any specific part of the process. If it takes one minute to fill the toilet bowl prior to a reflush, the time constant for that process is one minute. If you try to recycle the process before the time constant completes, you wind up with less than satisfactory results. To have an effective process control system, you must understand these time constants; otherwise, you risk creating a system that oscillates wildly around the set-point.

The hard part is identifying them in your process and accurately measuring them. This is part of what the metrics people are trying to do. The problem is that each enterprise has a different set of requirements and dependencies, and therefore the same process in a different environment has different time constants associated with it.

Let's look at the incident response cycle again. Every enterprise that has a decent security program has an incident response plan. It's triggered when something evil happens and an alert is sent "somewhere." Maybe the IDS has seen a suspicious packet stream and has sent out an alert, or perhaps the help desk has too many trouble tickets complaining of slow systems. In many cases, this alert is sent to the security group. Someone with a pager gets the alert and either runs to a computer or, if that person is off-site, makes a phone call. That call can be to someone close to the system or it can be to the data center. After the call has been made, the process of evaluating the event kicks into gear, and the decision process takes over:

- Is it a false positive?
- Is it a truly evil event?

- Is it internal or external?
- Are we hemorrhaging data?
- Can we recover?
- Do we need to call law enforcement?
- How much time has elapsed since the initial alert?

For most organizations, this time constant will probably be on the order of minutes.

By deconstructing the processes, you can discover how long each individual part of it takes, and thus identify where you should put your effort to improve it. Each breakpoint in the process is an opportunity to gather some information about the state of the process.

We can move from the alerting entity to the notification channel, through the analysis process, and into the resolution process, tracking the time it takes for each. For example, we examine our analysis portion of our hypothetical process and discover that the notification process takes more than 15 minutes. Clearly, 15 minutes is not a reasonable time to be notified that a critical condition exists on your network.

Another benefit of this effort is to identify exactly where the various control nodes in your network are, be they technological or human based. You now have a list that you can use or pass on to someone else. What you've done is move from a talent-based response to a role-based response that doesn't pigeonhole you as a resource. You'll also discover that the human-based process components are the ones with the long time constants and, by the way, the ones with the lowest level of repeatability and reliability.

CONTROL PATHS AND THE BUSINESS PROCESSES

You might be wondering what exactly a control path is. A control path is the path that the control and feedback signals take to change the set-point of the system. I believe that you need to map your control paths to the business processes to understand where the cracks in the security process are. Understanding how control signals are generated and understanding where they go, and possibly don't go, can prove critical to your success. This can also help you understand where a little bit of automation can make your life a lot easier (and identify some important metrics).

Let's start by looking at some of the information that passes through a control path. We'll call this our *control signal*. Perhaps that will help us understand how the business process affects our control process. Because we're talking about security, let's define a control signal as anything that is security relevant, such as the following:

- Failed login attempts
- Firewall rule violations
- IDS alerts
- New user requests
- User termination
- New software requests
- New protocol requests
- Software decommissioning
- Network access requests

Next, we have to ask ourselves how much of this information is made available to us by our control nodes as they were defined in the previous section, and how much is made available to us by the business process. As you can see, things such as firewall rule violations and IDS alerts are more like spam, because they're "made available" to us all the time in large numbers. However, the rest of them are made available to us through a business process that may or may not include the security group in the notification path.

The other sad part of this story is that all these processes are open loop—that is, there is no notification that they were completed, denied, or simply disregarded. How do you manage network access requests? Does a verification process occur prior to the decision to allow access? In most cases, the answer is yes, but only for that particular moment. After access has been granted, there is little follow-up to ensure that the system remains compliant with policy, so our control process breaks at the point where we hand the user his or her system.

Another good example starts with a question: Where do login errors go, and how are they processed? A large number of failed logins can indicate that someone is trying to break into your network. If that's the case, the behavior of the network should change in a way that attempts to eliminate those login attempts. In many cases, low-frequency failures are not noticed because they don't trigger the "three failed attempts per hour" rule. This kind of low and slow attack can easily be automated, but is difficult to detect. An interesting metric that you can use as a control signal is the number of failed login attempts compared to the number of successful attempts per user over a longer period of time (for example, a day). You can then compare that number to the preceding day and look for trends.

COMPLETING THE PICTURE

I'm starting this section with some questions: How do we capture the configuration information of our network and processes and do it in a way that enables us to share that information with other professionals? How do we gather all this process control information and represent it in a meaningful way? I suppose we have to start by asking this: What does our network look like?

Some people subscribe to an organic analogy and say that the network is a living organism. Others think that the network is better envisioned as a biosphere. I suppose people are comfortable with organic analogies because it's easier to identify with something that you're familiar with. We're organic, so why shouldn't our view of all things be an organic one? The short answer: because the random nature and boundless complexity of life simply doesn't exist in our networks. Our networks are designed by humans, built by humans, used by humans, and abused by humans. It stands to reason that humans should be able to understand and document them in a reasonable fashion.

Because I'm an engineer, I approach this from an engineer's perspective. Simply put, our networks are really just bits of electronic technology connected by electronic technology into larger and larger islands of electronic technology. The problem is that the islands have gotten so large that it's difficult, if not impossible, for the biological humans who manage them to visualize them.

Another problem is that to properly describe our problem, we need to be able to visualize it so that we can discuss it and share our thoughts with others. Therein lies another problem: Security people have no common nomenclature or iconology to describe our problem. Sure, we have firewalls and IDSs, but how do you draw a picture of it? Even the networking folks resort to drawing pictures of switches. Each vendor has their own clip art libraries that work with programs such as Visio that allow engineers to render network diagrams in great detail. However, no standard set of schematic representations exists.

In our world, if you put 5 people in front of a white board and tell them to draw a picture of a 22-user network that has a firewall, a DMZ, and 25 endpoints of which 20 are user systems, 3 are servers, and 2 are the firewall and switch, you'll get 5 different drawings! We've all been there, in a meeting, and someone draws a firewall as a box with some cross-hatching in it to represent the bricks. Or, they draw a wall and draw flames over it to signify a firewall. Then come the boxes and the notes that are supposed to add clarity to it. When you come back to the white board the next day, you have to spend some time reinterpreting the drawing. What if you get it wrong? "Was that 25 users and 22 endpoints, or was it 25 endpoints and 22 user systems?"

What I'm proposing is that we begin by defining some basic terms and icons so that we can talk about the process from a high level and drill down into more detail as needed. I'll start by saying that there are two basic kinds of endpoints: sources of data and sinks for data. This isn't an uncommon notion. If you have DSL, you probably have aDSL, which is *Asynchronous* Digital Subscriber Line. The aDSL protocol provides for faster download speed than upload speed because the assumption is that you're going to be sending things such as URLs and requests for email while receiving lots of data in Web pages and your now-abundant email.

Now that we have a basic endpoint definition, we need to add some control. Routers and switches essentially provide data routing services, whether that service occurs at Layer 2 or Layer 3. We also need a security gateway, a device that compartmentalizes the network into two or more trust domains. A firewall is a good example of this type of device. Let's add some networking icons. Figure 3-4 shows how we can start.

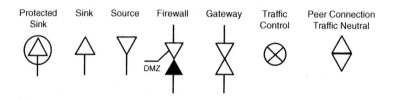

Figure 3-4   Basic security and networking diagram icons. Note that a source of data points toward the network; a sink of data points away. Sources and sinks of data can combine as gateways or peer connections.

Occam's razor principle states that simple is better, that the simple answer is probably the correct one. In our security world, things start to fail when they get overly complex, so the goal is to keep our nomenclature and iconology simple. But, having a workable set of icons is only half the problem. We need a way to connect them that helps us differentiate between the different paths of information and control. Looking at Figure 3-5, we see that we need three basic types of traffic: network, infrastructure, and process. So, now we have the basic elements that we need to be able to draw a network. Putting it all together, our 22-user network would look like our drawing in Figure 3-6. You can see that we added one additional icon: a diamond that represents the number of users on the network. (Some people have suggested to me that users should be represented by a rock, but I think a diamond is more appropriate because it signifies the creative potential that many users truly represent.)

Now that we have the basic network elements, we need to add the process control modes to our lexicon. I selected the icons in Figure 3-7 because I believe that they quickly and easily represent their function. The up arrow in the integration function shows the accumulation of error; the horizontal arrow depicts a stable set-point. Just to confuse things a bit, the device that performs the derivative function is also referred to as a differentiator (and thus the downward arrow as depicted in Figure 3-7). A bang-bang control is pretty much on or off, so I thought a simple switch would do nicely.

We have some good schematic icons, but we still haven't identified the summation or correlation points. I think that the icons in Figure 3-8 will work well because they visually represent their function. Okay, maybe the bull's eye is a reach for the correlation function, but I think it still works.

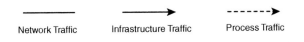

Figure 3-5   Path designations allow us to tell the difference between our network data, the infrastructure management data, and our control path data.

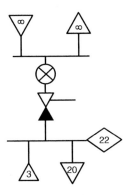

Figure 3-6   A complete schematic drawing of our 22 users, 23 endpoints, firewall, switch, and the Internet. Note that the DMZ network is empty.

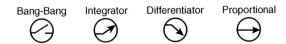

Figure 3-7   Icons for the four basic control modes. A differentiator provides the derivative data, and the integrator provides integral data for the summation function.

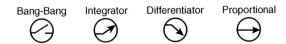

Correlation   Summation

Figure 3-8   Summation and correlation functions. Summation adds the PID signals to produce an output, whereas correlation provides either integral or derivative signal outputs.

Note that correlation and summation are *not* the same process. Correlation examines data looking for trends; summation adds control inputs in an attempt to provide a master control.

Now that we have some basic tools, let's look at a couple of drawings that pull it all together.

Examining our climate control problem and using the schematic icons outlined in this section, a drawing of our climate control system looks like Figure 3-9. Notice that the room is depicted as a sink and that it's between the thermostat and the control process.

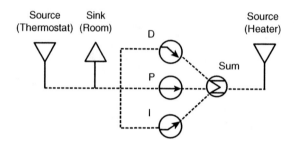

Figure 3-9   A graphic depiction of our climate control system using process control icons P, D, I, and S.

We need to discuss one more process control element: gain. Gain is the multiplier that acts to increase or decrease the impact of our control inputs. Think of it as leverage in the system. In this case, the gain of the system is fixed by the size of the room. If the heater capacity remains the same, and we increase the size of the room, it will take longer for the heater to move the temperature to the desired set-point. The implication here is that the gain of the system has been reduced.

So, now that we have a method and some nomenclature for depicting our control process, let's apply it to our network. Adding to the 25-user network we defined in the early paragraphs of this chapter, we can make some basic assumptions about our network:

- We have a system for probing our network for vulnerabilities.
- We have some way of identifying intrusion attempts.
- Gain is going to be controlled by how many systems we have.

Looking at Figure 3-10, we can see that our network has the following:

- 25 registered users
- 28 endpoints in total

- 3 server endpoints
- 22 user endpoints
- 1 firewall
- 1 probe system
- 1 security information manager
- 1 IDS
- 1 switch (infrastructure)
- 1 connection to the Internet

Looking at this in light of our control nomenclature, we have the following:

- 24 sinks (user endpoints, IDS, SIM)
- 4 sources (servers and probe)
- 1 integrator (IDS)
- 1 differentiator (probe)
- 1 correlator (SIM)
- 1 bang-bang (firewall)
- 1 control device

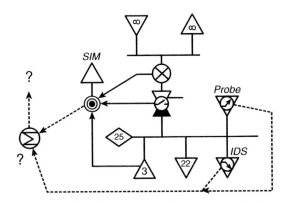

Figure 3-10 A process control depiction of our fictitious network. Note that the control outputs termi-
nate at a summation point that has no input back into the system.

It becomes pretty obvious that we're missing a few critical components. The control outputs from the probe, the IDS, and the SIM go to a summation function, which isn't
defined! We need to understand what this missing mystery function is. It's clearly not the

SIM, because the SIM is yet another provider of feedback into the system. The SIM doesn't affect the security set-point of the system, and the purpose of the summation process is to provide a control input. However, a great deal of valuable endpoint-related information gets sent to the SIM. Perhaps some of this information, in conjunction with something new, can help us identify this missing summation process.

KEY POINTS

The old way of modeling networks—that networks are living organisms that can't be controlled—is based on thinking that doesn't take into account basic science and engineering principles. Unfortunately for us, this kind of thinking has controlled our network designs and management techniques for too long.

WE NEED A BETTER IDEA

The fact that we're not gaining any ground in the security world tells us that we need a better idea. We need to understand how our systems interact and how the information that they produce can be used to our advantage. We need to apply basic engineering control principles to our network to control how risk is introduced so that we can predict how our networks are going to react when they are attacked.

TRUST VS. RISK

Although risk is an important factor in determining the overall state of security for a network, perhaps a better way of looking at individual endpoints should be based on trust. By setting a minimum level of configuration for each endpoint, you begin to build the element of trust into each system. You trust that a system will behave in a pre-described manner when faced with security stress.

PROCESS CONTROL HELPS BUILD A MODEL

The basic engineering principle that can help us is based on process control technology. Process control technology uses the PID algorithm to ensure that a predetermined set-point is achieved and maintained within identified limits.

All the devices on the network have a role, and that role can be associated with some form of control. By using this new model, we can more accurately set an acceptable limit of risk, build trust, and thus protect our networks more effectively. In addition, we can identify those elements of technology that are wasting our time and budget, because we will more easily understand their role and contribution in the solution.

BUSINESS PROCESSES CANNOT BE IGNORED

As you map control processes to control modes and feedback paths, you must remember to look at the business process that they affect (and vice versa). The human element plays a large role in those processes and in many cases is the most unreliable or variable element within it.

WE NEED A COMMON LANGUAGE

Like all other engineering disciplines, the information security discipline needs a universal set of icons and nomenclature that allows security professionals to exchange information effectively and reliably. Our present system of scratching out bricks with fire on them and clouds representing networks and the associated endpoints isn't working.

The set of icons presented in this chapter form the foundation for a schematic representation of our security elements and their associated control processes.

Missing Link Discovered

We've decided to take a different look at how to solve our problem, and in the preceding chapter we talked about how a different viewpoint can help shape what our solution will eventually look like. But, what is the link between having a secure network and having to deal with the traditional problems of security? In the preceding chapter, we clearly saw that as an engineering domain, security hasn't developed as quickly as we would have hoped. As a matter of fact, a great number of very smart people have developed a huge number of products, but we still have the same day-to-day problems plaguing us.

As engineers, we need to ask ourselves what common element we have throughout all of this that will enable us to solve this problem? It is the very thing that some folks are claiming has disappeared: the endpoints that define the perimeter. More specifically, it is the relationship between the endpoints and the network that has been ignored.

PRÉCIS

No network security solution can work in a vacuum. There is always something pulling security in one direction while users are pushing it in another. The solution du jour grabs our attention, and we hope upon hope that this is the one. But, always present in the corner of our minds is the knowledge that there is no silver bullet. Looming in that same dark corner is the reminder that we must solve the problem and solve it soon.

Our previous discussions regarding process control in Chapter 3, "Something Is Missing," led us in a direction that helps us unify our solution concept in a way that has never been done before. We saw in that chapter that a complex summation process was missing from our security solution.

We can now represent our networks schematically, as represented in Figure 4-1. Doing so enables us to focus on the functions rather than the artwork.

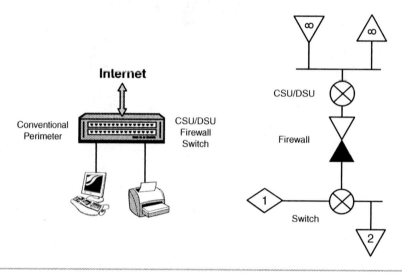

Figure 4-1   A pictorial and schematic representation of a typical network perimeter. We have represented one user, two endpoints, a switch, a firewall, and an Internet connection.

We're going to look at how the secure endpoint and process control can work together to form the backbone of our security process. By leveraging the endpoint's capability to self-assess and to communicate that assessment with the network, and the network's ability to dynamically reconfigure itself, we can form the foundation of a proportional control that will ensure that our networks are secure and reliable.

SPECIAL POINTS OF INTEREST

As we begin this chapter, keep your existing network architecture and your business practices in mind. As you begin to understand how the solution is going to work, you're going to have to manage the differences.

New technology will allow the endpoint to play a much more important role in ensuring enterprise security than it does today. Instead of being the source of malware, the endpoint can be the point at which a decision is made that prevents untrusted systems from gaining access.

While on the subject of trust, a slightly different concept of trust versus risk needs to be examined. Instead of using risk as a decision point, we will discuss how trust can be used instead.

Two Data Points Hint at a Solution

Chapter 2, "Why Security Fails," discussed how much damage there was and how worms and viruses were running rampant on our networks. In subsequent chapters, we examined what hasn't worked in conventional networks and have postulated a possible solution concept that might work to our advantage. Because we've been looking at the 50K-foot level, it's time we lost some altitude and begin looking at some of the details of our solution.

From the discussion in Chapter 3, we learned that an analysis of our networks based on process control tells us that we're missing a central proportional control that we can hang our other security tools off of. We have many security tools that can function as integral and derivative controls, but these tools are acting independently of each other and are not tied to a central controllable proportional process.

So, the question becomes, where do we find this proportional control? Are we going to have to completely reengineer our networks for them to work securely? Where should we start? Well, it seems to me that the logical answer is that we start with the endpoint itself, because all the other technology is there to support it. Yes, some networks are going to require some rework, but for the most part we should be able to make this work with what we already have (with some minor additions).

Because we're going to use a process control model as the basis for our solution, it stands to reason that we need to understand what the set point is going to be and how we're going to set it. In our examples, that was easy. We set a temperature on the thermostat, or we set a level of water in the bowl. It isn't going to be that easy here because of how many different interpretations there are for the proposed metric for our set point: risk. The nice thing about risk is that how much you're willing to accept is based on your particular situation. Some organizations are willing to accept more, whereas others aren't as predisposed to allowing as much as a camera phone into their facilities.

As the title of this section implies, we have two data points that we can use to craft our solution. First, we have a mechanism that acts as a source of "energy" for our system. If we think about how evil things are introduced into our networks, we can consider this as potential risk in much the same way that the plumbing represents the potential for water. Second, our network can function as a valve, controlling how much "risk" is introduced into the network.

ATTACK VECTORS

After much painful research, it becomes clear that the attack vector of choice is the end-point. I know that a bunch of you are laughing your heads off and saying that it's pretty obvious that it's the endpoint, but I hope that you appreciated the sarcasm nonetheless. The fact is that sometimes you just have to say the obvious thing for the record even if it sounds sarcastic. The thing that's not so obvious is how the endpoint will play a role in our process control model. I believe that it has something to do with risk entropy, or the introduction of risk into the network environment.

In the discussion of risk, we talk about ways to reduce it and ways of quantifying it, but we never talk about where the risk enters the environment. We kind of talk around it by saying that we're doing scans and patch management, but we never say it. And yes, many types of risk are associated with our information systems, but clearly the endpoint is above and beyond the largest contributor to loss and therefore risk.

Why? Because most endpoints are general-purpose computers equipped with the tools necessary to generate, manipulate, store, send, and receive digital data. Hackers use this general-purpose functionality to their own advantage, and there's no reason we shouldn't be able to use it to our advantage, too.

We shouldn't ignore the other potential attack vectors, such as social engineering and outright breaking and entering; but if we can force the evil ones to use these other vectors, we'll have succeeded in our goal of securing the endpoint.

PROCESS CONTROL ANALYSIS

I remember when I first started down the path of analyzing the network with process control eyes. When I started, it was with the intention of understanding *how* the network security process control function worked. I was astonished when I discovered that there was no underlying proportional control. What I found was a number of pieces of technology that were strung together with the good intention of solving the problem.

My work told me that we needed something capable of linking the side of the system that introduces risk pressure with the side of the system that controlled or mitigated risk to create a functional proportional control. In our present model, we allow the risk to be introduced onto the network, and then we try to identify it and eliminate it through the application of our security tools. The problem with that is that if there's a leak, the entire system breaks down. In short, we had no way of closing the loop in the process because we still really hadn't identified where that loop was and how it worked.

ENDPOINTS LOOK LIKE THE LINK

In all of our networks, whether they're Windows based, Linux, or Blackberrys, the one thing they have in common is the link between user and network. The endpoint is that link. It forms the interface between the user and the resources that the network represents. For that reason, the endpoint is also the starting point in our quest to find a proportional control.

We can't ignore that the endpoint is probably the smartest node on our networks. It has the capability to know more about itself than any other endpoint. Sure, network infrastructure devices know about operational statistics, and a few of them can tell you the fingerprint of the build on them, but how many of them can tell you whether they comply with corporate policy?

That knowledge—the knowledge of compliance—is what we need to have if we're going to build secure networks. We can secure an endpoint; but if we can't keep it secure, we're going to lose in the end. We need to use that inherent intelligence of the endpoint to our advantage if we're going to ensure that our endpoints, and thus our networks, stay secure.

TARGET OF MALWARE

We know that endpoints are definitely the link to introducing malware into the network. As you may recall from earlier discussions, the endpoint is the target of choice for most attacks. Some involve the user; some do not. Even if the user's not involved, the endpoints can wind up being the host of some pretty evil activity if the botnets get a foothold.

We usually only think about the network when we start thinking about security. We've gotten so used to hearing about how worms and viruses propagate that we've forgotten about the multitude of other ways that a system can be infected. For example, a little over a year ago, my CEO came to me with what he called a really cool toy. It was a secure USB drive that he'd received from the CEO of another company. It was in a really neat box and looked like a thick pen that I could picture in the pocket protector of a geek (before I could see it in the pocket of a $300 fitted CEO shirt). I asked him, "Did you stick this into your notebook?" He replied, "*No!* You've got me way too scared to plug anything into my USB." Because the system was designed for Windows, I figured that I could plug it into my non-Windows system and watch the fun. Imagine my surprise when all I could see was a mere 256K! Now my suspicion was aroused, and I had to find out what was going on. As it turned out, this cute little device automatically loaded a system driver that performed the duty of encrypting and decrypting data to a much larger, and otherwise invisible, 256M data partition. I thought to myself, what if this had been a malicious device? My CEO had heeded my warning and was glad he did after I showed him what I'd found. It was a legitimate product, but what if it hadn't been?

The security industry is starting to develop new tools that control just how the user interfaces with the system. USB drives and memory sticks have been used to install Trojans and viruses, so our reaction is to limit their use. Key-logging devices have been placed between the keyboard and the system to steal passwords. These, and their software cousins, have been responsible for all manner of havoc.

Embedded systems are also at risk here. As dedicated function endpoints, they tend to be the most overlooked systems. As the future rolls on, we're going to have to embrace a methodology that incorporates how we address the risk associated with these kinds of endpoints.

Medical systems also need to be included in this solution. I'm not going to go into the long, laborious process of describing the medical certification process, but suffice it to say that without some sort method for ensuring that they meet some minimal level of trust, we're going to have to segregate them from the rest of the endpoints.

ENABLE NETWORK ACCESS

I suppose that this is the "if you're a carpenter, every problem looks like a nail" kind of thing. It depends on your perspective as to where network access begins. If you talk to network engineers, they may tell you that it happens at the port on the switch. If you talk to Microsoft engineers, they may tell you that network access begins after you've been authenticated with the Active Directory.

There may even be those who say that network access begins when you can see bits from the network. Their argument is that, in essence, you have access to the digital data even though you haven't been authenticated. This is pretty much a security person's view of the world. If you can get physical access, all bets are off! I can't tell you how many times I've heard the phrase "if I can get to the keyboard, I can own the system."

The key point here is that you have to control access to the stream of bits somehow. We look at the endpoint as a way to do that by requiring authentication prior to giving access to the system. However, as we know from the previous paragraphs, we need the network to help if we're going truly prevent unauthorized access to the bit stream. We may not be able to prevent someone from gaining access to the keyboard, but we can surely prevent that keyboard from gaining access to the rest of the endpoint population.

WHAT NEEDS TO HAPPEN

For our solution to work, a number of things need to happen pretty much in parallel. We need to make sure that the system doesn't get infected with unwanted software, we need to ensure that the software that we want on the endpoint is installed and configured correctly, and we need some way of guaranteeing that the system complies with our stated policies. We need a way to ensure the integrity of the system.

As I stated early in the chapter, we haven't built our networks around the Proportional, Integral, and Derivative (PID) process, so we really don't have a basic proportional control. Add to that that defining risk is a series of books in its own right, and the problem begins to get complicated pretty fast. However, I think that we can craft a proportional control if we make the basic statement that we know what we don't want on our networks. At a minimum, we don't want the following:

- Viruses
- Worms
- Illegal software
- Spyware
- Unauthorized users
- Unauthorized endpoints

From these basic desires, we can start to drill down and get some details.

BASIC BLOCKING AND TACKLING

Before we go any further, we need to get the basics out of the way. These are the basic blocking and tackling drills that have to be done, and done properly, before we can even begin to think about complicating things. I'm going to assume that you have a basic build process (if you don't, you're going to need to buy another book). So, at the minimum, we need to make sure that each system has up-to-date antivirus software and that it's configured with the latest data files, that the system is patched and updated, and that the endpoint has a functioning firewall.

We can look at the huge number of worms and viruses and be safe in the conclusion that unpatched unprotected systems will be attacked, but for the most part we know that if our endpoints are patched, and we have detection and remediation tools, the exposure, and therefore the risk, is kept to a minimum.

When I say "minimum," there are some things that are difficult, if not impossible, to protect against. Closely guarded vulnerabilities, also called 0-days, are difficult to protect against because nobody knows that they're there until it's too late.

MANAGE HOST INTEGRITY

Now that we have something to work with, we can deconstruct our basic requirements a bit. When we do, we come to the conclusion that each endpoint needs to do the following:

- Ensure operating system integrity
- Validate system configuration
- Be remotely manageable

The aspect of remote management is a critical factor for success. You need to be able to designate and enforce a minimum configuration regardless of user protests. We need a policy that says that any endpoint that doesn't comply with our requirements is denied access to the network. I know that this is going to start many an argument, but the reality is that it only takes one noncompliant system to screw up our network.

Looking at Figure 4-2, we can modify our draconian rules a bit if we incorporate the notion of remediation and compartmentalization. Looking at this another way, we can ask this question: How does the network know that it can trust the endpoint?

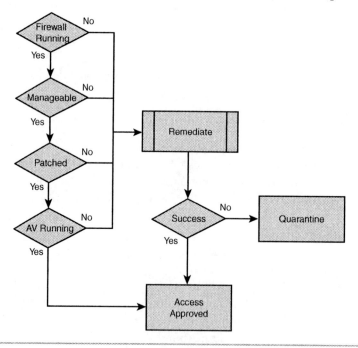

Figure 4-2   Basic network access should be quarantined if the endpoint can't pass four simple tests.

CONTROL ACCESS TO THE NETWORK

In short, if the network and the endpoint don't converse, there's no way that the network can tell whether a system is trustworthy. You have to manually get in the process to prevent rogue connections.

The "simple" way to accomplish this is a thing that many security people do already: They turn off any unused ports. I say "simple" because in theory all one has to do is to remove a patch cable from the wiring closet or send a command to the switch to "down" the port. In reality, this usually requires a call to the network folks, an email request, or the opening of the dreaded trouble ticket.

Disconnecting unused ports is one of those things that is deemed "best practices"—because our physical security systems aren't perfect, and anyone who manages to slip through the door can just plug into an unused jack. An additional benefit is that those who want to gain legitimate access to the network must verify with the security group that they have met the proper requirements and that the system they want to connect to the network is trustworthy.

Like I said at the beginning, this is a manual and sometimes time-consuming process. However, this is a small price to pay for the benefit of a decision point that we can use to control access to our network. The basic idea is referred to as network access control, or NAC, and there are some new ways to accomplish this same functionality without the manual labor.

NETWORK ACCESS CONTROL

The goal of NAC is to ensure that only systems that meet our stated level of trust gain access to our information resources. It relies on the idea that a system must comply with policy prior to connecting to the network. Present access control methodologies are varied, and some are proprietary, but the end result is that they all prevent unauthorized systems from connecting to the network.

Trusted Network Connect (TNC), Network Admission Control (NAC), Cisco Network Access Control (CNAC), and Network Access Protection (NAP) are all different flavors of the same idea.

The protocols from the TCG are a proposed open standard that many vendors are already generating products for. Although its core authentication mechanism is based on their notion of a "trusted platform"—that is, hardware-based system identification—the basic model is a good one that can be deployed across large enterprises.

The Cisco and Microsoft efforts are, of course, proprietary and are designed to leverage the strengths of their respective product lines. In addition, they use a version of the

Extensible Authentication Protocol[1] (EAP) called the Protected Extensible Authentication Protocol (PEAP) that was jointly developed by Cisco, Microsoft, and RSA Security.

The NAC method uses the 802.1x protocol and a client-side agent called a supplicant (see Figure 4-3). The supplicant communicates with an 802.1x-enabled network device, such as a switch or an access point, and the switch communicates with an authentication server running RADIUS.[2] If the RADIUS server can authenticate the user, it sends a message back to the switch, permitting the connection. Once connected to the network, the normal process of getting an IP address and authenticating with services such as Active Directory (AD) takes place. A quick peek at Figure 4-4 will show you how 802.1x and EAP sit on top of the Ethernet protocols. RADIUS is compliant with PPP, CHAP, PAP, and UNIX authentication protocols but must use EAP extensions to the RADIUS protocol to do NAC.

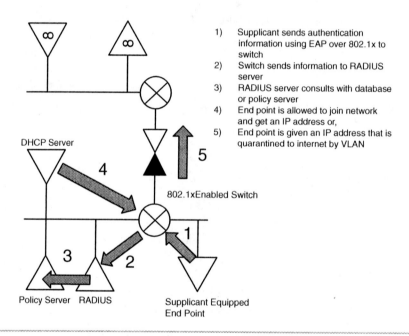

1) Supplicant sends authentication information using EAP over 802.1x to switch
2) Switch sends information to RADIUS server
3) RADIUS server consults with database or policy server
4) End point is allowed to join network and get an IP address or,
5) End point is given an IP address that is quarantined to internet by VLAN

DHCP Server

802.1xEnabled Switch

Policy Server   RADIUS

Supplicant Equipped
End Point

Figure 4-3   How NAC works on the network. A system can be allowed access, denied access, or directed to specific quarantined networks.

---

[1] RFC 2284, *PPP EAP*

[2] RFC 2865, *Remote Authentication Dial In User Service*

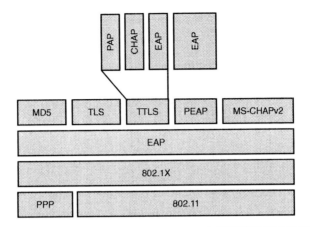

Figure 4-4 EAP can use Tunneled Transport Layer Protocol, thus simplifying the authentication overhead required from certificates in regular TLS.

Other methods of controlling access to the network don't require a change in infrastructure. Dynamic Host Configuration Protocol (DHCP) enforcement is another way to accomplish a similar outcome. The basic premise is simple: If the system doesn't meet the minimum standards, it isn't given an IP address.

VERIFY A MINIMUM LEVEL OF TRUST

Although we can authenticate the user, the 802.1x protocol by itself isn't sufficient to provide us with the detailed information that we need to determine whether we trust the requesting endpoint. 802.1x tells us about the user attempting to gain access to the network, and TNC associates the user to that endpoint, but it still tells us nothing about the state of the endpoint's security.

Prior to allowing a system to connect to our network, we must somehow verify some level of compliance with our policy. Some vendors have extended the functionality of 802.1x by using extensions provided in the RADIUS protocol and enhancing the amount of information sent to the network.

ALLOW ONLY TRUSTED SYSTEMS

Twelve years ago, Cheswick and Bellovin featured a comic strip by Wiley on the cover of their book, *Firewalls and Internet Security: Repelling the Wily Hacker*. The comic strip showed a bunch of barbarians standing in front of a carnival barker's stand. The barker had a sign that said "must be at least this high to storm castle." The height line was clearly set much taller than any of the barbarians, and was thus stopping them from sacking the king, who was peeking out the corner of a window. It was a valid notion then, and it's a valid notion now. "Trust, but verify" seems to be the catchphrase for security lately. However, I prefer the phase "comply and connect" because it really says what we want to happen. Show me that you're trustworthy, and you can come in.

Because the goal is to allow only trusted systems to gain access to our network, we need some way to determine whether the system is truly trustworthy. You might recall from Chapter 3 that the security information manager (SIM) can potentially contain some endpoint-related information. We could use this information, but why not go directly to the source of the information? Using an agent capable of examining the endpoint and sending the information via the extended protocol, we can determine whether the endpoint meets our minimum level of trust. We can ask the following:

- Are all the patches and updates installed?
- Is the firewall running and configured to policy?
- Is the antivirus (AV) running and updated?
- Are only authorized applications running?
- Is this an authorized user?

If these questions are answered "yes," we can permit the endpoint access to the network. But, what do you do if the answer to any of those questions is "no?"

REMEDIATION OF EVIL THINGS

Once again, I'm going to cite the manual process that we use so that we can examine ways to make it more efficient. If you come into work and your notebook won't connect to the virtual private network (VPN), you call the help desk. In the fullness of time, someone will show up in your cube with a disc that has the latest VPN client configuration on it. After a few minutes, you're back online. A good hour can go by before you're fixed.

Worse, you might have an endpoint that doesn't have the latest patch that prevents the "Want2HaveYourBaby" worm from sending itself and rude pictures of Paris Hilton to everyone in your address book. Which, by the way, your CEO has launched against everyone in your company.

Manual processes don't work here.

What if when you connect to the network an agent checks your policy against one that lives on a server? If there is a newer one, the agent downloads it and uses it to check your system. The agent can determine whether you have the required patch. If you do not have the patch, the network automatically redirects you to a remediation server that ensures that you are up-to-date before the worm has a chance to attack.

LEVERAGE TECHNOLOGY TO ENFORCE DECISION

When we have a decision about the level of trust we have in an endpoint trying to gain access to our network, we can enforce this decision through network configuration. Let's suppose that a rogue endpoint is trying to attach to your network. Because it doesn't have the requisite agent to tell the network that it's trustworthy, the network assumes that this rogue endpoint is hostile and either blocks its access completely or only allows limited access. I know of a few companies that have a policy that says any endpoint that connects to the network gets Internet access by default.

By taking advantage of how the Internet protocol works and how switches and routers operate, we can enforce quarantines and prevent untrusted systems from gaining access to our networks.

KEY POINTS

We can put together a solution that approximates a proportional control in our networks by using the endpoint and existing infrastructure that ensures that each and every endpoint complies with a minimum set of standards.

ENDPOINT IS KEY

The endpoint can be smart enough to check itself and communicate that information to the network. Our network technology is capable enough to automatically and dynamically change virtual LAN (VLAN) configurations in switches and assign and reassign IP addresses to endpoints, thereby ensuring that only trusted systems gain access to critical network services. Endpoints can take advantage of Web-based update capabilities to download and install patches and required software.

MUST-LEVERAGE TECHNOLOGY

The various pieces of technology exist to form a basic proportional control that moderates the introduction of risk into our networks. Protocols, hardware and software, must be connected in such a way that they automatically reconfigure themselves based on our dictated policy. Protocols such as 802.1x, EAP, RADIUS, and DHCP can be used to provide access, restrict access, or completely deny access to noncompliant systems.

THE NETWORK IS PART OF PROPORTIONAL SOLUTION

We have solutions for the endpoint. We have solutions for our network. What we need to do is embrace the fact that the endpoints and the network must be able to communicate with each other. The network is not the enemy of the endpoint, and the endpoint is not the enemy of the network. By taking some basic functionality afforded to us by our network devices, combining it with some functionality that exists on the endpoint, and adding a little glue, we now can build a functional proportional control.

Endpoints and Network Integration

Although this is a book about endpoint security, I hope that my point regarding closed-loop process control (CLPC) and how the endpoints need to work with the network to ensure complete security has been heard.

The network and the devices and people who connect to it must work as a team if predictable and reliable control is to be achieved. Although many of us are going to have to deal with the legacy hardware and software that has been added to our networks over the course of time, some of us are in the process of designing the networks of tomorrow.

No matter what your present network state, if you make decisions that drive your network toward a closed-loop process control model, you will be in a better position to address the security issues of today and those of tomorrow.

PRÉCIS

We start this chapter with a discussion about architecture and how your existing infrastructure can influence your decision on how to integrate CLPC into your enterprise. The question "do you need a forklift?" is discussed, as are some interesting alternatives to a complete reworking of your network.

We then move to a discussion about how the vendor community supports endpoint security and integrity. We discuss who some of the players are and what their strengths and weaknesses are.

Making a decision about permitting or denying access to the network without some form of remediation is clearly a nonstarter, so we discuss vulnerabilities and some remediation technology.

SPECIAL POINTS OF INTEREST

The discussion regarding what a vulnerability is seems to have sparked a vigorously contested set of definitions. Although this is a subject worthy of much discussion, we are going to take a pass on it for now. In this chapter, we use the term *vulnerability* to mean a way to attack the endpoint and the network.

We expand the definition of *authentication* a little bit to encompass the operating system and associated applications. This is key to the CLPC concept because trust is measured against a stated policy.

We've tried to solve this problem on the network and at the endpoint. Vendors, depending on their product, pick a direction and work from it à la Cisco and Microsoft. The plain fact of the matter is that the network needs to help the endpoint, and the endpoint needs to help the network. Only through this symbiosis can we provide the requisite controls needed to build a CLPC.

ARCHITECTURE IS KEY

When we start any design process, prudent engineering tells us that we should start with some basic assumptions that will drive our architecture. When we go down a specific architectural path, changing our minds or changing the basic assumptions usually means making compromises that reduce the effectiveness of our intended design.

There are three ways to architect our control solution. One is based on industry standards, and two are based on proprietary solutions offered by the leaders in their respective lines of business.

Cisco is a networking vendor that is trying to control and protect the endpoint, and Microsoft is an endpoint solution vendor trying to use parts of the network infrastructure to add security.

Some vendors, such as Juniper (through their Funk acquisition) and Symantec (through their Sygate acquisition), have expanded the capability of the 802.1x supplicant beyond simple authentication, and this is where we begin to see the foundation for a real proportional control standard that truly closes the loop.

These new products, such as Symantec's Enterprise Protection,[1] go beyond checking the endpoint to ensure that system-level policy issues have been complied with prior to allowing the system connectivity with the network. They also add some protection to the system that ensures that it's capable of protecting itself and the data it contains.

BASICS

To make CLPC work, you need to have an infrastructure that supports it. You have to have some mechanism that enforces your policy; otherwise, it's a voluntary participation model.

You can work from two basic choices if your intent is to actively enforce your policy: 802.1x and Dynamic Host Configuration Protocol (DHCP). Of course, you can realize a passive type of policy enforcement through compartmentalization. The downside of compartmentalization is that it adds complexity to your network architecture, and complexity means the increased possibility of failure. More on compartmentalization later.

HOW OLD IS OLD?

So, let's assume that we're going to use 802.1x as our enforcement mechanism. We've gone out and bought a product that supports our notion of CLPC and have installed the agents and supplicants on our endpoints.

Having clients that support 802.1x is great, but you also need the network infrastructure to support it. Much, if not all, of the older infrastructure doesn't support 802.1x. An easy way to tell is to look at when you bought your network equipment. If you bought your stuff before the days of wireless, you don't have the ability to do 802.1x. If you're lucky enough, you may be able to upgrade, but it's going to be expensive.

During the course of my day-to-day business, one of my clients, a major financial institution, did a survey of their equipment and determined that it would cost more than a million dollars to upgrade their network to the point where they could support 802.1x.

Oh, and there's all those pesky embedded systems that we look at in Chapter 12, "Embedded Devices," such as printers and respirators, that don't speak 802.1x (or antivirus for that matter) that still need to be addressed.

---

[1] Symantec bought Sygate in 2005. SEP, Sygate Enterprise Protection, was renamed to Symantec Enterprise Protection.

COMPARTMENTALIZATION IS STILL EFFECTIVE

As you work through the pains of designing a new network architecture, you realize that the real fun is going to start when you begin the cutover. Few of us have had the opportunity to build a brand new network from the ground up. You usually have to transition from the old architecture to the new one in some controlled manner. This transition represents a huge problem for mergers and acquisitions people.

This is where compartmentalization can be utilized as a migration tool as well as a security tool. By placing security gateways between your enforced network and your legacy network, you can reduce the security risk to your entire network. Notice that I didn't say "eliminate"; I said "reduce."

But how do you compartmentalize? Do you do it based on the classification of systems and data, or should you break your network into functional zones? It makes a difference, especially if access from zone to zone is managed by access control lists (ACLs) in your routers or firewalls. Making the incorrect choice can mean that the business processes are impacted in significant ways.

For example, Figure 5-1 depicts a basic method of compartmentalization that is predicated on use. It is the classic concentric architecture. The users from the Internet have limited access to extranet services based on business needs and requirements. The dotted line surrounding them suggests a certain level of porosity that must be tolerated with such a service. However, when you get to the corporate network perimeter, you're greeted with a classic firewall, antivirus (AV), and intrusion detection. Moving to the intranet services, we encounter some access controls that limit how we interact with the supplied service. We might not have write access, and the service might not be available to all areas of the network.

The user area of the network is our next layer. It will have access to the Internet, intranet, and possibly the extranet. It will also have limited access to critical internal services. Critical internal services are protected by access controls such as ACLs, authentication, and authorization services. In the Windows world, these controls are enforced using Active Directory (AD) and groups. In non-Windows worlds, this means Remote Authentication Dial In User Service (RADIUS) and Lightweight Directory Access Protocol (LDAP).

The downside of this architecture is that it is fairly promiscuous, and if you're not up-to-date with your AV data files or you get hit with some zero-day exploit, you'll have quite a bit of damage to address.

At the other end of the spectrum is a method used to compartmentalize your network that is based on carving it into containment zones, as shown in Figure 5-2. By creating numerous zones and controlling all communication between the zones through the use of a firewall, you hope to prevent the spread of viruses and control the movement of data.

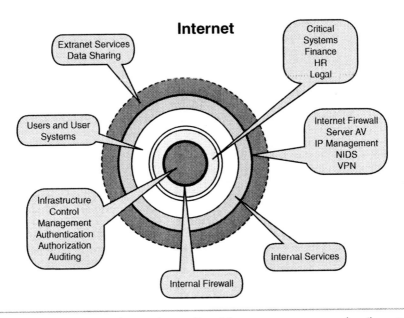

Figure 5-1 Classic compartmentalization by use. Core infrastructure systems are heavily protected and managed.

Unfortunately, the underlying message is that you don't trust your endpoints or the people who use them. You don't trust the endpoints to protect themselves, which implies that you don't have much faith in your security program. I can understand the "belt and suspenders" approach, but the rules, ACLs, and complex procedure that must be in place to support them begins to look like a ripe place for errors and failure.

As you can see from Figure 5-2, each zone has a firewall and therefore a firewall ruleset associated with it. You must explicitly allow traffic to leave a zone, and you must explicitly allow traffic to enter a zone. That means that if you want the folks in User Zone 1 to be able to access Corporate Services, you must tell the User Zone 1 firewall to allow traffic to pass outbound, and you must tell the Corporate Services firewall to allow the inbound traffic. I know what you're thinking: "The firewalls allow all outbound traffic by default." The firewall will allow outbound traffic unless you don't trust the systems on the inside and you configure the firewalls such that they stop all traffic by default. Remember that one of the purposes of such a design is to prevent the spread of viruses.

It's been my experience that such a zone-based architecture can become overly complex fairly quickly if not managed properly. It's easy for this type of architecture to develop a life of its own and in the process become quite a nightmare for the users and the security team. I've seen examples of this architecture where every change to the network required security group approval because a firewall rule change was necessary.

This created quite a bottleneck. A special group had to be created just to address the changes to the firewall that were required on a daily basis just to keep the business going. The result was the inability of business groups within the organization to innovate at the speed of business.

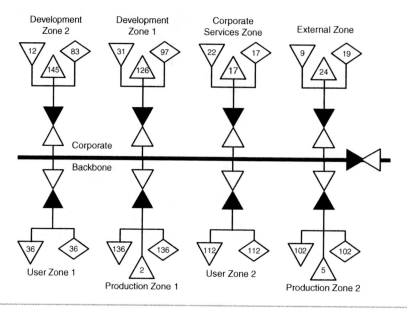

Figure 5-2   Zone-based compartmentalization can grow to be very complex.

Another victim in a complex zone-based architecture can be service level agreements (SLAs). SLAs are there to ensure that a basic level of functionality is always present so that business can be processed. SLAs ensure that file servers are always running with minimum delays and that Web services provide their proscribed function to your user community. In a complex zone-based architecture, the tools required to measure and gauge service levels can be severely hampered (if not completely cut off).

To be fair, this type of architecture usually results from numerous mergers and acquisitions and the requirement that the security people have to manage the overall security of a patched-together network. I guess that means that it's the financial guys' fault that the network is overly complex.

I will concede that compartmentalization, if done properly, is also an effective tool for controlling the spread of malware. It gets back to the question I asked before, however: Do you want to compartmentalize by data classification or by function? If you're a government agency or the military, this question already has one answer: You've compartmentalized by data classification. This seems easy enough until you need to connect services or share data between classification zones. As shown in Figure 5-3, the Bell/LaPadula rule states that you can have no "write down" and no "read up" capability.[2,3] What this means is that systems with a higher classification can't write data to a lower classification system nor can a lower classification system read from a system with a higher classification. If you consider your network a "higher" classification level than the Internet, you break that rule every time your email server receives email.

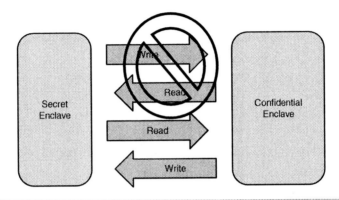

Figure 5-3 The Bell/LaPadula rule prevents the migration of high classification data to lower classifications.

There must be some middle ground, and I believe that is to compartmentalize by function and monitor traffic patterns. We have seen this type of compartmentalization in our demilitarized zone (DMZ). We put systems that act as data bridges in our DMZ so that external users can access the data while not getting access to the internal network services. We even give it a fancy name and call it an extranet.

Some security architects take this idea a bit further by breaking up the network into smaller compartments—not as extreme as a zone-based architecture, but not quite as open as a classic security architecture. As you can see in Figure 5-4, a logical demarcation point is the difference between user endpoints and server endpoints. This segregates endpoints based on their function as sources and sinks of data.

---

[2] D. Bell & L. LaPadula, Secure computer systems: Mathematical foundations. Technical report ESD-TR-73-278, The MITRE Corp, Bedford, MA, 1973

[3] http://en.wikipedia.org/wiki/Bell-LaPadula_model (The original paper at MITRE is hard to get.)

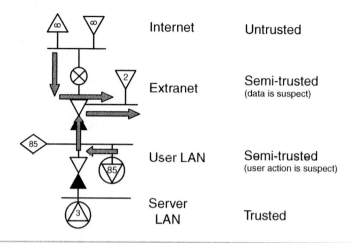

Figure 5-4 The extranet allows Internet users to exchange data with internal users.

The added advantage to this is that you can track flow information and when it looks like a system has changed roles—a sink becomes a source, for instance—you can take appropriate action. An example of this is a user's system spewing data to the Internet. It's either been hacked and is spamming the universe, or a large amount of data is being extracted from it.

I will take this opportunity to remind you that it is for this reason that our endpoint icons are triangles. If the pointy end is connected to the network, this is a source of data and network traffic, such as a file server. If the flat end is connected to the network, it is a sink of data.

There is a third possibility: that the identified endpoint is being remotely accessed for legitimate purposes. I would counter that if you have a network with any sensible level of restrictive policy, chances are that you're not allowing remote access to ordinary desktops.

DO I NEED A FORKLIFT?

As I pointed out earlier, not all network infrastructure devices can support your decision to rely on 802.1x. As our networks have grown and expanded over the years, most of us have accumulated different vendors and different versions of each vendor's equipment. Not all of them are going to have the same capability. Add to that the fact that there are hundreds of thousands of "dumb" switches (or worse, simple hubs), and you begin to see how the problem can get out of hand quickly.

Some of us are going to have to rip out and replace a lot of equipment.

UPGRADES ARE EXPENSIVE

Hardware vendors love change. Change means that they get to sell more hardware! When people stop buying new hardware or upgrading the hardware they have, the "network iron" companies are going to go out of business. We saw this happen when the "bubble" burst. Folks were waiting on the "killer application," and in anticipation other folks went crazy installing lots of fiber and infrastructure. One day someone woke up and said, "Hey, we have a lot of dark fiber out there and no killer application to fill it with bits. Maybe we should stop buying stuff."

Stall, spin, crash, burn, die.

The resulting crash didn't really lower the price of equipment, unfortunately. My most recent data on this comes from a financial customer who was planning on upgrading to all 802.1x-capable devices. He called his network hardware vendor in for a chat and told him what he was planning on doing. The vendor told him that all his hubs would have to be replaced because 802.1x only allows one connection per port and each new connection would need authentication and would kill the last connection. Most users would classify that as "bad." Some of my friend's switches were a couple of years old, and they didn't have the memory capacity for the new code; and because they were so old, they couldn't have more memory added. They would have to be replaced. However, a good number of the switches could be upgraded and would have to be to support the 802.1x-capable code. Yay! Now, you probably need some professional services people to help with such a huge upgrade. After all, a lot of details and configuration changes need to be accounted for. Oh, and he needed a "good solid project manager" to pull all those PS people together. By the time it was over, my friend was looking at a $2 million plus, one year to complete, "you get to keep the forklift" upgrade.

Let's not mention the time and potential for disaster as far as the user is concerned. New devices become the excuse of choice. "Because your fill-in-the-blank burped, I missed my delivery date!"

The good news is that he was able to convince his board that it was more important to be a leader in the security space than tomorrow's headlines, and they're well on their way to implementing a CLPC-enforced network.

A LESS-EXPENSIVE WAY

So, you don't want to help your local network rep make the payments on his shiny new BMW? There is a cheaper way. It's not as effective, but it does work. I say "it's not as effective" because it relies on voluntary participation.

Instead of relying on the switch to make the decision, you can use the fact that Internet Protocol (IP)-based endpoints use the IP address and its associated subnet mask to accept traffic. You can use this to your advantage in a kind of bastardized implementation of the IP protocol. By using DHCP, you can control if and how an endpoint talks to the network. This works because switches operate at Layer 2 and routers operate at Layer 3. By using switches to make connections between individual endpoints based on Media Access Control (MAC) addresses and by using the routers to control how networks communicate using the IP address, you can gain a great deal of control over all the endpoints on your network.

Let's take a look at how this works by starting with the DHCP protocol. The Dynamic Host Configuration Protocol,[4] DHCP for short, evolved out of the Bootstrap Protocol (BOOTP) that was used in the early days of the Internet. DHCP is backward compatible with BOOTP and supports the idea of a lease. Instead of being given an IP address in perpetuity, DHCP lets you use the IP address only as long as the lease is valid. When the lease expires, the DHCP client on the endpoint "releases" the IP address back to the DHCP server.

If your endpoint isn't configured with a static or fixed IP address, it's usually set to ask a DHCP server for an address. You usually get your first DHCP lease when the endpoint first joins the network, but there are other times when you can get one. Many operating systems come out of the box with the network configured to talk to a DHCP server.

The complete protocol exchange is fairly elegant. The requesting endpoint sends out a broadcast packet with a destination address of all 1s and a source address of all 0s. A listening DHCP server responds with a packet that has the IP address, the subnet mask, the default gateway, the length of the lease, and at least one DNS server, as shown in Table 5-1.

Table 5-1   A Simple DHCP Network Scope

Parameter	Setting
IP address	192.168.168.21
Subnet mask	255.255.255.0
Default gateway	192.168.168.1
Duration of lease in seconds	7200
DNS server	192.168.1.25

It can send more information, especially if you're a Microsoft endpoint, but we'll stop at this level of detail because this isn't a book about the DHCP protocol. After the

---

[4] RFC 2131

endpoint has received the IP address information, it sends a message back to the server acknowledging that it's going to use the address.

Using the information in the table, we can see that our endpoint is now equipped to access the network for two hours. When two hours is up, it will have to ask the DHCP server again for an address.

So, why is this cool, and how can we use it to our advantage? To start, it's cool because most of us are lazy and DHCP makes it easy to support an IP-based network, because you don't have to configure static IP addresses and mess around with all the information that goes with them. Each time you touch an endpoint is an opportunity to screw it up, and you eliminate that with DHCP. The downside is that if you misconfigure the DHCP server, you can really "screw the pooch" for all of your users.

How can we use this to our advantage? Easy, most DHCP servers can manage multiple scopes. A *scope* is a geek term that defines each set of parameters for each set of IP address ranges that the DHCP server will be giving out. One scope may say that the IP address range has the parameters depicted in Table 5-1, whereas another scope has the parameters defined in Table 5-2. In Table 5-2, the top scope serves as the remediation scope; the bottom scope allows connections to the production network.

Table 5-2 Two DHCP Scopes

Parameter	Setting
IP address range start	192.168.168.2
IP address range end	192.168.168.31
Default gateway	192.168.168.1
Subnet mask	255.255.255.224
Duration of lease in seconds	7200
DNS server	192.168.1.25
Parameter	**Setting**
IP address range start	192.168.2.2
IP address range end	192.168.2.127
Default gateway	192.168.2.1
Subnet mask	255.255.255.128
Duration of lease in seconds	14400
DNS server	192.168.1.25

Scopes are usually associated with networks, but this can be worked around with third-party software, hardware, or magic.

If you figured that one scope was for a trusted network, and the other was for an untrusted network, you understand what we're trying to do here. When an endpoint starts up, it gets an address in the untrusted or quarantined network. When it can prove to the DHCP server that it can be trusted, the DHCP server gives it an address in the trusted enterprise network.

The magic part has to do with how routers handle DHCP requests. Because a DHCP server might not be on the same network segment as the client, the router has to tell the DHCP server what network the client requesting the DHCP request lives on. So, when a router sees the DHCP request, it appends what network the packet came in on to the packet. The DHCP server uses that information to decide which scope to serve an address from. DHCP enforcement uses that to select what network the endpoint is going to be assigned to. The network access control (NAC) client appends compliance information, the router appends network information, and the information is taken apart and sent to the DHCP enforcer/server. There are multiple ways to do this, and it depends on the vendor what method is used. It could be a change to the DHCP software, or it can be a proxy server in front of the DHCP server.

Why does this work? Because routers can support multiple IP address ranges on their interfaces, thereby allowing routable and unroutable IP address ranges on the same network. For that matter, if a router doesn't know about an IP address range, it would look like spoofed addresses and drop the packets. Instant containment! In Figure 5-5, the endpoints inside of the dotted box will not have access to the rest of the network because their IP address won't be passed by the router.

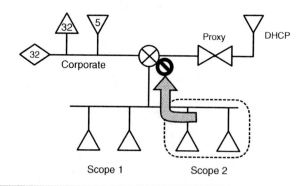

Figure 5-5   DHCP enforcement. Through clever use of proxies and routers, DHCP NAC enforcement provides containment.

Now that we've looked at why DHCP works, let's consider why it doesn't work. It's voluntary. If I decide that I'm going to manually assign an IP address from an observed list of IPs, I can defeat DHCP enforcement. You should consider DHCP a migration mechanism, but completely relying on it probably isn't the best idea in the long run.

TECHNOLOGY PROMISES AND FUTURES

Technology got us here, and technology is going to save us. I can prove it! Technology has been getting us "here" for the past 50 years. Since the first computer, technology has been promising us a better future, and it's going to save us sometime real soon. Any moment now technology is going to ride up on a big white horse and save our butts. I'm not holding my breath, however.

Just as technology provides a savior, technology will also provide three new adversaries. We'll add enforcement to our solution, but like a water balloon that you squeeze in the middle, our problem will pop out somewhere else. If we continue to treat technology as a series of point solutions designed to solve our problem of the moment, we're going to be disappointed for a long time to come.

So, what does the future hold? Not much if we don't change our ways. We can't continue to let the vendors drive our solutions through marketing and the threat du jour. The future of security is hinged on turning it into an engineering domain complete with processes and postulates. From these postulates, we will be able to craft specific tests, run the tests, analyze the test results, and see whether they agree with our postulates. If they do, we're one step closer to better security. If not, we can reexamine and reformulate our postulates.

We can set some milestones, but when we get to them, we need to be ready to move on to the next one. As we secure our environment, we need to turn our attention to the data that we're generating.

In the previous paragraphs, we talked about compartmentalizing our networks to protect them. One of the methods was the compartmentalization of the network based on the data classification. Using our present operating system architectures, that's about all we can do. We don't have labels, and we can't make decisions based on the classification of the data. Sure, third-party data protection solutions do exist, but they're bolt-ons and as such aren't a part of the consideration put into the operating system.

ENDPOINT SUPPORT

How well our solutions work is going to be based on vision, simplicity, and common sense. Each endpoint is going to have to receive a different kind of support because each endpoint type has a different user profile associated with it. Some endpoints, such as our industrial controllers, don't have users per se; they have "actors," such as "bots."

AUTHENTICATION

Authentication used to be about identifying the user. In recent years, the definition has expanded to encompass the system to a certain degree. Through the use of certificates, you can be fairly certain that you're really talking to the server that you intended to talk to.

The Trusted Computing Group (TCG) has expanded the authentication mechanism such that it now includes the hardware. This is a great thing because it should reduce the incidence of notebook theft in the future by making it easier to trace (and therefore harder to sell) the stolen property. However, it should be said that all the Trusted Platform Module (TPM) really is, is a secure place to store keys and certificates. As we are so painfully aware, each security solution that we've come up with in the past has been bypassed or otherwise broken, thereby keeping us on the wheel of pain.

For the purposes of CLPC and NAC, we're going to include a trust element in our authentication protocol. This trust element will include a determination regarding the state of the endpoint. In short, it will examine whether the endpoint meets a preset level of compliance and thus an implied level of trust.

VENDOR SUPPORT

As I've said, there aren't a lot of options out there to help with integrating our endpoints and our networks. We're counting on NAC (in whatever form) to help, but vendors are working to get into the market. A bit of a warning here: The following information was accurate as of this writing. Vendors change directions fairly quickly, and although there are the expected offerings from Cisco and Microsoft, both pushing their respective solutions, this could change the day after publication.

Hardware vendors such as Enterasys, Foundry Networks, Extreme Networks, and Juniper Networks presently provide some, if not all, parts of the solution.[5] Juniper bought Funk and the Steel Belted Radius product line; and with that, combined with

---

[5]   www.juniper.net/products/aaa

their existing product line, they seem to offer something that has everything except endpoint integrity compliance.

Enterasys literature shows them doing a remote scan of the system, and they claim that their agent solution, Trusted End-System Solution, works with their other products that manage policy and authentication, authorization, and auditing (AAA).[6] A deeper look into their products indicates that Enterasys relies on Sygate (now Symantec) and Zone (now Check Point) agents to check integrity.

Foundry has taken the same approach that Enterasys has—not too strange considering Foundry is a hardware vendor.[7] To make their solution work, you need a good agent on the endpoint, and that means Symantec or Check Point. The combination of Foundry and Symantec is a solution that I've personally seen work. It took a bit of work to get the remediation part to work because it had to have some custom scripts, but it did work.

Extreme has also teamed up with another vendor (in this case, StillSecure) to provide a multitude of NAC solutions.[8] They claim to provide agentless testing through the StillSecure Safe Access solution. This process uses Windows Remote Procedure Call (RPC) and credentials to interrogate the endpoint, so each endpoint must be configured to accept StillSecure access to accomplish testing. Your endpoint firewall will have to be configured to allow this type of access. Thankfully, we haven't seen any buffer-overflow vulnerabilities in RPC that allow an attacker to execute arbitrary code since late 2003.[9] But, if using Windows RPC makes you nervous, you can always use the browser-based ActiveX tool! If you want to avoid the remote execution of code that MS06-014 says is possible (unless you patch "at the earliest opportunity"),[10] however, you can always use the StillSecure agent.

Symantec now has a NAC offering thanks to its purchase of Sygate. The Symantec Sygate Enterprise Protection (SSEP) solution is an agent-based solution that leverages 802.1x (an additional module), DHCP, or network compartmentalization. The agent is capable of doing self-enforcement, thereby eliminating reliance on 802.1x or DHCP. However, a basic rule of security is that if you can put your hands on it, you can break into it. Self-enforcement is a last resort if you have no other options and you don't have a very sophisticated user community. SSEP does have an integrity component that ensures

---

[6] www.enterasys.com/products/ids/NSTAM/

[7] www.foundrynet.com/solutions/security/NAC.html

[8] www.extremenetworks.com/products/securityappliances/

[9] www.kb.cert.org/vuls/id/568148

[10] www.microsoft.com/technet/security/Bulletin/MS06-014.mspx

that the system has the required software and patches and actively prevents malware from infesting the machine. Operating system protection examines how system calls are made; if they exhibit unknown behavior, the call is terminated.

The Symantec/Foundry combination is also a solution that I have seen work. By using the 802.1x capability of the Foundry FastIron switch, noncompliant endpoints were switched to a remediation LAN where they could be repaired. SSEP provides remediation services as well as interfacing with third-party remediation and patch-management products.

Check Point Integrity has a similar set of features with respect to NAC, but it wraps VPN support and integration with other Check Point security products into the mix. Integrity also has an endpoint integrity option that can be used to evaluate the security state of the endpoint and, if needed, initiate remediation actions or quarantine.

Cisco and Microsoft, as of this writing, have yet to completely deploy their solutions. They seem to have a good set of visions, but the implementation side is a bit slow.

Infoblox[11] is an interesting solution because it's a toolkit that only addresses DHCP-based NAC. Let me draw an analogy here. You walk into a pet shop and ask for a dog. The clerk asks, "What kind of dog do you want?" Check Point and Symantec products are kind of like that pet shop. Do you want DHCP, 802.1x, compartmentalization, or do you want a mutt? On the other hand, you can walk into a pet shop, ask the clerk for a dog, and the clerk can hand you some DNA and tell you that you can make any kind of dog you want. Toolkits are like that.

VULNERABILITIES AND REMEDIATION

As mentioned earlier, an incredible industry is devoted to just identifying and classifying vulnerabilities on your network. Companies such as Qualys and nCircle have successfully implemented a business model that feeds on vulnerability detection and analysis.

I suppose that I should be clear when I make this next point because I'm about to poke some folks in the eye with a stick. The marketing model for the vulnerability assessment (VA) industry is predicated on two things:

- Eliminating exposed vulnerabilities will make you secure.
- The scan, repair, scan model is effective.

I submit that there are more problems with this "hacker's eye view" than vendors would lead you to believe.

---

[11] www.infoblox.com

First, your network is changing faster than you can scan it. At best, a scan is a snapshot of a very quickly moving set of scenes. Imagine trying to figure out what a movie was about by looking at every ten thousandth frame!

Second, the mere act of scanning a network can create problems by itself. If you have any kind of intrusion detection software, it's sure to alert on the fact that the endpoint is being scanned. Sure, you can add exceptions to your network-based intrusion detection system (NIDS) and your host-based intrusion detection system (HIDS), but you have to do that every time your scanning source changes. Even with that, some applications don't like being scanned and may behave by crashing or slowing down to the point where service levels are affected.

Third, although they can be configured to, these scans don't scan every port. They only scan a comparatively small number of ports. If someone wanted to hide an illegal application, it wouldn't be hard.

Scans are also insensitive to where the endpoint is on the network. A vulnerability is a vulnerability.

So why scan at all? Well, a simple answer to that is that it helps an organization meet the regulatory requirements of outside assessment. Sarbanes-Oxley (SOx) is a perfect example of this. You can have the best security in the world, but you still need an outside assessment to fill a check box. Am I opposed to outside assessments? No, I'm not. I just think that if you're going to spend your money, there are better ways to spend it. Get an occasional scan, but be careful how much you pay for it. This type of service is now a commodity. And remember that you still have to remediate what you find at some point in time.

DETECTION

Now that I've completely bashed the VA market, we can talk about how to detect vulnerabilities in your endpoints. You can use a couple of methods to detect vulnerabilities. The first I talked about in the previous pages: You can scan and hope for the best. But as I discussed, scanning does have its downside. Besides the reasons I mentioned before, I believe that scanning is reactive and inaccurate.

Another, and I believe more effective way, is to keep track of what's added or removed from the endpoint. If you know what's on the endpoint, you can compare that to a known list of vulnerabilities and make a determination of risk and exposure.

That means that you have to have access to the endpoint either through a smart agent that provides an inventory function or via a remote protocol.

Another way to do that would be to install inventory software that keeps track of what software is loaded on the system. It doesn't operate at the frequency that NAC requires, but it does give you some feedback as to what's living on your endpoints.

VULNERABILITY TRACKING SERVICES

Multiple services track vulnerabilities, and you can use that information to check your endpoints for vulnerabilities. Most sites use a naming format called the Common Vulnerabilities and Exposures, or CVE, to name their vulnerabilities. CVE allows publishers of vulnerabilities to use a common dictionary of terms in the hope that it will allow us to more effectively communicate. You can find these databases as follows:

- Secunia, http://secunia.com
- SecurityFocus, www.securityfocus.com
- NIST, http://nvd.nist.gov

VULNERABILITY MANAGEMENT

So, what's the difference between vulnerability management (VM) and vulnerability scanning? Commitment to the process. VM is about taking information that you have about the state of your endpoints, their vulnerabilities, and understanding what type of mitigation to employ. Once again, there is a subtle tone to what I'm trying to say here. *Just because you have a vulnerability doesn't mean that you have to rush out and install a patch.* VM is not blind faith in the ability of vendors to perfect their offerings. It's about understanding how the vulnerability, potential exploits, and your business processes intersect to form a workable solution.

VM is based on a process that constantly reassesses your vulnerability posture while applying controls to ensure that business objectives are appropriately met. You can use the scan, evaluate, assess, prioritize, implement, verify cycle as a basis for your process. Most of us recognize this as the basic test, analyze, fix process, albeit with some needed controls to ensure success. As you read the next few paragraphs, use Figure 5-6 as a reference.

1. **Scan.** Using either the hacker's eye view of a VA scanner or the system owner's view of an agent or inventory control tool, generate a list of your vulnerabilities based on all your installed software.

2. **Evaluate.** Determine your level of exposure based on available exploits and proximity to attack. What is the risk of the exploit being used successfully against your vulnerability? Does the vulnerability have any nasty interactions with other vulnerabilities? What is the proscribed course of action?

3. **Assess.** Determine how the patch or fix is going to impact your production processes. Is the patch going to require the rewriting of custom code? Does the fix really mitigate the vulnerability? Is the fix worse than the risk?

4. **Prioritize.** Determine which systems are going to get your critical resources based on their value to the organization, risk of successful attack, and ability to act as a jumping-off point.

5. **Implement.** Install the patches, change the procedures, or remove the offending object. It could be code, as in the case of Windows needing a patch, or it could be a case of something like a Napster, which needs to be removed. Or, as discussed in the section "Penetration Testing," it could be that a procedure has to be changed.

6. **Verify.** You need to ensure that the dictated remediation has been accomplished. This could be a rescan or it could be an audit. For that matter, it could be a full-up penetration test. At any rate, you need to verify that the fix really has been implemented. I recommend that whatever process you use that you keep the verification out of band, or outside of, the normal VM process. This will act as a check and balance to your overall VM process.

7. **Start again.**

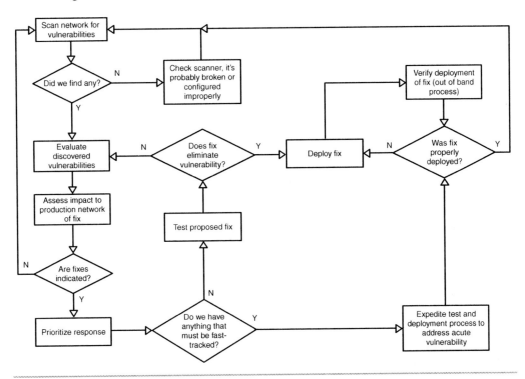

Figure 5-6   The VM process defines a set of procedures that discover and manage vulnerabilities in a network environment.

REMEDIATION

Painless. Transparent. Those two words, in my opinion, accurately describe the two most important qualities of a remediation process. Sure, remediation has to be reliable and accurate, but remediation has to be painless or transparent; otherwise, people will find ways around it. If it's too restrictive or time-consuming, remediation will be viewed as "one of those productivity-sucking security processes" and will eventually get bypassed by management at crunch time.

When AV first came out and files were quarantined such that the email admin had to release them, people went around the process by copying files to floppy disks (remember those?). The viruses of the time still spread because people just afforded the malware a different carrier via removable media. The AV vendors had to include a new feature that allowed the AV engines to scan floppies. And thus, the typical weapons escalation profile continues.

To address this problem, some vendors have built what they call "automated" remediation tools. The notion is that when the user connects, a determination is made regarding the user's patch level. I say "patch level" because most of the remediation vendors are either in the vulnerability management space or the patch management space.

PENETRATION TESTING

Let's start this section by saying that social engineering is a method of circumventing technology controls through the manipulation of people. We'll get back to this in a few paragraphs.

It is the goal of penetration testing to see how resistant your enterprise is to attack. The process starts by learning about the target. So you start by asking a few simple questions:

- What does the target do; what is their business?
- What is the target's threat profile?
- Does the target rely on network technology?

From these basic questions, many more can be asked, but you really need to start from there.

By finding out what the target company does, you learn more about how the company is organized and what business processes they're going to have in place. Business processes can be attacked.

A bank is going to have a different threat profile from that of a car dealership. Because banks deal with currency and funds, you can skip a great deal of risk (as an attacker) by going for the money rather than the painful and labor-intensive activities required to sell or to part out a stolen car.

If you have a bank and the bank relies heavily on the Internet for account transfers or funds management, you have a remote target. Once again, our car dealership is going to rely on the Internet for fleet orders, customer inquiries, and the occasional car sale. Really big thinkers are going to find some way to manipulate the system to have cars delivered to some fictitious business where they can be "disappeared." However, even that doesn't come close to being in the same league as a financial institution. Different businesses, different threats, different return on, well, nefarious investment.

While someone on your team is off finding out about business profiles, someone else from your team has done some research and discovered that the target has a network assigned to it. So, what is the next step? To scan it, of course! Let's get the low-hanging fruit out of the way and see whether they have any endpoints that we can touch from the Internet. That means a scan. The very same kind of scan that an organization is going to do in the course of a VA scan.

Now we come to the conclusion that there is no low-hanging fruit, and attacking the technology directly isn't going to work. So what do you do? You attack the people and the processes that they rely on to get their jobs done. Chat with some employees and get the help desk number. With a little more ingenuity and some dumpster diving, you can learn quite a bit about a small number of employees. People are generally very proud of what they do or very angry with someone "inside," and both emotions can be used against them.

You can also intimidate them if you're really good. We used the information that we learned from a company newsletter and some intimidation to get a help desk engineer to change the virtual private network (VPN) password of the CIO of a Fortune 100 company *over the phone*. We were then able to access the network via the CIO's VPN connection. How did this happen? The help desk person didn't follow procedure.

The purpose of this discussion is to underline the fact that not all vulnerabilities have to do with technology. Human-driven processes are the next target on the list when the technology pushes an attacker to try something else. Because human-driven processes can take more time, the fact that they have been penetrated will also take more time. Some vulnerabilities merely make the technology available to attackers.

CONTRACTORS AND VISITORS

What good is a solution if it doesn't address your real-world needs? Well, one of those needs for many of us is the requirement that contractors and visitors must have some sort of Internet access. In some, if not many cases, contractors and visitors will be reluctant to install your client-based solution onto their system. I know that I would have some heartburn installing a remotely managed client on my private notebook!

The good news is that CLPC-based solutions such as those discussed in this chapter allow for this very condition. When you configure your process, you can say that systems that don't comply will be relegated to an Internet-access-only network if they fail the remediation process. Systems are given a chance to participate, and those that choose not to cannot access internal resources but can still access the Internet.

KEY POINTS

KNOW YOUR ARCHITECTURE

You must be keenly aware of your network infrastructure and what capabilities it represents before you decide on a CLPC path. If you have an older network infrastructure, you may have to turn to other technologies to implement a CLPC solution. Older infrastructure may not be capable of supporting 802.1x without a sizable infusion of budget, so you may need to turn to DHCP or other forms of compartmentalization in the interim.

You must also keep in mind that there are going to be devices on your network that won't be able to operate properly if they are isolated, such as printers, so you must plan your solution around them. With that in mind, other network enclaves must also be considered when you start forcing them into a new access control model. Different security controls might have to be placed on these systems.

THREE BASIC NAC MODELS

The three basic NAC models are 802.1x, DHCP, and compartmentalization. 802.1x has the benefit of being a standard and forms a nice proportional control that is difficult to bypass. However, some of the tools needed, mainly a host integrity checker, are only offered by a few vendors. In addition, 802.1x-enabled devices may not be completely deployed throughout your network, creating "attack holes" that can be used to gain entry.

DHCP offers the advantage of being easy to implement while being relatively inexpensive to deploy. All enterprise endpoints have a DHCP client that can be easily configured and managed. The downside to DHCP enforcement is that it is easily bypassed by a skillful attacker.

The last method is compartmentalization, or the breaking up of your network into security zones. Many networks already use this design philosophy to separate production, development, intranet, and extranet networks. Although it does require a modification to the network fabric, it does reduce the speed that viruses and worms can spread at by forcing them through chokepoints such as ACLs.

You need to keep in mind a dark side of compartmentalization: When you have a secure compartmentalized network, you need to address the reality that different users and different applications are going to require access between compartments for business purposes. You're going to have to build an exception process that evaluates these requests based on a balance between security and business need.

It gets darker when you realize that at some point the complexity of your security architecture will create a situation in which the processing of exceptions becomes a major task that requires a small army to manage. At this point, the complexity and lack of visibility has completely eroded the security you were seeking. You will have to craft a solution that just manages the exception process, and I say that's when exceptions become the rule—thousands of firewall rules, to be exact.

You also have to consider that over compartmentalizing will break some basic functions on your network. For example, a basic element of large networks is that they have a group that monitors service. Most of us have to live with service level agreements (SLAs) that dictate how fast we respond or how often service is provided. In a large network with lots of applications separated by lots of firewalls, you can find yourself with service monitoring problems.

SELECT VENDORS CAREFULLY

NAC is still young, and vendors are still wrestling with the "model." By "model," I mean the marketing and messaging model. When you consider a vendor, make sure that the components they sell will work and play well with the components on your network. Will the proposed solution work with your RADIUS server? Will you need to build a proxy? How will the supplicants and host integrity modules get on the endpoints?

DON'T BELIEVE IN FUTURES

Lots of ideas never make it from marketing to engineering. I know because I've been stung by them as well as been the one pushing them. For this reason, you need to stick with what's in front of you today. Make plans that can incorporate proposed features, but don't stake the security of your design on futures.

ALLOWING CONTROLLED ACCESS IS IMPORTANT

In some cases, you will have to provide access to contractors and guests. It's best to provide this access in a way that reduces or eliminates the exposure your network has to unknown threats. By effectively using the automated features of a NAC solution, untrusted systems can be allowed to attach to your network and gain restricted access to services such as the Internet.

VM HAS A PLACE IN THE PROCESS

For a VM solution to work properly, it must have controls that ensure that the correct decision is being implemented and that the implementation is correct. Simple discovery and patch methodologies can present problems for existing applications and even introduce new vulnerabilities. They also don't ensure that the critical patches have been reviewed and implemented on the critical systems. By layering a control process that incorporates the build and regression process onto your VM process, you can be assured that patches and fixes are being implemented in an auditable and repeatable fashion.

Penetration testing can also be a useful tool for verifying that procedures are being followed and to discover vulnerabilities in your processes. Keep in mind that many of our processes are driven by people, and people have short memories. These memories can be "updated," however, through training and regular exercise such as that provided by penetration testing.

TECHNOLOGY, PROCESS, AND CLOSING THE LOOP

Closing the loop means more than just throwing some technology at the problem. NAC does have a place, but if you don't understand where your vulnerabilities are (both technical and nontechnical), you're leaving a very critical portion of the loop wide open.

Knowing where your vulnerabilities are and understanding how they affect your overall security processes is critical to understanding exactly where all the loops that need to be closed are. Some methods are faster and more closely approximate real time than others, whereas some operate at a much lower frequency, such as vulnerability scanning. Some processes, especially those with humans in them, are very slow and are potentially the weakest link.

However, by effectively merging the technologies associated with endpoint security into a well-engineered, self-managing, trust-based CLPC solution, you can mitigate many of these problems before they become liabilities.

Trustworthy Beginnings

We've often heard the phrase "don't shoot the messenger." But if you can't trust the messenger, can you trust the message? Our crypto-savvy readers will all shout "*Yes!*" But like any tool, cryptography can only be part of the solution; it can't be all of it. Cryptography can tell us whether the results of a system check differ from the last test, or they can hide the results from prying eyes. However, cryptography isn't going to tell us whether our systems are secure in the first place. I've been asked whether I think virtual private networks (VPNs) are the answer. The reasoning goes something like "if I only allow authorized individuals to connect securely to my systems, how can I be harmed?"
I tell the person asking that question that hackers love VPNs because it gives them a secure channel between them and the victim. VPN solutions are based on software, and software has flaws. I have trouble basing a solution on a tool that I know has flaws in it from the outset.

We need to know that we have a good starting point. How many times have you been assigned a project only to think that it would have been easier to just start over? You looked at it and said, "I have no idea what they were thinking," and thought that if given the option you would scrap the whole thing and start over.

Well, that's what this chapter is about. We're making the admission that trying to fix something that we had no control over is a losing proposition and one that we can't live with. Someone's going to ask us whether we can trust the solution, and if we didn't craft it, there's always going to be that lingering doubt in the back of our mind about the security posture of our endpoints. Your boss is going to ask whether you trust what you've been given, and he or she will detect the hesitation in your response.

This chapter removes that hesitation.

PRÉCIS

This chapter takes us through the processes and procedures of generating and maintaining a secure baseline. This part of the operational process is probably the most boring, because after the process is in place, it should be static and self-maintaining. It's the tried-and-true process of test, analyze, fix.

I'm going to repeat myself a bit here: This must be a repeatable and verifiable process; otherwise, you're wasting your time. If you can't look back and see where a system came from and how it should be configured based on your records, the system is not verifiably secure.

We're going to start with building a secure build environment, defining a secure baseline, include some basic tools, and finish off with the testing process. We're also going to cover some of the basic pitfalls that many people fall into because they've never had to generate and maintain a secure build.

SPECIAL POINTS OF INTEREST

Although this chapter discusses a number of different security technologies and how they work together, how they work as a team is an important issue. But like any team, if the foundation is weak, so is the team's performance.

The process used to put your foundation together is a critical component to ensuring that the rest of the team, the other pieces of your security solution, has a snowball's chance of being successful.

START WITH A SECURE BUILD

We're never going to be able to trust our systems if we're always trying to fix the security on-the-fly. If you're not sure whether a system has been compromised, the quick thing to do is to re-image it and start over. It's also the safe thing to do.

I realize that this isn't always practical, because in some instances the system contains legacy applications that can't be easily ported over to the newest operating system. In those instances, other processes are more appropriate, such as compartmentalization. I mention it here just so we know that we can't always start over.

For the purposes of what we're trying to do, which is to secure the endpoint, we're not going to worry about those legacy systems at the moment. We're going to generate a process that is safe, reliable, and most of all, secure, for generating endpoints that we're going to deploy moving forward.

PROCESS IS KEY

I wish I were getting paid based on the number of times I use the word *process*. If you don't have a repeatable process, you have no way of knowing whether someone hasn't inserted something evil into your systems. Even a process that has some quality controls can be affected. For example, Creative Labs, a fairly well-known organization, managed to release an MP3 product with a worm in it![1]

As I've said earlier, security is about control, and you can't control something you don't understand. The best way to understand it is to try to describe it in words or draw it in a picture. To start with, you have to have a process that enables you to generate known secure builds.

Starting from scratch, that process would look something like what I've depicted in Figure 6-1. When you first start, I recommend starting from known good sources (such as vendor DVDs or CD-ROMs).

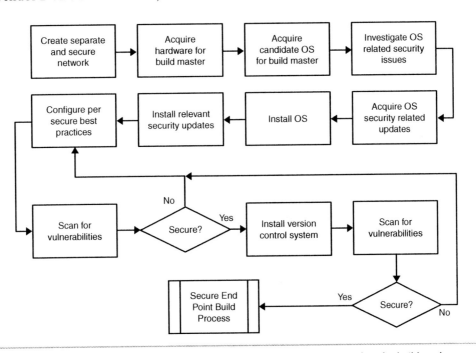

Figure 6-1   The process used to create your build environment must ensure that the build tools themselves are secure to begin with.

---

[1] The Register, 9/1/05, www.theregister.co.uk/2005/09/01/creative_mp3_player_virus_flap/

A SAFE, WELL-LIT PLACE FOR BUILDS

Where are you going to build your endpoints? It makes a difference. A long time ago, at the beginning of the DEFCON capture-the-flag games, one of the people in my security group decided that it was more fun to lurk than to hack. He had discovered that one of the popular operating systems had a vulnerability that he could exploit while the system was being installed. He wrote a scanner that would wait for new systems to come onto the network; if they had this vulnerability, he would attack them. It was great fun watching script kiddies as they tried to figure out what was happening. It was one of those things that was just obvious when you saw it. They'd try a few tentative keys, and their heads would pop up over the hunched-down heads of the other participants. Then came the banging on the keyboard of their notebook when they realized that they'd been hacked even before they could get their systems up!

This happens in the operational world, too. I had a very large customer that had the policy that any user could have a server and that they could load any configuration of Windows that was supported by the company. Web servers, email servers, application servers—all were allowed by the company *at the desktop*.

Then CodeRed hit.

They couldn't rebuild systems fast enough. A new system would come on the network, and all the others would attack it so fast that they couldn't keep up. It was a nightmare. Even the patched systems created packet storms that brought the network throughput to near zero.

In the first case, our script kiddies were trying to build systems in a known hostile environment. In the second case, system administrators were trying to rebuild systems in an infected environment. The moral here is that you can't produce a trustworthy build on an untrusted network.

Your build network must be isolated from your production networks. For this reason, I support a minimum of four networks, as shown in Figure 6-2:

- Corporate
- Engineering and QA
- Security testing
- Build

The corporate network is separated from the engineering networks by a firewall. There are controlled exchanges of email and files through an intranet demilitarized zone (DMZ) network. The engineers need a bit of autonomy if they're going to generate security software, but the business has to survive, so we protect the corporate network from the development network.

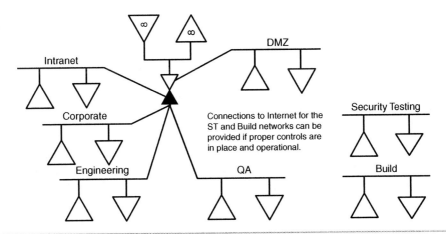

Figure 6-2 A corporate network is protected from the security testing network, and the build network enclave is protected from all of them.

The security-testing network is an isolated, stand-alone network because we load some pretty evil things on this network, and if they got out, it would be bad for everybody.

For the inverse reason, our build network is isolated from the rest of the network. We don't want anything getting in, so we keep an air gap between it and the rest of the world.

Now, I can hear all the system administrators shouting about not being able to get to things that they need to download from the Internet. "I need the latest drivers!" Well, that's exactly my point: What you need should be on your build network and under some form of code control. The only things that go on your secure build are those things that have been tested and included in the secure baseline.

I have seen build environments in which they have successfully maintained a network connection to the Internet so that they can download drivers, but they also maintain a rigid policy of control. The connection is only there to facilitate the downloading of drivers, and the firewall enforces this policy by denying any traffic to unauthorized networks. It is a default deny all with explicit permits based on requirements. When a driver, or any application for that matter, is approved to include into the build, it's added to the source control tree.

I've also seen the connection implemented with a cable that's only plugged into a switch or the firewall after the security posture of the build network has been verified and there's a reason to connect to the Internet.

NEED A SECURE BASELINE

We're going to be hanging a lot of different applications off of our operating system, and the last thing we need to worry about is whether the foundation of our endpoint is secure. Having a secure baseline allows us to evaluate the security of these additional applications based on their own merits. We will be more easily able to understand how our security is going to be affected because there will be no equivocation regarding the security posture of the endpoint to begin with.

If an application has a flaw, and our operating system is configured properly, and the application is configured properly, we should derive some amount of containment when that flaw is exploited. For example, suppose that AIM has a flaw that allows an attacker to drop a Trojan on our system. If the operating system is secure, and the user doesn't have administrator privileges, the Trojan will only have limited access to the system. Any attempt to change system files will be met with a privilege violation.

Yes, that's a lot of "ifs," but the very first one is "if" the operating system is secure. It's where we have to start.

CONTROL YOUR SOURCE

Software engineers have known for years that they need a way to keep track of their source code. It's so ingrained in the UNIX world that they have a free tool for managing the files. On the system I'm on, the tool is called cvs (for Concurrent Versions System). On some systems, it's different applications called sccs (source code control system) and rcs (revision control system), but the purpose is the same: to control versions and ensure that the user has the pertinent version. Notice that I didn't say contemporary. Sometimes you need to go back a few revisions to understand how something changed.

Version control systems can keep track of a number of things, but at a minimum, here are some things that you should include in control:

- Application name
- Size
- Version number
- Creation date
- Modification date
- Path

Having this information makes it easier to determine whether a system has been compromised, because you can compare your archived list with one you pull off of suspect systems. You can also use this information to determine whether you're vulnerable to specific threats. It's a lot easier to search a list for a name and version number than it is to try to find just the right dynamic link library (DLL) in a crisis.

INCLUDE SOME TOOLS

A secure build isn't enough anymore. Today, you need some additional tools to help keep your endpoints secure and reliable. At a minimum, you should have the following:

- Firewall
- Antivirus
- Patch management

If you're a more advanced shop, you could also add these:

- Intrusion detection
- Intrusion prevention
- Host integrity
- Encryption

Keep in mind our earlier discussion in Chapter 4, "Missing Link Discovered," regarding process control. Without some form of host integrity checker, your systems may or may not be what you think they are.

SOFTWARE FIREWALL

Most desktop- and notebook-based endpoints come with some form of software-based firewall on them. If you have a Windows or Macintosh, getting to the firewall configuration window is fairly easy. If you're using a Linux variant with a window manager, they also make getting at the firewall an easy process.

As you can see in Figure 6-3, the firewall lives between the operating system and the network and is there to filter network traffic coming into and leaving the endpoint. Most software firewalls can filter on the type of transport and the port being used. For most of us that means filtering on TCP, UDP, and ICMP traffic and ports 1 through 65,535. To illustrate, most Web traffic is initiated on TCP on port 80. Your firewall may be set to allow outbound TCP traffic as long as it's on port 80 but may block everything else. The upshot of this is that many firewalls are direction aware. They can impose rules based on what direction the traffic is going.

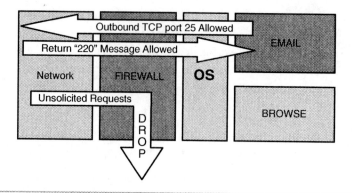

Figure 6-3   The firewall protects you from unsolicited incoming traffic while permitting outbound connections and the resulting returning packets.

Most firewalls will also maintain session "state," ensuring that all inbound packets are there due to an outbound request. Because there is no outbound request to match up to, unsolicited inbound requests are dropped at the firewall.

Not all firewalls are created equally. Some firewalls don't do outbound traffic filtering, and some firewalls have an application programming interface (API) that allows them to be turned off remotely. Keep in mind that just because it's there doesn't mean that it's turned on or configured properly. We cover this later in the sections on each operating system.

ANTIVIRUS

Although Microsoft is saying that they're going to include an antivirus (AV) feature in their new Vista operating system (I'm sure that's going to create some litigation), it still hasn't happened yet. That means that you have to turn to a third party to get it. AV has been around so long that folks are referring to it as a commodity. I guess that puts it squarely in the realm of gas and oil. Lots of people sell it, everybody needs it, and it's a real pain when we don't have it. Unlike oil, AV is relatively cheap at the enterprise level.

I said this before and I'm going to repeat myself here. Just because you happen to have an operating system that doesn't have a large malware muzzle aimed at it doesn't mean that you should ignore the threat. I've talked to a number of folks who believe that because there haven't been any viruses observed in the wild that they don't need AV on their system. Good security is about getting out in front of the problem. The other side of that coin asks, "What does a virus or worm look like in modern non-Windows systems?" This is also a good question. To answer, let's look at the applications supported on these other systems. Many, if not all, sophisticated software allows for the generation and application of macros to automate repetitive processes. Macros can read files, save data, and generally take any action that a user can take. A virus macro running through Word on a Macintosh could read your address book and send out spam hawking the latest erectile dysfunction drug, and you wouldn't know it without an AV program.

On another branch of the same tree, I suppose that's why many of the AV vendors talk about using heuristic analysis to "stop known and unknown treats." By understanding a little bit of behavior, they can stop malware without a predefined signature. At that point, they begin to look a little more like intrusion detection systems in my opinion, however.

AV comes in two flavors: server and desktop. The idea is that the email server will scan for things coming through the firewall and from the Internet and the desktop client will check any media inserted into the endpoint and scan against incoming email and chat. Figure 6-4 shows how AV is positioned in a typical desktop endpoint so that it can intercept inputs from the network, applications, and peripherals.

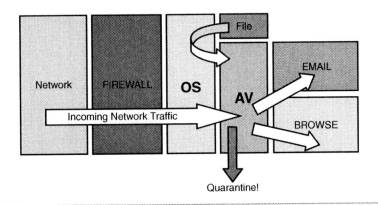

Figure 6-4 An example of an endpoint equipped with endpoint AV. Quarantined files are generally made available through the AV user interface.

Most organizations use a hybrid solution as depicted in Figure 6-5 that takes advantage of the strengths of both types of solutions.

The religious argument here has to do with what's called a "belt and suspenders" approach. Some hardcore security people will tell you that the server AV software and the desktop AV software should be from two different vendors. The argument is that a failure by one product won't necessarily mean that the malware gets though. The second product would be the last line of defense against attack. Nice argument, but it doesn't work against zero-day viruses. Chances are that neither vendor will catch them if all they're using is signature-based AV. You'll be really ticked off when the latest "Oh day" rips through not just one, but two AV systems.

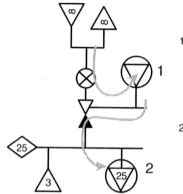

1. Incoming email is examined at the server prior to distribution

2. Desktop AV checks incoming packets from email, web, and removable media

Figure 6-5   Some networks scan for viruses at the incoming email server and at the endpoint itself. This is called a "belt and suspenders" solution because one system is supposed to catch what the other misses.

Also consider this: There's something to be said for enterprise pricing and only having one neck to choke!

Another nice thing about AV at the desktop is that it can scan data and files that don't originate from the enterprise network. Most endpoints have removable media in the form of CD-ROMs, DVDs, and USB memory. Desktop AV can be set to ensure that any document or file that comes from one of these sources is checked to ensure no evil content is present.

There are a number of vendors in this space, but I believe the top players are as follows (in alphabetical order):

- Computer Associates
- F-Secure
- Kaspersky
- McAfee
- Panda Software
- Sophos
- Symantec
- Trend Micro

PATCH MANAGEMENT

One thing that is also certain besides death and taxes is that all software will at some point need a patch or an update. Until recently, this fun little task was left up to the desktop administrator, or worse, the end user. Either you popped in a CD or DVD or you went to a Web site, but it was a manual process fraught with error and pain.

This spawned a whole new industry bent on making sure that you have all the updates that you can stand. There are two flavors of patch management: stand-alone and enterprise. The stand-alone versions are products that provide patch management services only. Enterprise versions include other management services such as security policy management.

The nice thing about Microsoft is that there is a built-in feature for updating it. We've all seen the little window pop up that tells us "updates are available for your computer." Yay! I could go on a tirade about how it took Microsoft forever to get it right, but I won't. Because they haven't. They're close, but third-party systems are still superior to the free Window Server Update Services (WSUS).

Apple also has a similar function for their operating system that automatically looks for updates. It's a part of the basic preferences, and the nice thing is that updates can be turned off or disregarded by the user.

Third-party patch management (PM) vendors will install an agent onto the endpoint that checks with a policy server at boot time and at preprogrammed intervals. If a patch is available, the patch is downloaded and installed onto the target endpoint. The agent usually runs as a system process with administrator privileges. This makes sense because the agent is going to have to modify the system DNA when critical patches to system executables or configurations are required.

As you can see from Table 6-1, more than a few companies can provide you with a solution to meet most of your patch and update needs. This is not an exhaustive list, but you get the idea that there are different levels of complexity among the vendors.

Table 6-1 Patch Vendors' Diverse Offerings (Some Are OS Specific)

	Microsoft	Apple	AIX	HP-UX	Solaris	Novell	Linux
Patchlink	Yes	Yes	Yes	Yes	Yes	Yes	
St Bernard	Yes				Yes*		Yes
Kaseya	Yes						
Bigfix	Yes	Yes	Yes	Yes	Yes		Yes

*Microsoft products only

INTRUSION DETECTION

If you walk into a bank, you see cameras, motion detectors, window-break detectors, and in some banks, guards. This is all about detecting intruders. For somebody to penetrate the bank after hours, he must first get past the perimeter detection system to get to the vault. You would have to defeat the locks on the doors, then somehow turn off the motion detectors and the alarm, and then make your way to the vault. If the vault does what it's supposed to do—delay intruders for a specific period of time—other parts of the security process will compensate to foil the would-be bank robbers. In this case, it would be a roving security guard making rounds on foot.

That's why banks are usually robbed during the day. It's easier.

In this real-world case, the intrusion detection system (IDS) forces the evil ones to choose a different, more daring attack method. In our case, things happen so fast that an IDS system is more of an alarm trigger for the forensics and recovery teams. But an IDS system can detect a great deal of things that you would want to know about but wouldn't normally see. For example, maybe someone is "casing" your network by scanning it for known vulnerable ports. An IDS would tell you this, and you could prepare for it. The IDS would tell you which ports the attacker was looking at or maybe the operating system being targeted. This is good information if you need to mount a defense.

Like AV, most IDS solutions rely on signatures and pattern matching to identify undesirable activity. These databases must be updated at regular intervals to stay current. There are two forms of IDS: network based and host based.

For a network-based IDS (NIDS) to be effective, it must have read access to all the network traffic. A NIDS is usually placed on span ports or taps for this reason. A span port or tap is a special port on a switch that is configured to see all the packets that the switch sees. As you might imagine, on a busy network this can be a great deal of traffic! This can generate quite a few false positives, so a NIDS generally requires a bit of tuning to be effective.

A NIDS is important, but we're interested specifically in the host-based IDS (HIDS). A HIDS performs the same basic function as a NIDS, but a HIDS does it at the endpoint. By being an integral part of the endpoint, a HIDS can tell whether other methods are being used to attack the system, such as the USB port.

Check out some of the products from the following vendors (yes, in alphabetical order):

- Computer Associates
- Internet Security Systems (ISS)
- Lancope
- McAfee

- NFR
- SonicWALL
- Sourcefire

If you're the "grow your own" type, you can always consider snort.[2] Snort is an open source IDS solution that runs on dedicated hardware that runs on various versions of Windows and Linux.

INTRUSION PREVENTION

Intrusion prevention systems (IPSs) are a relatively new product group and based on the idea that one can stop the attack before it does any damage. Like IDS, IPS comes in two flavors: network based and host based.

In the case of network-based IPS (NIPS), the device is installed as a "bump in the wire," as shown in Figure 6-6. The IPS will intercept all the packets, inspect them for evil, and either allow them to pass or shunt them to a bit bucket while the alarm is sounded. They function in much the same way as a firewall does, except whereas a firewall examines where traffic goes and the protocol used to send it, a NIPS examines the syntax of the packets and in some cases how the packets are put together. The downside of a NIPS is that it usually requires you to modify your network to allow for the insertion of the NIPS device, because it does have to be between the source and destination of traffic.

Most NIPS systems are still signature based, but many are adding heuristic elements to their rule-set. From a NIPS perspective, this may involve a learning period during which your NIPS product tries to sort out what is normal behavior and what is abnormal and potentially harmful behavior. A clerk in the mailroom isn't going to be accessing the finance network under normal conditions, so you probably want to know if this kind of activity is happening. A NIPS will identify this type of behavior and send out an alert.

In the host-based IPS (HIPS) products, the software examines how other software and applications are accessing system-level drivers, relying on behavioral quirks to trigger them. Take a look at Figure 6-7, for example. Your word processor wouldn't be trying to write to critical system files, so the HIPS will stop it if it tries. Another example is if a JPG file tries to access your email address book, the HIPS will flag that as "bad," stop it, and notify you.

---

[2] http://www.snort.org - open source IDS solution

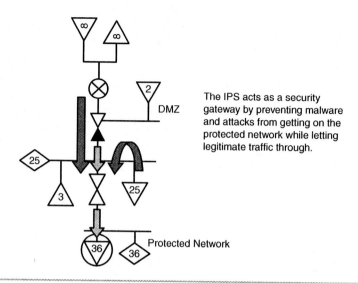

The IPS acts as a security gateway by preventing malware and attacks from getting on the protected network while letting legitimate traffic through.

Figure 6-6 A network-based IPS must live between the protected network and the outside, in much the same way that a firewall does.

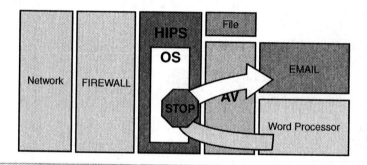

Figure 6-7 A HIPS prevents actions that shouldn't be occurring, such as your word processor accessing your address book.

You can think of a HIPS as an internal firewall with automatic rules. Hackers are exploiting flaws in software that allows malware to misbehave. A HIPS adds an additional layer to the operating system that identifies when this misbehavior occurs and stops it before it can do any harm.

Figure 6-7 shows another way to think about HIPS. HIPS acts as a wrapper around the operating system, examining things that affect it and the file system.

If you're interested in an IPS solution, you might want to consider examining the following vendors' products:

- AirTight Networks (WiFi IPS)
- Cisco
- Computer Associates
- eEye Digital Security
- ForeScout
- McAfee
- TippingPoint

HOST INTEGRITY

All the preceding technology is great, but it's only effective if it's turned on and configured correctly. The first thing that a savvy virus or worm writer does is turn off the AV.

I recently helped a friend troubleshoot his computer because he complained that it was running too slowly. I asked him when was the last time that the AV had updated itself? I could hear him banging on the keyboard and wildly clicking the mouse over the phone, so I asked him to tell me what he was doing. This should have taken two, possibly three mouse clicks. The horrible reality was that his computer had been attacked and the AV had been turned off!

A host integrity (HI) checker would have discovered that the AV had been turned off. Actually, an HI check would have revealed that my friend didn't have a critical patch that would have prevented the Trojan horse from being loaded in the first place.

The HI function is really a key element of our control solution because it's the component that makes the determination on the client side that the system meets our designated level of trust. As you can see in Figure 6-8, an HI process first checks itself to ensure that it hasn't been tampered with and then checks to see whether the other processes are running, whether the system is at the required patch level, whether forbidden processes are running or installed, and whether certain process are not running, such as AV or IPS. If the system isn't at the required level of trust, they'll report this to the network for appropriate action. This might mean being directed to a remediation network or the opening of a trouble ticket.

If I were to follow the pattern from the previous four sections, there would be a list of HI vendors here. Sadly, however, none meets my criteria at this time.

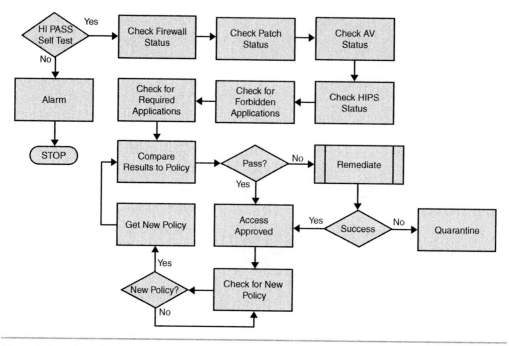

Figure 6-8 A basic host integrity process checks itself and checks to ensure policy compliance.

ENCRYPTION

Now that you have a clean, well-lit place for your data, you need to think about what you're going to do with it. Me, I like to hide it from the world, and that means encryption. Most operating systems come with a built-in file encryption tool, so this isn't a problem.

If I were talking about individual endpoints I would tell you that the built-in encryption tool will be just fine. That's what I tell my friends. However, an enterprise is different, because all the data belongs to it. You need a way to protect yourself from extortion and other illegal activity.

If you're going to use an encryption tool, and I highly recommend it, the tool must provide a key escrow service or some form of key extraction service to address the eventuality that the person who knows the key becomes unavailable for any reason.

There are some really good vendors in this space. Here's a short list:

- Information Security Corp (Secret Agent)
- PGP

- PointSec
- WinMagic

Taking this notion to a higher level, there are now products that specialize in what is called *intellectual property management* (IPM). The nice thing about IPM products is that they tend to focus on the data, who creates it, who is allowed access to it, and where the data is distributed. Virtually all IPM products have an endpoint client that communicates with a database where meta data about the documents is stored. Some IPM products integrate with Windows networking, whereas others operate as stand-alone products. I mention them not so much as an alternative to encryption but as a tool that the enterprise security professional should consider if the ultimate goal is to protect the information.

Digital rights management systems are also considered a form of IPM systems but tend to be more focused on the creation and management of enterprise-type data. I think that the difference is really just a marketing ploy designed to focus attention on specific market verticals. At any rate, here's a list of vendors that supply some form of digital management:

- Innovation Asset Group
- Liquid Machines
- Microsoft
- Verdasys
- Vontu

TRUST, BUT VERIFY

Now that you have your tools collected and you think that you have a good understanding of how you want them to behave, it's time to make sure that they do. The engineering process is a simple one: test, analyze, fix. In a manner similar to the scientific method, we postulate how our system is going to behave, test against that postulate, and fix what doesn't work.

TEST, TEST, TEST

Did I mention that we need to test? The first thing that we need to consider is a test plan that takes us step by step through the process. The test plan must address the security of the endpoint and the functionality of the endpoint. Some basic, high-level steps are as follows:

1. Verify that our test rig hasn't been altered.
2. Verify the build number on the system with the most recently approved build.
3. Execute the test plan.
4. Compare the results with the policy.
5. Approve/disapprove.
6. Document the results.

You must include basic set of tests in your test, such as port scanning, operating system identification, and network application availability. If the system is a server, you might want to do some Web service application testing to make sure that things haven't crept into your build. The number one killer of Web services is poor coding techniques that introduce exploitable flaws. This is your last chance to find them before someone else does.

From a service and application perspective, what you allow depends on what your security policy allows, but my recommendation is that the less you allow, the better off you're going to be. For example, I see no reason to allow a Web server on an endpoint destined for the desktop. There are other applications that you probably want to explicitly test for, such as the presence of known Trojan horses and peer-to-peer (P2P) programs that will get your legal department up in arms.

You also want to make sure that your security and management tools can connect so that you can remotely manage your endpoints. This is more of an operational test, but it ensures that when the endpoint is deployed you can remotely verify its state and security posture.

Something else you want to consider here is that the person who builds the endpoints can't be the person who tests the endpoints. Once again, this is a division of roles that ensures that our system isn't abused through collusion or carelessness.

Track Your Results

Trends can develop over time, and you need to be able to identify them. Are you getting more secure or less secure? Are more things being added to your builds, or are you taking things out? How many patches have been added over the course of an endpoint's life?

You can use your version control system to keep track of your test results, too. That way you can pull up a configuration along with the pertinent test results.

Also of great importance is the fact that you are keeping track of what is going into your build process.

KEY POINTS

I used to sign my email with "security is a process, not a solution." The more time I spend in the security world, the more I believe that it is more about developing a reliable process than anything else. We must develop a process that ensures that each endpoint we deploy is as secure as it can be. That process begins with a known entity and ends with a level of documentation that enables us to track trends and verify results.

We must have a secure area for our build process to live, and we must have a system that tracks our build configuration and test results. We must also have a separate place for the testing process to occur.

START SECURE

The area that we build and configure our endpoints in can offer an attacker the opportunity to hide Trojans or viruses. To reduce if not eliminate that possibility, you must have a dedicated stand-alone network that contains all the tools you need to build your target endpoint. I believe that the process starts with a known secure system and that all other changes must begin with that point.

TOOLS ARE NEEDED

Although you can generate a secure baseline, it won't stay that way if you don't protect it. The operating systems of many devices have only a minimal capability to protect themselves from outside threats, and none of them can protect themselves from well-crafted attacks. For that reason, we must include other tools such as AV, firewalls, and patch management into our basic builds. For those of us who teeter on the paranoid side, IDS, IPS, HI, and encryption are also required additions.

CHECK YOUR RESULTS

Simply building something that you think is secure isn't good enough. You need to verify that the endpoint that you're building will stand up to the attacks that it's going to see on the network. You also need to use this test process to ensure that the decisions you're making regarding application selection and software engineering don't introduce flaws into your build that can be exploited later.

From the vantage point of a secure, stand-alone network, you can launch viral attacks, port scans, and other vulnerability assessment tools that validate your build and the process that generated it.

Threat Vectors 7

One can attack an endpoint in numerous ways, but for the most part the truly devastating methods leverage the power afforded by the operating system. If you "own" the operating system, you can do anything you want. If you're the system administrator or the root user, you can turn off the firewall, kill the intrusion detection system (IDS), and clear out the logs. When attackers have that kind of access, they can cover their tracks and make it very difficult for you to find them.

Many operating systems are pretty loose with who they allow to run programs with administrative privileges, whereas others don't allow any to run with executive status. Minimizing the list of applications, and users, that run with that level of privilege is a key step to ensuring the security of your endpoint.

Having said all this, the next critical threat vector involves the applications that run on top of the operating system. Peer-to-peer networking and chat protocols have evolved faster than the security tools that protect them. This deficiency, coupled with a low level of user knowledge, can conspire to make the very applications that we rely on a significant threat to the endpoint's security posture.

PRÉCIS

The combination of operating system and applications and the relationship to the security of the endpoint is the topic of discussion. We're going start with a discussion of the operating system and how it can protect itself, how it can be dangerous to itself, and then move to a discussion about user privilege levels and high-risk applications. The goal is to run the endpoint at the lowest privilege possible. We'll examine how the operating system can protect itself, but we'll also look at some of the weak points that inhabit most operating systems. We're also going to explore a couple of applications that represent the largest threat to your endpoint's security now and in the future.

SPECIAL POINTS OF INTEREST

The operating system that is the core of every endpoint can also be the weakest link in the security chain. The general nature of most operating systems creates a situation in which the lowest common denominator drives overall system security.

Having said that, some of the applications that we use on our endpoints can actually make it worse. Peer-to-peer networking applications and instant messaging applications, while creating a collaborative environment, also enable the spread of malware and abuse.

PROTECTING THE OPERATING SYSTEM

As I said earlier, if you lose control of the operating system, you've lost the game. Hacker tools such as rootkits are designed to hide the fact that a system has been exploited. Introduced into the system via an exploit that exercises a vulnerability, these tools are designed to enable a hacker to maintain access to a system in a completely undetectable manner.

Because the operating system controls how applications interface with the hardware and other applications, it stands to reason that if you can control its behavior you can successfully hide inside of it. However, you can do some basic things to protect it if you plan for it.

SOME BUILT-IN PROTECTIONS

Most operating systems support different levels of user privilege, where, for instance, an administrative user has complete control over the system while common users have control only over their own environment. This basic stratification of system privileges ensures that a common user can't delete system files or change the configuration significantly.

We see this instantiated in Windows systems that use NT File System (NTFS) as administrator, power user, user, and guest. There are other user groups in Windows, such as backup operators, interactive, network, and terminal server user. The last list of users is intended to provide administrative access with the exception of the terminal user.

In the UNIX world, it's a similar situation. Superuser, or root, is the system administrator in the UNIX world and the holy grail for hackers. UNIX uses user identifications (UIDs) to identify various users, with the UID of 0 being reserved for root. UNIX generally reserves UIDs from 1 to 9 for system functions such as daemon, agent, and FTP. Human UIDs usually start at 20 and work their way up to 65,535.

Another interesting feature of most operating systems is their capability to associate owners with files. This association makes it harder for unauthorized users to diddle with your documents. It also makes it very hard for nonowners to modify or eliminate system files.

In Figure 7-1, you can see something called the "mode" on the far left side of the list. The mode denotes what kind of file it is and who has access to it. Because this isn't supposed to be a chapter on the UNIX operating system specifically, I focus on the principles that the mode represents. The purpose of the mode is to tell you what kind of file you're dealing with and who gets to do things to it. You can read a file, write to a file, or execute a file. That ability is assigned to the owner, the group, and the world (or, as most of us know it, guests).

The operating system uses the user and group information to enforce access controls on the files. In the case of our example, if I were logged in to the system as "guest" and tried to read the directory "movies," the operating system would tell me, "No, you can't read that directory because you're not markkadr." Being able to associate files with users is a great way to protect system files and other sensitive files from inadvertent modification or deletion.

The message that I want for you to take away from this particular section is to pay attention to how you create users and groups. It's been my practice to install users with the lowest level of privilege as possible, no matter how much they complain.

The ability to be able to associate users with groups is a big help in reducing the amount of workload on the administrative side. Microsoft has built-in support for network-based groups through Active Directory services. The UNIX world also has directory-based services through Lightweight Directory Access Protocol (LDAP) and Network Information Service (NIS). LDAP is a standardized method of storing and accessing just about any kind of information and is especially good at the user and group information used in the authentication process.[1] NIS has been around just about since the dawn of time and is a way that UNIX systems use to share information files. NIS+ moves away from the flat files used by NIS to a database architecture.

Hiding files is also another way to protect them, although it is a pretty weak way that will only thwart the less experienced. Most operating systems can designate a file or

---

[1] http://www.ietf.org/rfc/rfc2251.txt

directory as viewable or hidden. The attribute that controls whether a file or directory is hidden is different between the operating systems. In the case of UNIX, simply putting a leading dot or dash will prevent the file or directory from being displayed when a user uses simple commands such as **ls** to see the file list. However, adding **–a** to the **ls** command will provide a listing of all files:

```
>ls -a
```

To get the additional file detail as seen in Figure 7-1, I added the **l** switch.

In Windows, the ability to hide the file is coded into the file attributes. Basic Windows attributes are as follows:

- **Read-only.** The file can only be read.
- **Archive.** The file has been backed up.
- **System.** The file belongs to the operating system and not a user.
- **Hidden.** The file shouldn't be displayed in a normal file list.

```
[StarBlazer12:~] markkadr% ls -al
total 4456
drwxr-xr-x   48 markkadr  staff     1632 Feb  8 22:28 .
drwxrwxr-t    8 root      admin      272 Dec  9 15:15 ..
-rw-r--r--    1 markkadr  staff        3 Dec 31  1969 .CFUserTextEncoding
drwxr-xr-x    3 markkadr  staff      182 May  5  2003 .CodeByDesign
-rwxr-xr-x    1 markkadr  staff    12292 Feb 28 13:08 .DS_Store
-rw-r--r--    1 markkadr  staff        0 Mar 27  2003 .MCXLC
drwxr-xr-x    3 markkadr  staff      182 Apr 14  2005 .SygateTmpYY
drwx------  140 markkadr  staff     4760 Mar  8 16:47 .Trash
-rw-------    1 markkadr  staff        0 Apr  1  2004 .Xauthority
-rw-------    1 markkadr  staff       49 Apr  1  2004 .bash_history
-rw-r--r--    1 markkadr  staff       24 Jul 12  2003 .cshrc
drwxr-xr-x    4 markkadr  staff      136 May 21  2003 .datastudio
drwx------    5 markkadr  staff      170 Sep 14 11:56 .gnupg
drwxr-xr-x    2 markkadr  staff       68 Aug 12  2004 .java
drwxr-xr-x    4 markkadr  staff      136 May  8  2003 .jpi_cache
-rw-r--r--    1 markkadr  staff       34 Nov 25 19:24 .lpoptions
-rw-------    1 markkadr  staff        2 Sep 11  2003 .mysql_history
drwx------    4 markkadr  staff      136 Jun 12  2003 .ssh
-rw-r--r--    1 markkadr  staff        0 May  5  2003 .strt
-rw-------    1 markkadr  staff      741 Apr  4  2005 .viminfo
-rw-r--r--    1 root      staff    26923 Sep 18  2003 .xftcache
-rw-r--r--    1 markkadr  staff   652288 Apr  6  2005 4-5-05, TNC draft 1.doc
-rw-r--r--    1 markkadr  staff    28992 Jun 12  2003 Database tools review.doc
drwxr-xr-x   30 markkadr  staff     1020 Mar 18 09:43 Desktop
drwx------   63 markkadr  staff     2142 Mar 11 13:38 Documents
-rw-r--r--    1 markkadr  staff    22016 May 28  2003 Don.doc
drwx------   49 markkadr  staff     1666 Nov  4 08:41 Library
-rw-r--r--    1 markkadr  staff    26848 Apr 13  2005 LinuxMacCC.log
drwx------    9 markkadr  staff      306 Oct 30 13:12 Movies
drwx------    8 markkadr  staff      272 Aug 30  2005 Music
-rw-r--r--    1 markkadr  staff        0 Feb  8 22:28 Opera 7 Preferences.new
```

Figure 7-1   File list from an Apple Macintosh showing the file mode, number of links, owner name, group name, size of file in bytes, last modified date, and path.

Actually listing all the file information on a Windows endpoint is a little trickier than it was in our Mac environment because you can't get all the information from one command. To get the same information in DOS, it requires three commands: **dir**, **dir /q** (owner information), and **attrib** (show me file attributes), as shown in Figure 7-2.

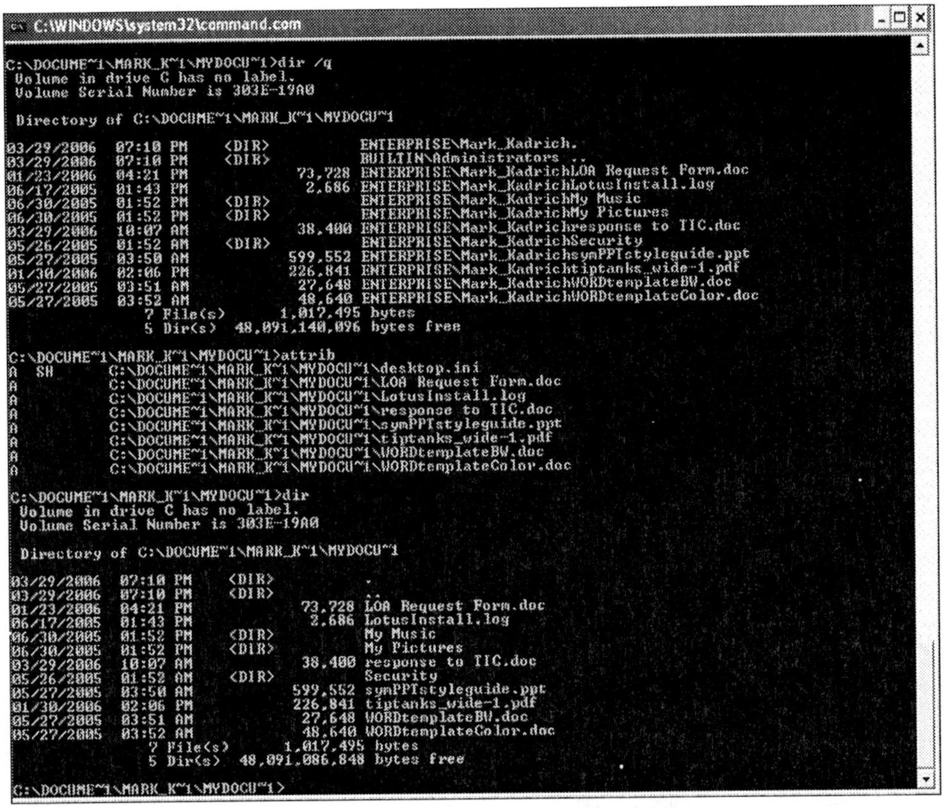

Figure 7-2   Directory listings using **dir /q** (owner), **attrib** (file attributes), and a standard **dir** command.

SOME BUILT-IN WEAKNESSES

The strength of modern computers is their capability to do or be just about anything we can program them to do or be. With that general-purpose functionality, however, comes a price: Some things they just aren't very good at. They're designed to provide access, so the converse of that, restricting control, can be a problem.

Take file sharing, for example. If I encrypt my files but make them available to the network via a file share, anybody who can gain access to the network can potentially get at my protected information. Let's not even mention that we're now extending a part of our file system to the network via some fairly complex and vulnerable code that can be and has been attacked successfully numerous times.

There is also the problem of intellectual property management and the loss of control that uncontrolled file sharing represents. Chapter 6, "Trustworthy Beginnings," explained how intellectual property management (IPM) software can control this if you have the money. Backup also becomes a bit of a problem in a noncentralized data environment.

Support for back-rev programs can be a problem because sometimes they bridge security functionality in ways that the programmer never intended. In many cases, you have to make changes to certain permissions to get them to run, and that can be exploited. For example, if you run terminal server user and you're running a legacy program that requires administrative privileges to operate correctly in Windows XP, you may be able to exploit a flaw in the legacy program and elevate your privilege to administrator. If the legacy program has a vulnerability and you successfully exploit that vulnerability, when the system breaks, it will break leaving you with the highest privilege possible: administrator.

Another built-in weakness is that the operating system doesn't check to see whether the file it's about to execute is really the file that it thinks it is. This is how viruses are able to infect executable files. A virus modifies the code, adding programming that helps propagate the code and infect other computers. When the operating system loads the executable, it doesn't know that the file has been changed. In most cases, you can change the name of the file completely, and the operating system *doesn't even care.* Many third-party security applications check themselves using a cryptographic tool called a *hash* or *message digest.* As shown in Figure 7-3, a hash is a fixed-length nonreversible representation of a string of bits. According to Wikipedia, the most utilized hash functions are MD5 and SHA-1. The U.S. government seems to be enamored with SHA and as such has specified SHA-1, SHA-256, SHA-384, and SHA-512 as the secure hash standard for the Federal government.[2] The nice thing about a hash function is that changing 1 bit in the original document results in a completely different hash output.

To illustrate how this could prove useful, I used the MD5 hash function that resided on my Mac and made a hash of this chapter. The result was this:

```
MD5 (Chapter 6.doc) = c67d3e3cbdaf2a16338043f8cd692342
```

---

[2] Federal Information Processing Standards Publication 180-2

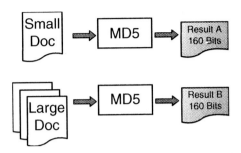

Figure 7-3   A message digest produces a different and unique result for each file. The result is always the same length.

I changed the chapter by adding a space at the end of the previous paragraph, changing the ending of the sentence from

"results in a completely different hash output."

to the very similar

"results in a completely different hash output. "

I saved the file again and ran it through my MD5 function. The resulting MD5 hash was this:

```
MD5 (Chapter 6.doc) = b2935f4b0f5ce826a735c83251f90272
```

You can see that the addition of the space at the end of the sentence completely changed the resulting MD5 output! This would be a great way for operating systems to check file integrity.

Having demonstrated how useful hash functions are, I should point out that collisions, different files with the same hash value, are possible. Research work by Wang, Yin, and Yu has demonstrated that both MD5 and SHA-1 (among others) are susceptible to collision attacks.[3,4] So, although these attacks do exist, it doesn't decrease the general usefulness of hash functions, although it does mean that for sensitive security applications, a "belt and suspenders" approach (one that uses two hash functions) may be in order.

I'm going to finish this section by saying that a significant built-in weakness is guest access. Guest access is a big problem because it's designed to allow anyone access to the system if even in a restricted way. In much the same scenario that we talked about with

---

[3]   Collision Search Attacks on SHA-1, Wang, Yin, Yu, 2/13/2005

[4]   Collisions for Hash Functions MD4, MD5, HAVAL-128 and RIPEMD

legacy code, if I can get onto a system at any level, I have increased the probability that I'll be able to successfully break into it further.

"KILLER" APPLICATIONS

Everyone is looking for the next killer app—the one application that will take the industry by storm and make folks a bunch of money. The problem with killer applications is that they usually solve some vexing problem or add some new type of functionality that is so wildly popular that it's impossible to hold back the tide of clandestine user installations. From a hardware perspective, we've seen this in cell phones and the cameras that now come as a standard feature. The camera was so popular that people changed phones to get that one feature.

On the software side, the two classes of applications that fit this description are peer-to-peer file-sharing programs and the ubiquitous chat applications. Figure 7-4 shows that this is a many-to-many connection relationship.

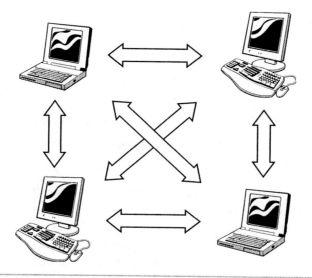

Figure 7-4   Peer-to-peer networking model connects all computers to each other.

Networking comes in two flavors: peer-to-peer (P2P) and server-based. All the endpoints that have network-based operating systems have the ability to share files on a P2P basis. However, P2P file-sharing applications (such as Napster and Kazaa) aren't integrated into the operating system and have the ability to mask their operation in a way that makes it extremely difficult to find and control them. This has created significant problems in the past.

Chat applications are of the server-based type because they need a server to relay their messages, as shown in Figure 7-5. Chat applications provide for more than simple text messaging. They also provide file exchange services and, in some instances, audio and video services.

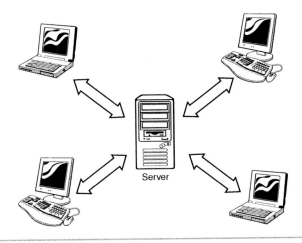

Figure 7-5 Chat applications use a central server to relay messages between clients.

PEER-TO-PEER ATTACKS

An interesting twist to this is that hackers understand the value of P2P networks and the power that they represent. In 2002, the slapper worm ran through the Linux world *creating* a P2P attack network.

Ignoring the fact that these little beasties can be used to attack other folks, how about the risk to you and your network?

Let me ask this question another way: Is the P2P application the only thing that you're getting in the download? How do you know that the downloaded application doesn't have a Trojan horse in it? How about a good old-fashioned security flaw? Well, as recently as last year, the fading Kazaa P2P application was still getting security flaws posted against it that allowed for successful attacks against the endpoint.[5]

---

[5] http://www.mp3newswire.net/stories/5002/KaZaaSecurity.html

File-distribution tools such as BitTorrent, which use a P2P distribution model, can actually act as a network-based denial-of-service attack if allowed to grow uncontrolled. Recent evidence also indicates that the files that P2P networks are sharing can hide malware. VitalSecurity.org reported in 2005 that music tracks, TV episodes, and porn that were distributed via BitTorrent were being bundled with adware.[6]

So, download and install a rogue P2P application, use it to download questionable content, and get a nasty piece of malware for free!

There is a bit of good news/bad news. The good news is that these programs can use just about any port to establish a connection to other hosts. The bad news is that one of the most popular, port 80, our HTTP port of choice, is routinely allowed to pass outbound through our firewalls with no restrictions.

LET'S "CHAT" ABOUT IT

Instant messaging (IM) chat applications such as MSN Messenger, AOL Instant Messenger, and Yahoo! are the human-driven equivalent of P2P networks. They're also one of the largest growing points of viral attack and information leakage on your network. Using these protocols, you can exchange files and share information. According to IMlogic, the first eight months of 2005 saw an astounding 1,968 percent increase in IM and P2P threats as compared to the same period in 2004. Assuming a self-serving factor of 10 to 1, that still leaves us with a near 200 percent increase in the number of threats in the IM world. Not to pick on Microsoft, but they lead the pack with more than 60 percent being aimed at MSN Messenger.

My research showed that virtually all the chat programs had at various times supported vulnerabilities that enabled an attacker to successfully execute code on the target endpoint. All of them have also been successfully used to send viruses and Trojans. That part of the equation boils down to stupid users doing stupid things. You send a Trojan file to a chat room and tell folks that it's the latest Paris Hilton video and see how many morons open it up.

As threat vectors go, chat applications are about as target rich an environment that you can get. They are ubiquitous, and they support the exchange of real-time messages and files. You can even get some chat services that support video. My Mac comes equipped with iChat. Plug a camera into it and you're good to go. Combine that with a rootkit and you have a great tool that will enable you to steal critical intellectual property or record video chat sessions of board meetings.

---

[6] http://www.securityfocus.com/news/11215

KEY POINTS

The endpoint is a combination of an operating system and the applications that use it. Because a computer is a general-purpose device, it is a compromise in a number of areas. Being the focus of that compromise, the operating system must do its best to balance the requirements of managing hardware and providing a suitable and hospitable environment for the applications and the people who use them.

THE OPERATING SYSTEM IS YOUR BEST ENEMY

Most operating systems have a number of built-in features to control how users and groups interact with the system. These features can prevent unauthorized users from gaining access to other users' information while ensuring that authorized users and groups are allowed to freely exchange information.

However, if not properly configured, these same features can be bypassed or manipulated in a way that makes it much easier for an attacker to get a foothold on the endpoint. How users are added to the system and the privileges that they have must be controlled in such a way that they have only the minimum level of access to system resources and other users' environments.

Two major sections of the operating system, the file system and networking, are designed to connect users and thus increase productivity by supporting collaboration and sharing. However, it is these features that support connectivity and collaboration that are usually exploited to the detriment of the enterprise.

THE APPS ARE YOUR WORST FRIEND

The applications that exist on the endpoint are the tools that give users the power to generate and manipulate the information that our enterprises rely on. However, some applications represent significant potential for abuse through security flaws or misuse.

P2P applications and chat applications have found and filled a requirement for exchanging large amounts of information and for providing personal communications. Unfortunately, these applications also represent a significant and dangerous threat and infection vector if not managed securely.

Microsoft 8 Windows

In this chapter, we get specific by starting with the Windows environment. Most of you have picked up this book and turned to this chapter because this is where most of your pain is, so we'll start with things that you can do to Windows in general to improve your security posture. We're not going to concern ourselves with anything prior to Windows 2000 because those early versions of Windows weren't really capable of protecting themselves or the data on the system.

Microsoft has been much maligned over the years, but although much can be said of Microsoft, being stupid isn't one of them. Microsoft has done a Herculean job of turning a huge organization into a huge security-aware organization in a fairly short time. As you'll see in this chapter, we can do many things to improve the security posture of Windows while integrating it into our closed-loop process control (CLPC) environment.

PRÉCIS

The first thing we're going to do is talk about checking our system for beasties. Before we can even begin to discuss improving our security, we need to know that our security hasn't already been breached. We'll cover some methods and tools that will help you assess the security posture of the endpoint. Included in that section is a lively discussion on rootkits and ways to detect them.

Microsoft breaks their security into three different modes, so that's how we're going to look at it. In the Microsoft world, there are systems that are connected to Active Directory, those that aren't (considered stand-alone), and what Microsoft refers to as "an extremely high level of security in which application compatibility or usability may be constrained," or specialized security—limited functionality (SSLF).

We walk through how to lock down the file system from a stand-alone endpoint's perspective to what I consider the minimum level of security that a system should have. We then "crank on the screws" to further enhance our stand-alone endpoint's security posture. Armed with the knowledge of what you can do to secure a Windows endpoint, we move to the methods and processes you should follow to generate a security policy and to lock down the enterprise.

Our stand-alone procedure makes the assumption that you're the administrator of the system; our enterprise approach assumes that the end user is not the administrator.

The final level of security leverages our CLPC to ensure that the system stays secure.

Aside from the CLPC security function, Windows security has a number of different reference sources to quote from. Because I'm not trying to reinvent the wheel as far as securing Windows, I quote from a number of different sources. A great place to start, however, is with the Microsoft TechNet Threats and Countermeasures site, located at www.microsoft.com/technet/security/topics/serversecurity/tcg/tcgch00.mspx.

SPECIAL POINTS OF INTEREST

Windows NT is probably the exception to the claims of early Windows insecurity made in the preceding section. Windows NT 4 actually got to be pretty well trusted after a while, but it took a basic change from the DOS file system to the NT File System (NTFS) and many years of trial and error to get a workable security profile for Windows NT.

The NTFS and years of beating on Windows NT worked to the advantage of those who were using the operating system. Yes, we whined mightily about security problems, but in the end, Windows NT security was quite workable.

I know that I said that starting with a clean image is really the best way to ensure that your entire population of endpoints is secure, but I also said that for some of us that isn't practical. For that reason, we're going to start off by checking the endpoint to see whether it's infected or corrupt in any way. There's no point in locking down a system that has a rootkit on it!

Chapter 3, "Something Is Missing," discussed our iconology and nomenclature. Drawing on that for the purposes of this chapter, in our final security configuration we will be creating a protected endpoint. Not only is the endpoint secure, it's also capable of assessing and remediating itself when it discovers that it no longer is secure or up-to-date. Figure 8-1 shows the symbol for a protected endpoint.

Desktops Notebooks	Hardened OS Firewall Antivirus Host Integrity Patch Management Enforcement Remediation Remote Management	Servers
Data Sink		Data Source

Figure 8-1 Protected endpoint iconology. User systems sink data, whereas server systems act as a source of data.

If you think that you might have a serious breach and want to involve law enforcement, *stop right now!* Changing any portion of the file system may render the endpoint *useless as evidence.* Many of the things that we're going to do from this moment on have the potential to damage evidence; so, if you suspect that a crime has been committed, call your legal advisor (yes, I just said get a lawyer) and determine a plan of action.

Finally, another thing that I want you to be aware of as you read this chapter is the fundamental process associated with ensuring that a system is secure. If you have any questions about the trustworthiness of a system, you will have trust questions associated with your network. If the system can't be trusted to start with, the role that it would play in a CLPC solution would be that of a potential hole. We end this chapter with a discussion on how Windows, and Windows tools, can play a role in our CLPC system.

A WORD ABOUT VISTA

The *American Heritage Dictionary* defines *vista* as two things: a distant view or prospect, especially one seen through an opening, as between rows of buildings or trees. Or, an awareness of a range of time, events, or subjects; a broad mental view: "the deep and sweeping vistas these pioneering critics opened up" (Arthur C. Danto).[1] Only time will tell which definition is correct when referring to Microsoft Vista. Either it will be a narrow and distant prospect or it will be a broad and sweeping view. But, the future of Microsoft isn't what we're discussing here. As security professionals, we have real-world, deploy-it-today concerns. Vista is tomorrow.

On the security side, Vista supports memory randomization, technically referred to as *Address Space Layout Randomization* (ASLR). ASLR is a feature that should reduce the impact of malware by making it difficult to predict where system libraries are located.

---

[1] The American Heritage Dictionary of the English Language, Fourth Edition.

In addition, users are given more latitude to make some operational settings, such as setting a Wired Equivalent Privacy (WEP) key, without the need to be an administrator. Windows service hardening restricts services from doing things that they shouldn't be doing, such as Remote Procedure Call (RPC) replacing system files.

However, on the downside, Vista seems to be a bit chattier as far as warnings are concerned. Between having discussions with Vista testers and my experience with Vista, my concern as a security administrator is that users would tend to "click through" the fairly content-free messages. I say "content free" because the information contained in the warning dialogs doesn't contain information that would support effective troubleshooting of security-related issues.

As of this writing, Vista, and Microsoft, are still fighting the world with regard to features and functions. Some of the major security vendors have complained that Microsoft is preventing them from integrating with Vista in an effort to expand the Microsoft market share at their expense.[2] I suspect, and this is just my opinion, that some of these complaints will wind up in court. This means that Vista is going to change, so detailing anything here would be pointless.

Vista does have some nice features, such as the Microsoft version of network access control (NAC), NAP or Network Access Protection. Be warned, however, this is a Microsoft-specific solution, with all that implies.

But, as of this writing, Vista hasn't been deployed in large enterprises, and we don't know what the true security posture of Vista is going to be in the real world. When we understand how enterprises are going to use Vista and we have grappled with the practical implications of deployment, I will be happy to add it as a separate chapter.

INITIAL HEALTH CHECK

Before we start to crank down the security of our Windows endpoints, it's a good idea to make sure that we still "own" the box. There's no point in spending the time to secure an endpoint if all we're going to do is secure it for the hacker who has already got rootkit running on it.

First, we're going to look at the system the way a hacker would: through the eyes of a port scanner. This is pretty much just to see whether there is something obviously wrong and to make us a little more familiar with the system. Next, we're going to see whether we still own the system: We're going to check for rootkits. Then we're going to look in a

---

[2]   Adobe, Symantec Behind Complaints to EU about Vista, Paul Thurrott, WindowsITPro, 9/21/06

few of the places that hackers stash things such as hidden files, the Registry, alternate data streams, and services.

SYSTEM SCAN

A fairly simple thing to do is to look at the system the way a hacker would: from the outside. Because Trojan horse programs use the network to connect to the hacker, they sometimes leave a port open, and that can be detected.

A great tool that you can get to do this type of detection is called nmap.[3] Nmap, short for Network Mapper, is a free program available in versions that will run on Linux, Windows, UNIX, FreeBSD, and MacOS, just to name a few. I have the Mac version, and I can attest to nmap's speed and accuracy. I run nmap on my network segments to see whether any new endpoints have popped up while I wasn't watching. The nice thing about nmap is that it tells me a great deal about the endpoint:

- IP address
- Operating system type (Windows, Linux, and so on)
- Port number (1–65,535)
- Transport type (TCP or UDP)
- Port state (open, closed, filtered)
- Service (SSH, FTP, HTTP, and so on)
- Version (if the service provides it)
- Uptime (time since last reboot)

This can be very useful information because things such as Trojan horses show up as additional network services. The downside is that the Trojan services tend to use legitimate service ports to hide behind. Therefore, if it looks like the SOCKS service is running on port 1080, you really need to check the endpoint to make sure that it really is SOCKS and not some Mydoom variant. If you check the process list or service list and SOCKS isn't listed as running, you have a Trojan horse that is hiding behind that port. More on this in the following section on finding rootkits.

On Windows systems, you can usually expect to find a couple of ports operating that support standard Windows networking features such as file sharing and RPC. You may find some other services, such as Remote Desktop Protocol (RDP), that will definitely turn on a siren or two. Table 8-1 lists some common Windows services.

---

[3] www.insecure.org/nmap

Table 8-1   Common Microsoft Windows Ports

Port	Description
123	Network Time Synchronization
135	RPC (Remote Procedure Call) and DCOM (Distributed Component Object Model)
137, 138, 139	File and Print sharing using NetBIOS over TCP/IP (name service, datagram service, and session)
445	File and Print sharing for Windows 2000 and above
500	IKE (Internet Key Exchange) support for IPSec
1900	Universal Plug and Play (UPnP)
3372	Microsoft Distributed Transaction Coordinator (MSDTC)
3389	RDP (So you want to remotely control a computer?)
5000	SSDP (Simple Service Discovery Protocol), works with IKE

Think of a scanner as the first step in identifying whether something is amiss on your endpoints from an external perspective. You still have to do the legwork.

FINDING ROOTKITS

Rootkits are tools designed to allow hackers to keep the system that they have hacked. There are numerous methods, especially in userland, that hackers use to cover their trail. They're hoping that with all the stuff that goes on in Windows, that a simple EXE or a tiny process isn't going to be noticed. Rootkits take covering your tracks to a new level. They modify the system so that the services and applications that the hacker uses are protected from detection.

There are three basic types of rootkit: kernel, library, and application. Kernel rootkits modify the system kernel by adding a device driver or a loadable module. The method really depends on the target operating system. In our case, device drivers seem to be the vector of choice—specifically, VxDs (virtual external drivers).

Library rootkits typically modify a library by patching, hooking, or replacing a system call. By intercepting system calls, rootkits can do things such as tell Windows Explorer not to display the directory that contains the rootkit or to not list the process in the Task Manager.

Application rootkits use similar methods but target the somewhat easier-to-modify applications.

But rootkits aren't perfect. We actually have a great deal of the information that we need to determine whether a rootkit is running on our system. The problem is that the information being provided to us is under the control of the rootkit, so we have to have an external source to compare against.

One method is to compare the results of the external scan with the information provided by internal tools such as netstat. Netstat can provide a great deal of information on connections, routing tables, sockets in use, and which applications are using them (**netstat –b**). However, if there is a back door on the system, netstat may not report it, and the extra open port would become obvious in the scan. You might have to connect a sniffer to the system, capture lots of packets, and sort though them looking for anomalous traffic.

You can pull the disk out of the system and examine it using a known good system.

Another method to discover rootkits is through the use of a third-party tool such as F-Secure's Blacklight[4] or Rootkit Revealer[5] from Sysinternals.[6] Another tool, RKDetect, uses the Windows Management Instrumentation, or WMI, and the Windows Services Manager to query the system. RKDetect compares the results and reports the differences. This is similar to the manual process described in the previous paragraph.

Now comes the hard part. You've come to the conclusion that the system has been rooted and you want to fix it. You're mad, and you want to cut the bleeping hackers off. You want to beat the hackers at their own game, prove that you're as smart as they are, and find all their code and rip it out.

Don't bother.

By the time you spend the time to detect the rootkit and install the tools to detect all the bits, you've spent the time that you could have used to re-image the system. It's a critical resource, you say? All the more reason to make sure that you can trust it, and you can't trust a system after it's been rooted.

For those who are determined to "fix" the system, there are some things that can be tried, but they all have their drawbacks.

---

[4] http://www.f-secure.com/exclude/blacklight/index.shtml

[5] http://www.sysinternals.com/Utilities/RootkitRevealer.html

[6] Microsoft bought Sysinternals in July of 2006.

Some tools purport to identify and remove rootkits. RKdetector runs on the local machine and attempts to identify hidden processes.[7] After hidden processes are identified, RKdetector tries to kill the processes. RKdetector has an internal MD5 database of rootkits and other hacker tools. Another tool, unhackme, has a free evaluation download but will require $19.95 after that expires.[8] I haven't used these tools, but there are reports that both of them suffer from false negatives, so be careful when you use them.

There is a manual method, but it only works if you know what rootkit has been installed on your system. By using the Windows Recovery Console, and the knowledge you gained from your scans and netstat, you may, and I repeat *may*, be able to remove a rootkit.[9] The basic steps are as follows:

1. Insert the Windows operating system installation CD.
2. Boot. (You may have to modify your BIOS to boot from CD/DVD.)
3. Choose R to enter the Recovery Console.
4. Choose the Windows installation you want to clean from the list.
5. Enter the Administrator password.

The Recovery Console enables you to list services that can be enabled or disabled. This is where the tricky part comes in: You have to know the name of the service you want to disable. Hopefully, the research you did earlier has provided you with the correct name. After the service has been stopped, you can reboot and finish removing the rootkit. Make sure you take good notes just in case something quits working so that you can go back and start it up again.

I've left off version numbers because they change so often. Furthermore, other tools are available, but I didn't want to write a book about rootkits.

One last note about removing rootkits: Of all the scenarios that remind me of weapons development, rootkits and rootkit detectors have all the characteristics of a traditional arms race. Unlike worms and viruses, rootkits have a human intellect constantly tweaking and refining their methods. If it were I, and I detected or even suspected that a rootkit was on my endpoint, I'd re-image it in a minute—minus the original vulnerability that allowed the jerk to root me in the first place!

---

[7] http://www.3wdesign.es/security/

[8] http://greatis.com/unhackme/

[9] http://support.microsoft.com/?kbid=314058

SYSTEM FILES

Later versions of Windows, starting with Windows 2000, come with a nifty tool called sigverif. This tool will scan your drive, checking the digital signatures of the files to those on record, and will notify you of incorrect or missing signatures. Having good signatures is part of the basic block and tackling of system integrity. If the signature is good, that application can be trusted. Running sigverif on my XP systems produced the result in Figure 8-2.

Signature Verification Results

The following files have not been digitally signed:

Name	In Folder	Modified	File Type	Version
atprint.gpd	c:\windows\system32\spool\drivers\w32x86\3	3/23/2006	GPD File	None
hpcljx02.hlp	c:\windows\system32\spool\drivers\w32x86\3	11/15/2001	Help File	None
hpcprd02.dll	c:\windows\system32\spool\drivers\w32x86\3	1/10/2002	Application Extension	2.0.12.2
hpcps02.ini	c:\windows\system32\spool\drivers\w32x86\3	6/19/2001	Configuration Settings	None
hpcstr02.dll	c:\windows\system32\spool\drivers\w32x86\3	1/10/2002	Application Extension	2.0.12.2
hpcui02.dll	c:\windows\system32\spool\drivers\w32x86\3	1/10/2002	Application Extension	2.0.12.2
hplj5m_4.ppd	c:\windows\system32\spool\drivers\w32x86\3	1/9/2002	PPD File	None
ps5ui.dll	c:\windows\system32\spool\drivers\w32x86\3	3/24/2005	Application Extension	0.3.3790.1830
pscript.ntf	c:\windows\system32\spool\drivers\w32x86\3	3/24/2005	NTF File	None
pscript5.dll	c:\windows\system32\spool\drivers\w32x86\3	3/24/2005	Application Extension	0.3.3790.1830
stdnames.gpd	c:\windows\system32\spool\drivers\w32x86\3	12/31/2001	GPD File	None
unidrv.dll	c:\windows\system32\spool\drivers\w32x86\3	3/23/2006	Application Extension	0.3.0.0
unidrvui.dll	c:\windows\system32\spool\drivers\w32x86\3	3/23/2006	Application Extension	0.3.0.0
unires.dll	c:\windows\system32\spool\drivers\w32x86\3	3/23/2006	Application Extension	0.3.0.0

Figure 8-2 Sigverif will find and display files that have bad or no crypto fingerprints.

I have to admit that I was moderately annoyed at the fact that these drivers weren't signed, so I went to the Internet to verify their authenticity. The INI and the GPD file I looked at with a text editor and decided they were harmless. The PSCRIPT.NTF file is a binary "mini driver" that contains descriptions of fonts for PostScript printers.

I figured that anything that started with "hp" would probably be found somewhere on the HP Web site. Using HP's internal search engine, I popped in hpcps02, hpcprd02, hpcstr02, and hpcui02. My results? Not very rewarding. As a matter of fact, I spent more time on the HP "try again" page than anywhere else. However, an Internet search did turn up references to the files, so I felt a little better.

I went through the same process for the rest of the files, taking about an hour to sort through the entire list. The final judgment was that they were indeed part of my printing subsystem and, although not signed, were okay.

ALTERNATE DATA STREAMS

Streams can be evil. Streams not as in babbling brooks filled with trout, but as in alternate data streams, or ADSs. Attackers can hide executable files in another executable's data streams. Originally devised to enable compatibility between Windows and the Macintosh Hierarchical File System (HFS), ADS allowed data to be sent to other applications. The thing about this feature is that hackers use ADSs to hide their tools and the fact that they are running on your system. The usual file browsing tools such as dir and Windows Explorer don't detect ADS-infected executables. Unfortunately, you have to use a third-party tool to audit and detect ADSs on your system because most antivirus (AV) and intrusion prevention tools don't catch them.

Some useful tools for detecting ADS can be found at the following Web sites:

- www.adstools.net/
- www.crucialsecurity.com/products/index.html

A bit of warning before you use these tools: If you're running AV software, you may want to check with the AV vendor to see how they deal with ADS. Some AV software adds an ADS to each file that it scans, so you may have to add an exclusion to keep the output from being a bit verbose. I could add an exception with command-line based adstools but not the GUI-based crucialads. Adstools also allow you to do the following:

- Include subdirectories
- Debug ADS
- Generate verbose error messages
- Get a summary of all bytes used in the scanned directories
- Exclude any ADS name
- Read a parameters file as input

The last one is nice if you have lots of exclusions.

Crucialads has a nice GUI, so it is a little easier to use so long as you don't mind that it does the entire drive. I also noticed that mixed in with the results were lots of "error 32 open" notices from trying to open files that were in use. You have to sift through the data to pick out the nuggets of information. The good news is that the information that they found was the same.

REGISTRY CHECK

For those of you unfamiliar with the Windows Registry, it is the DNA of the Windows operating system. The Windows Registry is a database of information that Windows uses to manage tasks, services, user profiles, how document types are related to applications, and so forth. It replaced the INI files that used to be used in older versions of Windows prior to Windows 95.

Under the system name (usually My Computer), the Registry is broken into five logical sections:

- **HKEY_CLASSES_ROOT.** Information about registered applications, file associations, and OLE object class IDs
- **HKEY_CURRENT_USER.** Settings specific to the current user
- **HKEY_LOCAL_MACHINE.** Information that is general to all users on this system
- **HKEY_USERS.** Information about all the authorized users of this system
- **HKEY_CURRENT_CONFIG.** Information gathered during the boot process

HKEY is shorthand for Handle to a KEY.

Before we start, because the Registry is the heart of your Windows system, screwing it up can hose your system. You need to back it up before you make any changes. You can do this by running REGEDIT. Select Export, click My Computer, click Export, and follow the prompts to save the file. You can find a complete set of instructions on how to back up, restore, and edit the Registry at http://support.microsoft.com/kb/322756#E03E0ACAAA.

As you can see in Figure 8-3, these five basic hives explode into a considerable number of subkeys. I didn't expand on HKEY_CLASSES_ROOT because it is a very large list of things.

For the purposes of our exercise, we're going to look at just a few keys, because they are predominantly the keys that are going to be modified. Under HKEY_LOCAL_MACHINE, check these subkeys:

- \Software\Microsoft\Windows\CurrentVersion\Run
- \Software\Microsoft\Windows\CurrentVersion\RunOnce
- \Software\Microsoft\Windows\CurrentVersion\RunOnceEx
- \Software\Microsoft\Windows\CurrentVersion\RunServices
- \Software\Microsoft\Windows\CurrentVersion\RunServicesOnce
- \Software\Microsoft\WindowsNT\CurrentVersion\Winlogon

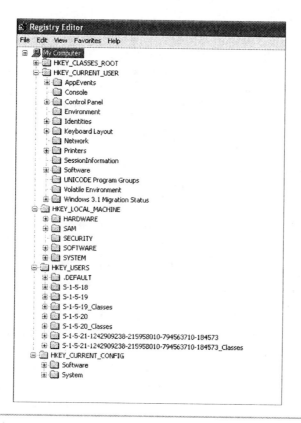

Figure 8-3   The Windows system Registry is broken into five sections or keys.

When I checked my Windows Registry, I discovered that there were 21 additional entries under \Software\Microsoft\Windows\CurrentVersion\Run.

- \Software\Microsoft\Windows\CurrentVersion\RunOnce
- \Software\Microsoft\Windows\CurrentVersion\RunOnceEx

were empty and

- \Software\Microsoft\Windows\CurrentVersion\RunServices
- \Software\Microsoft\Windows\CurrentVersion\RunServicesOnce

didn't exist.

Do this same check for these keys:

- HKEY_CURRENT_USER
- HKEY_USERS\.DEFAULT

If the subkeys are empty or do not exist, you should be in fairly good shape as far as the Registry is concerned. I spent some time checking out the 21 entries in my Registry to see whether anything evil lurked. Google and Yahoo! are great resources for checking things out. For example, if you pop "ccApp" into Google, you'll get a list of potential sources of data. I clicked the first one, http://www.liutilities.com/products/wintaskspro/processlibrary/ccapp/, which took me to a page that told me that this was the Symantec Common Client CC App. You have to go through this for all the entries in the Run subkey to be sure that they're all legitimate.

Because my Windows laptop was really the property of my employer, I figured that the security folks would get a little peeved if I published copies of the Registry, so I asked a friend who didn't mind getting fired from her job, and the result is in Figure 8-4. This is from a pretty vanilla Windows XP system.

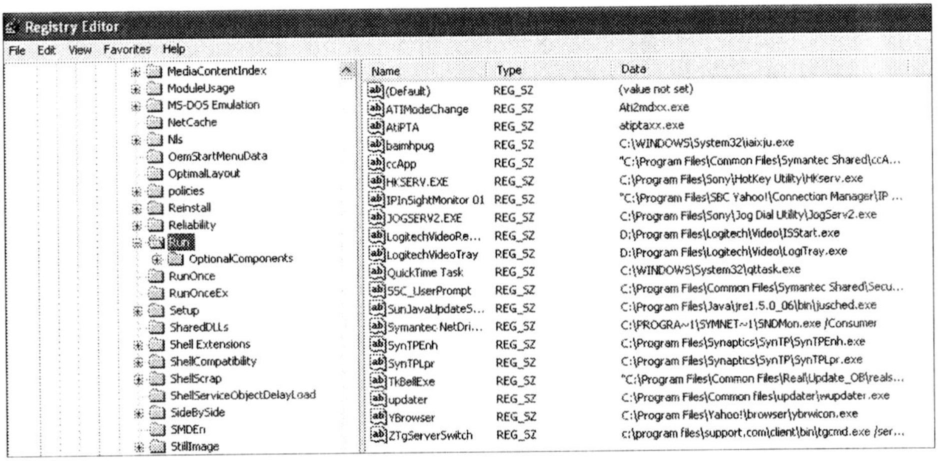

Figure 8-4 Registry subkeys under \HKEY_LOCAL_MACHINE\Software\Microsoft\Windows\CurrentVersion\Run.

IT'S ABOUT THE PROCESSES

Another way to examine your system is to see what processes are running. You have to go through the same drill that you went through above, checking each one to see if it's a legitimate process.

To check what processes are running on your XP system, go to Start > Control Panel > Administrative Tools > Services.

You will be presented with a list of processes, their description, status, startup type, and how they log on to the system. This is a long list, on the order of 100 or so individual processes, so plan on taking a couple of hours to check out everything.

Most of the services may be legitimate, such as Event Log, which was started automatically and running as a local system service. Some of them are a bit more obscure, such as SSDP Discovery Service (UPnP discovery), which was started manually as a local system service. You can eliminate those processes that aren't started or disabled, such as TELNET and routing. The truly paranoid will check all the services because a rouge service wouldn't be called "evilservice"; it would probably be called something quite innocuous, like Event Log.

As with most Windows utilities, you can click the column heading to re-sort the entries. I clicked Startup Type to see a list of disabled services, as shown in Figure 8-5.

Name	Description	Sta...	Startup Type	Log On As
IPSEC Services	Manages IP security policy and starts the ISAKMP/Oakley (IKE) and the IP security driver.		Automatic	Local System
Security Center	Monitors system security settings and configurations.		Automatic	Local System
Alerter	Notifies selected users and computers of administrative alerts. If the service is stopped, program...		Disabled	Local Service
ClipBook	Enables ClipBook Viewer to store information and share it with remote computers. If the service is...		Disabled	Local System
Human Interface Device Access	Enables generic input access to Human Interface Devices (HID), which activates and maintains th...		Disabled	Local System
Messenger	Transmits net send and Alerter service messages between clients and servers. This service is not...		Disabled	Local System
Network DDE	Provides network transport and security for Dynamic Data Exchange (DDE) for programs running ...		Disabled	Local System
Network DDE DSDM	Manages Dynamic Data Exchange (DDE) network shares. If this service is stopped, DDE network ...		Disabled	Local System
Routing and Remote Access	Offers routing services to businesses in local area and wide area network environments.		Disabled	Local System
Telnet	Enables a remote user to log on to this computer and run programs, and supports various TCP/IP...		Disabled	Local System
.NET Runtime Optimization Service v2.0...	Microsoft .NET Framework NGEN		Manual	Local System
Application Management	Provides software installation services such as Assign, Publish, and Remove.		Manual	Local System
ASP.NET State Service	Provides support for out-of-process session states for ASP.NET. If this service is stopped, out-of...		Manual	Network Service
COM+ System Application	Manages the configuration and tracking of Component Object Model (COM)+-based components....		Manual	Local System
Distributed Transaction Coordinator	Coordinates transactions that span multiple resource managers, such as databases, message qu...		Manual	Network Service
Fast User Switching Compatibility	Provides management for applications that require assistance in a multiple user environment.		Manual	Local System
HTTP SSL	This service implements the secure hypertext transfer protocol (HTTPS) for the HTTP service, usi...		Manual	Local System
IMAPI CD-Burning COM Service	Manages CD recording using Image Mastering Applications Programming Interface (IMAPI). If this...		Manual	Local System
Indexing Service	Indexes contents and properties of files on local and remote computers; provides rapid access to...		Manual	Local System
iPassConnectEngine			Manual	Local System
Logical Disk Manager	Detects and monitors new hard disk drives and sends disk volume information to Logical Disk Man...		Manual	Local System
Logical Disk Manager Administrative Ser...	Configures hard disk drives and volumes. The service only runs for configuration processes and t...		Manual	Local System

Figure 8-5   The services admin tool list services, their startup type, and who owns them.

SPYWARE

Spyware, the programs that collect information and send it back to the mothership, is a little easier to deal with. Anti-spyware is quickly becoming a commodity in the same way that AV has. Popular programs such as Ad-aware[10] from Lavasoft and

---

[10] http://www.lavasoft.de/software/adaware/

Spyware Doctor[11] from PC Tools promise to identify spyware and Trojan horses. A recent review[12] of 10 anti-spyware tools by TopTenReviews placed Ad-aware and Spyware Doctor sixth and eighth, respectively. Spy Sweeper[13] from Webroot placed number one.

To be fair, in a similar report by About,[14] Ad-aware took the number one spot, with the free Spybot Search and Destroy[15] snagging the number two spot.

My experience with anti-spyware told me to run a "belt and suspenders" operation by manually running two different detectors. There was enough overlap then to catch everything. However, if the recent reviews are any indication, improvements in the for-fee versions of anti-spyware programs have greatly improved their utility, accuracy, and reliability.

LOOKING AT THE LOGS

Windows does have a system of logs that an endpoint owner can use to keep track of the system. However, unlike other operating systems, Windows logs aren't readable unless you use the Windows log viewer. If you're sending the logs to a central log host, such as a syslog server, the logs must be converted before they're sent over using a tool such as winlogd.[16]

NETWORK STUFF

The Windows hosts file is the last reference used by a Windows endpoint. However, this is one of the files that can be modified by attackers. By associating a rogue IP address with an attacker's Web site, an attacker can fool users into going to a phishing site. If attackers can associate their URL with something like the Bank of America, they can convince your browser to go to a rogue Web site that looks like the Bank of America site. Check the hosts file for any entries other than the local host at 127.0.0.1 and a broadcasthost at 255.255.255.255.

---

[11] http://www.pctools.com/spyware-doctor/

[12] http://anti-spyware-review.toptenreviews.com/

[13] http://www.webroot.com/land/spysweeper-tt/index.html?rc=3815

[14] http://netsecurity.about.com/od/popupsandspyware/tp/aatp082804.htm

[15] http://www.safer-networking.org/en/spybotsd/index.html

[16] http://www.edoceo.com/products/winlogd.php

MOP UP

The last thing that I want to mention here is that you probably know what should be on these systems and what shouldn't. After a while, you'll be familiar enough to be able to spot something that shouldn't be there. A quick check of batch files using the search function of Windows may turn up something suspicious enough for you to dig further using the aforementioned tools. There aren't that many of them anymore, and maybe you'll get lucky and spot something unusual.

A review of the file system may uncover other things, such as porn, movies, or music, that could place you and your organization square in the sights of law enforcement. Make sure that you have administrative privileges, turn on hidden file viewing, and look for the following:

- JPG
- MOV
- MP3
- AVI
- MPG
- MPEG
- WMV

Be suspicious of any media that you find in out-of-the-way places, but don't forget to start with the usual location of My Documents, My Pictures, My Music, and My Movies. We already know from the earlier chapters that the very mechanism used to protect intellectual property has been hacked, so checking on a user's pictures, music, and movies would be a good place to start.

HARDENING THE OPERATING SYSTEM

Regardless of how we got here, either through a fresh image or an unhacked system, we have a good foundation that includes the latest operating system patches, and we're ready to start the hardening process. However, like everything else in the security world, we're really only ready to start asking more questions.

You must consider a number of things when hardening a Windows endpoint. You can't just rush off and start applying security templates to all your Windows endpoints until you understand what it is they're going to do. Some things you want to know before you start the hardening process are the following:

1. Is the endpoint running NTFS?
2. Is the endpoint going to participate in an Active Directory?
3. Is the endpoint going to be remotely managed?
4. Is the endpoint going to be a server?
5. Is it going to be a stand-alone system?
6. How much security can you tolerate?

Knowing these things about the endpoint will enable you to decide just how much security you're going to wrench into your endpoint.

STAND-ALONE SYSTEM

Because this is the easiest configuration, we're going to start with it. It's also either the least secure or the most secure, depending on how you approach the problem. If I want a general-purpose system that doesn't give me any hassles when I install stuff, it's probably going to lean toward the least secure side. As such, a stand-alone system is probably best considered to be the most similar to your home computer. As an endpoint, it's not part of any Active Directory or domain and operates pretty much independently of all the other endpoints on the network. One other requirement for a Windows system is that it must be running NTFS for many of our protections to work properly. Without NTFS, there is no concept of file ownership, and that's a key element to restricting access to them.

As a stand-alone endpoint, you are probably going to be the administrator for the system. The administrator has significant power over how drivers are installed and which services are running. This is the first thing that we're going to fix. We're going to create a new user for your day-to-day use that isn't in the administrator group. As you follow the instructions, refer to Figures 8-6 and 8-7:

1. Right-click on My Computer.
2. Click Manage.
3. Click Local Users and Groups.
4. Right-click Users.
5. Click New User.
6. Fill in the new user information.
7. Click Create.

Now we need to check to see who's an administrator:

1. Click Local Users and Groups.
2. Right-click Groups.
3. Click Administrator.

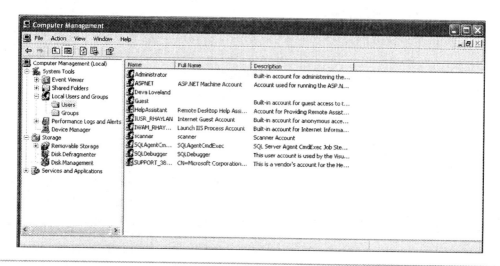

Figure 8-6   The list of users on a Windows XP endpoint.

You should see a list of users, and you shouldn't be surprised by the members on the list. If you are, you need to go back to the beginning of the chapter. In your stand-alone system, there shouldn't be a long list of users on this list, and I wouldn't expect anything other than administrator and possibly one user.

Your new user shouldn't be in the administrator group list. When you log off, you can begin using this new user account. The reason that this is safer has to do with how the system gets compromised. If, by some chance, you're online and someone takes advantage of your browsing habits, that perpetrator will gain access only to the user portion of the system rather than the administrator.

The next thing we're going to do is check to make sure that guest access is turned off. Although many new systems come with the guest account disabled, it's a good idea to check it anyway. Going back to our open management window, follow these steps:

1. Right-click Users.
2. If the Guest user is displayed and it doesn't have a little red X in the lower-right corner of the icon, double-click Guest.

3. Click the Disable check box.

4. Click Apply.

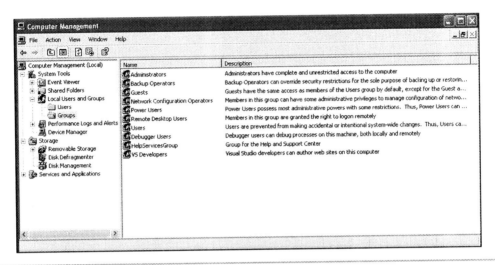

Figure 8-7 A list of typical groups on a Windows XP endpoint.

Now we're ready to deal with the local security policy. Go to Start menu > Settings > Control Panel > Administrator Tools > Local Security Policy.

1. Once there, click Account Policies. You should see Password Policy and Account Lockout Policy.

2. Click Password Policy.

What you should see now is a screen similar to that in Figure 8-8. For settings, I recommend the following:

- Enforce password history set to 3 passwords remembered
- Maximum password age set to 180 days
- Minimum password age set to 0 days
- Minimum password length set to 8 characters
- Password must meet complexity requirements set to Enabled
- Store password using reversible encryption for all users in the domain set to Disabled

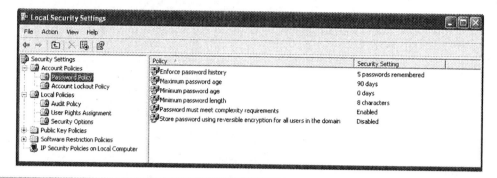

Figure 8-8   Local Security Settings window. Password policy controls complexity, lifetime, and reuse of passwords.

Next, click Account Lockout Policy. You should see a display similar to that in Figure 8-9.

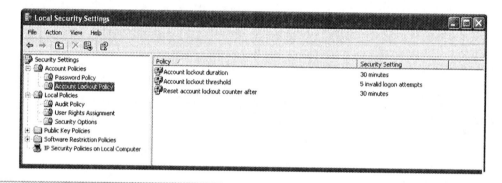

Figure 8-9   Lockout parameters. Lockout prevents automated attacks against the system.

I would set the account lockout parameters as follows:

- Account lockout duration to 30 minutes
- Account lockout threshold to 3 invalid logon attempts
- Reset account lockout counter after to 30 minute

The next thing we're going to do is check to see whether the firewall is running. If you have Windows XP SP2 or later, it comes with a built-in firewall, and until such time that you get a third-party firewall, it's better than nothing. The Windows firewall will prevent external connections, but it can also be turned off externally through the built-in API. If you have an earlier Windows system, you need to get a third-party firewall. To check to see whether your firewall is running, go to Start menu > Settings > Control Panel > Windows Firewall.

In the General tab, you should see that the green "firewall good" radio button has been selected, as in Figure 8-10. Next, select the Exceptions tab. I recommend that you uncheck the following:

- File and Printer Sharing
- Remote Assistance
- UPnP
- Remote Desktop
- Windows Media Connect

Because this is a stand-alone working (versus gaming) computer, I can't imagine needing to provide exceptions for any of these services.

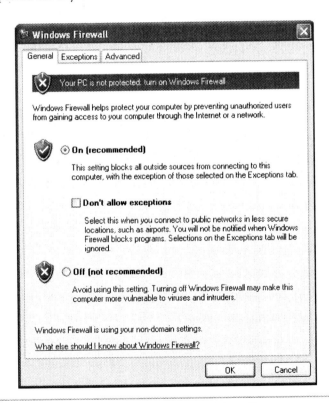

Figure 8-10 Microsoft recommends that you run the included firewall.

This next part pretty much depends on what your AV vendor is, so the instruction is going to be pretty general:

CHECK YOUR AV

Ensure that your AV is running by starting the GUI. Just because the icon is in the system tray doesn't mean that your AV is up and running. I once had a project where the goal was to "whack," as in kill, the competition's security product as part of a demonstration. Whacking the product was fairly trivial, but the interesting thing was that a quick look in the system tray indicated that the product was still running, even when it wasn't! A mouse over the afflicted product's icon in the system tray made it disappear, and one marketing person actually asked if I could add a whooshing sound!

After you've determined that your AV is running, you also need to check to make sure that it has the latest DAT file update. Figure 8-11 shows an example AV status screen. If you have a subscription, it shouldn't be an issue, but it does require a connection to the Internet to get the updates. Also, if your subscription has expired, you may have absent-mindedly clicked on the "don't bother me with this again" dialog window. I have the Symantec AV on my system, and the GUI tells me that the program is running and that the last update was today.

One last check that you should make is to ensure that the schedule feature of your AV is enabled. Having it set to run at 2 a.m. won't take any cycles from your day or your system's productivity.

Before we finish with this section, there is one more thing that we need to do. We need to go back into Computer Management and change the passwords of the administrator and our new user so that we can be sure that they comply with the new password policy:

1. Right-click My Computer.
2. Click Manage.
3. Click Local Users and Groups.
4. Right-click Users.
5. Select Administrator and then your new user.
6. Change the passwords.

There is one extra thing that I recommend: changing the name of the administrator to something innocuous and creating a new user named administrator with no privileges.

Although this won't slow an experienced hacker down, if a rookie hacker does happen to get onto the system and gets to the administrator account, it'll drive the rookie nuts trying to figure out what's wrong with the system.

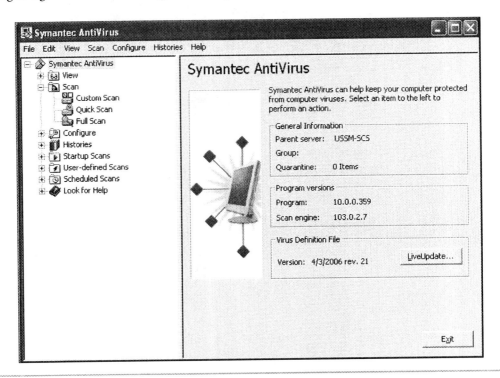

Figure 8-11   The GUI for the Symantec AV shows status and last DAT file update.

The last thing that we're going to enable is the ability of the system to automatically check for updates. Go to Start menu > Settings > Control Panel > Automatic Updates.

You should see the window shown in Figure 8-12.

I like to get the updates, but I review them prior to blindly installing them. As I mentioned in the first chapter, sometimes the cure is worse than the illness! Before installing an update, I want to make sure that there aren't any surprises.

We're ready to proceed to the next step if you're interested in increasing your level of protection.

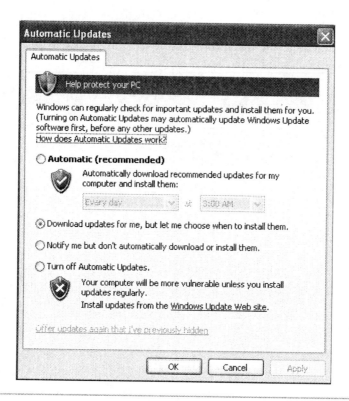

Figure 8-12   Automatic Updates will download and install operating system patches and hotfixes.

CRANKING DOWN THE SCREWS

We've used a manual process to get at some low-hanging fruit, and we have improved the basic security of the endpoint. This manual process is good for those who are loath to get into the deep DNA of Windows or just want to spend a couple of minutes improving their basic security posture. To sum up, at this point we have a system that has

- All operating system patches
- Secured administration access
- Antivirus
- Firewall

Although this is a great start, it is really only the minimum, and we can do much better; but to do so means going a little deeper into the toolbox. Because this isn't intended to be a complete course on configuring Windows, we're going to go over the method that should be used to identify and modify those critical security parameters that are important to you. I'll also say that at this point I'm going to make some recommendations and one of them is to get two documents from Microsoft:

- Windows Server 2003 Security Guide
- Windows XP Security Guide

You can find these documents at www.microsoft.com/technet/security/topics/serversecurity/tcg/tcgch00.mspx.

I'm making the assumption that the system is functioning as a stand-alone system in support of a single user, so many of the security recommendations, such as turning off the user's ability to write to removable media, aren't applicable here. Also, this is still a manual process. We get into the automated process description in a later section.

The next thing we're going to do is to disable autoplay on the CD-ROM/DVD player and the USB. Autoplay is a feature designed to be a convenience, but in reality it can act as an attack vector because Windows reads a part of the media automatically. To turn off this "feature," follow these steps:

1. Double-click My Computer.
2. Right-click DVD/CD-RW Drive. (Yours may only say CD-ROM, depending on how your computer is equipped.)
3. Select Properties.
4. Select the AutoPlay tab.
5. In the drop-down menu, select Music CD.
6. Click the radio button Select an action to perform.
7. Select Take no action.

Repeat Steps 5 through 7 for DVD Movie and all other removable media such as the USB.

Now we're going to protect our data from theft by encrypting it. You can encrypt the entire file system if you want, but I prefer to just protect the data. To create an encrypted folder, follow these steps:

1. Right-click the folder that you want to encrypt.
2. Click the Advanced button.
3. Select the Encrypt the contents to secure data check box.
4. Click OK.

5. Click Apply.

6. Click OK on the last window.

Because we're not connected to the domain, we're going to have to produce our own recovery agent. Go to the Start menu and open a command window. Then enter the following:

```
Cipher /r:yourcertname
```

Replace *yourcertname* with a name that is meaningful to you and nobody else. You will be asked for a password and to reenter the password. When you're done, you will have two files, one with a .pfx extension and one with a .cer extension. Protect these files carefully; they are your public and private certificates. If someone else gets them, they can become a recovery agent for your data. I suggest that you put them on a CD, DVD, or USB drive for safekeeping.

Now we need to import the certificate and create the recovery agent. From the Microsoft Management Console (MMC), follow these steps:

1. Select Local Computer Policy.

2. Select Computer Configuration.

3. Select Windows Settings.

4. Select Security Settings.

5. Select Public Key Policies.

6. Select Encrypting File System.

7. From the Action menu, select Add Data Recovery Agent.

8. You will be presented with an Add Recovery Agent Wizard window. Click Next.

9. Browse to the folder with your CER file, select it, and click Open. You should see the window shown in Figure 8-13.

10. Click Next.

11. Click Finish.

You should have an entry in the Encrypting File System window similar to the one in Figure 8-14.

Next, we're going to disable the good Doctor Watson. Dr. Watson is an automatic debugger that collects information and sends it back to Microsoft when applications crash. A knowledgeable hacker could exploit the Doctor, so we're going to cut off his practice.

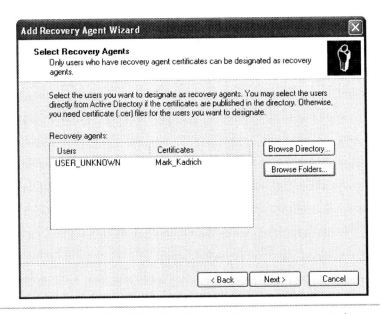

Figure 8-13 The Add Recovery Agent Wizard makes generating a recovery agent a breeze.

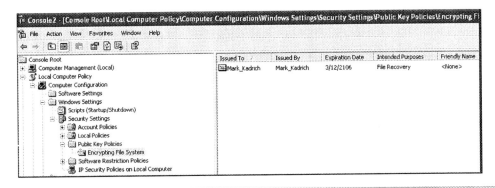

Figure 8-14 The recovery agent certificate is added to the local computer policy through the MMC.

WARNING

We're playing with the Registry again, so make sure that you export it and save it somewhere safe!

Go to Start menu > Run and enter **regedit:**

1. Heed the aforementioned warning.

2. Select the Registry key HKEY_LOCAL_MACHINE\Software\Microsoft\Windows NT\CurrentVersion\AeDebug.

3. Delete the AeDebug key.

APPLICATIONS

Before we get into the next section, I want to discuss another important aspect of the Windows endpoint: the applications that run on them. In the next section, we discuss the process that you use for setting security parameters on an enterprise, so I think that it is important to discuss the application software and some of the security settings that you should consider as you're formulating your enterprise security policy. In many cases, it is the applications that run on the endpoint that are the targets of attackers. The recommendations that follow are pretty consistent no matter what the level of security you're trying to achieve.

SOFTWARE RESTRICTION POLICY

Software Restriction Policy (SRP) is the single most powerful tool in the Microsoft arsenal because it uses a policy-based process to decide what software will be executed. It is executed either through Active Directory (AD) and Group Policy or on stand-alone computers. You have two ways of implementing SRP: unrestricted or disallowed. If you select the unrestricted mode, all software can run on the endpoint, and you have to enter specific rules to block applications. However, if you select disallowed, all software execution is prevented unless there is an explicit permit rule.

SRP isn't just for applications either. It also prevents Visual Basic, Scripting Edition (VBScript), JScript, and other scripting languages.

As a security professional, I like the fact that this policy has an explicit "deny" for all software. SRP uses four rules to identify software. You identify what software is allowed to run and associate a rule with it:

- **Hash rule.** Uses MD5 or SHA1, file length, hash algorithm ID number
- **Certificate rule.** Uses digitally signed certificates from the publisher to identify files
- **Path rule.** Uses the local UNC (Universal Naming Convention) or Registry path to identify the EXE file

- **Zone rule.** Uses the Internet zone where the EXE originates if it was downloaded by Internet Explorer

Each rule type has different advantages and disadvantages. Hash rules work well if you're not updating software continuously, because each time you do you must recalculate the hash value and update all the endpoints with it.

Certificate rules require that each software vendor has a registered code-signing certificate on the endpoint. Considering the present state of PKI and the fact that not every vendor has a code-signing certificate, this can be a crap shoot. It tends to be the method of choice for verifying trust in ActiveX controls, however.

The path rule relies on the location of a file to determine trust. If it's in the right folder, it must be the right software! Registry path rules seem to be an extension of the basic path rules but applied to the Registry. This is the method that Windows uses so that when you set SRP to disallowed it doesn't lock itself out of the operating system. Four Registry path rules are created:

- %HKEY_LOCAL_MACHINE\SOFTWARE\Microsoft\Windows NT\CurrentVersion\SystemRoot%
- %HKEY_LOCAL_MACHINE\SOFTWARE\Microsoft\Windows NT\CurrentVersion\SystemRoot%*.exe
- %HKEY_LOCAL_MACHINE\SOFTWARE\Microsoft\Windows NT\CurrentVersion\SystemRoot%\System32*.exe
- %HKEY_LOCAL_MACHINE\SOFTWARE\Microsoft\Windows NT\CurrentVersion\ProgramFilesDir%

INTERNET EXPLORER

Internet Explorer, besides being at the heart of international lawsuits, is at the heart of many exploits. For this reason, we're going to give IE a bit of attention when we consider our enterprise security policy. If I were to characterize what our approach is going to be, it would be to reduce the possibility that the user can download something evil or change the security settings such that the browser security can be bypassed. So, when we configure our administrative template in the Group Policy Object Editor, we're going to enable the following:

- Disable Automatic Install of Internet Explorer Components
- Disable Periodic Check for Internet Explorer Software Updates
- Disable Software Update Shell Notifications on Program Launch

- Do Not Allow Users to Enable or Disable Add-ons
- Make Proxy Settings Per-machine (not per-user)
- Security Zones: Do Not Allow Users to Add/Delete Sites
- Security Zones: Do Not Allow Users to Change Policies
- Security Zones: Use Only Machine Settings
- Turn Off Crash Detection
- Internet Explorer Processes (MK Protocol) (This blocks the legacy MK protocol from being used.)
- Internet Explorer Processes (Consistent Mime Handling) (This prevents MIME types from masquerading as text files when they're really executable.)
- Internet Explorer Processes (MIME Sniffing) (This prevents IE from promoting a file type to executable.)
- Internet Explorer Processes (Scripted Window Security Restrictions) (This prevents Web sites from hiding other windows and generating pop-ups.)
- Internet Explorer Processes (Zone Elevation Protection)
- Internet Explorer Processes (Restrict ActiveX Install)
- Internet Explorer Processes (Restrict File Download) (Non-user-initiated download prompts are disabled.)
- Deny All Add-ons Unless Specifically Allowed in the Add-on List
- Add-on List (needed for the previous rule)

Although we've done a great deal of "enabling," we need to disable some things. Some things seem pretty intuitive, and I believe that the following falls squarely into that category. In the administrative template in the Group Policy Object Editor, disable the following:

- Internet Explorer\Internet Control Panel\Advanced Page—Allow software to run or install even if the signature is invalid

NetMeeting

NetMeeting is a collaboration program that enables users to have video teleconferences from the comfort of their cube. It also has the ability to chat, whiteboard, and, of course, point-to-point audio and video. What it also supports is the ability of the remote user to share his or her desktop! If you have a secure environment, you want to turn this feature off in your domain by setting the administrative template in the Group Policy Object Editor to enable Disable Remote Desktop Sharing. I know it sounds a bit confusing to enable something to disable something, but this is Windows.

TERMINAL SERVICES

Terminal services allow users to remotely access another computer just as if they were at the console. This is a handy method for doing remote management of other computers and, as you would expect, a handy way to break into a computer. Therefore, in the administrative template in the Group Policy Object Editor, enable the following:

- Client/Server Data Redirection—Do not allow drive redirection (Prevents the local drive from being shared with Terminal Servers.)
- Encryption and Security—Always prompt client for password upon connection
- Client—Do not allow passwords to be saved

WINDOWS MESSENGER

I'm going to "step in it" here and go on record as saying that IM, or instant messaging, is the universe's way of getting even with mankind. IM, or chat, is the single largest growing threat to users of the Internet and your enterprise. Files can be exchanged, malware can be downloaded, your systems can be hacked, and you can lose control of your intellectual property. So, I'm very happy to say that in the administrative template in the Group Policy Object Editor, enable Do Not Allow Windows Messenger to be Run. It felt very good to type that.

WINDOWS UPDATE

Windows Update is the automatic service that Microsoft uses to download patches and hotfixes to your system. You've probably seen the window pop up near the system tray telling you that "updates are ready for your computer." To make this work, your system must talk to a server and download the update. This can obviously be used in a nefarious way to install malware onto your Windows endpoint.

Microsoft has expanded this service to the enterprise by combining the Software Update Services (SUS) with the Windows Update service to create the Windows Server Update Services (WSUS). WSUS is an infrastructure service that lives on your network, accepts updates from Microsoft, and makes them available to your clients, thus eliminating the need for them to go to the Internet for updates. Another interesting feature of

WSUS is that it eliminates the manual update steps, providing an automatic way to distribute and install updates on your endpoints.

Anything automatic can be subverted if not configured properly, so in the administrative template in the Group Policy Object Editor, we're going to enable the following:

- Configure Automatic Updates
- Reschedule Automatic Updates Scheduled Installations (Previously scheduled installations will be delayed for a short period of time after system startup.)
- Specify Intranet Microsoft Update Service Location

Some things also need to be disabled in Windows Update, as follows:

- Do Not Display "Install Updates and Shut Down" option in Shut Down Windows Dialog Box
- Do Not Adjust Default Option to "Install Updates and Shut Down" In Shut Down Windows Dialog Box
- No Auto-restart for Scheduled Automatic Updates Installations

ENTERPRISE SECURITY

Until now, we've been treating our operating system hardening effort as a one-off kind of procedure. We started with the assumption that you were just doing this to your computer and not the entire enterprise. Now that you have an idea of what it takes to secure a Windows endpoint, we're going to take that to the next level and leverage this across the network.

Microsoft has two levels of security that it discusses in the security guides that it imposes against three types of clients. These three clients are called stand-alone (SA) client, enterprise client (EC), and specialized security—limited functionality (SSLF). I said two levels of security because the SA and EC clients are pretty much at the same level, and the SSLF is pretty tightly sealed. In the SSLF environment, you'll get a much better level of trust, but at the expense of flexibility and functionality. This is a perfect example of the traditional security balancing act, only this time the balance tips a bit to the paranoid side. If you decide that you're going to go with an SSLF enterprise client, be ready for the additional administrative burden that will be imposed on you and your team.

Because most of you will be connecting your endpoints to an Active Directory, we need to change our perspective on what is permissible by the user and what isn't. Because you were the system owner, the assumption was made that you willingly set up a day-to-day use environment that didn't have the broad access and power of the administrator. In an enterprise environment, that assumption no longer applies. Users don't need to have the sweeping power of administrator privileges; in fact, it is those very privileges in combination with poor user awareness that attackers prey upon.

We also need to get comfortable with the fact that the best way to do this is via templates. Because there is a lot to do and you need to be sure that you do it right, this is where we depart from me giving you a list of things to do. Until this point, it was fairly easy to give you a list of things to do because it was a "onesie-twosie" kind of thing. Now we're going to be pushing things out to hundreds of endpoints, and we need to make sure that we get it right and do it in a way that doesn't inconvenience users any more than we need to. After all, they're probably not going to be happy with the new restrictions placed on them.

To get to this level of security, Microsoft says that you should at least:

- Be an MCSE with more than two years of security-related experience or equivalent
- Have an in-depth knowledge of your enterprise's domain and AD environments
- Know how to use MMC, secedit, gpupdate, and gpresult
- Have experience with administration of Group Policy
- Have experience deploying applications and client computers in enterprise networks

The security guide has a great deal of information in it and is a 200-plus page document all by itself. It walks you through the choices that you as a security administrator need to make before you deploy a new policy to your endpoints. Although I believe that I've given you a flavor for what has to be done to secure the operating system, there are nearly a hundred settings that need to be reviewed and could be a separate book all by themselves. At a high level, you need to give thought to the following:

- Update services
- Logon services
- Autoplay
- Remote assistance
- Error reporting
- Remote procedure calls
- Internet access settings
- Network connections
- Firewall
- User services
- Applications

After you have a good idea of the security level that you're going to pursue, you can begin planning for deployment. The basic steps outlined in the security guide are as follows:

1. Configure the AD domain infrastructure.
2. Configure the settings for Windows XP clients.
3. Create the templates for Windows XP.
4. Deploy the templates.
5. Wait for complaints.

Okay, the last step was one that I added based on my experience with such matters, but it is an important step. Critical applications may break, and you'll have to revisit your policy when they do.

SERVERS

I've talked quite a bit about workstation endpoints, so now it's time to talk about servers. Because servers are a much more tightly controlled environment, or should be, I'm going to go straight to the Group Policy method of imposing security controls. This method enables you to track changes and enables you to map policy to action.

Microsoft has happily provided us with a document to secure our Windows Server 2003 called, surprisingly enough, Windows Server 2003 Security Guide. The guide covers many of the same points that were covered in the Windows XP security guide but adds information specific to a server environment, such as the following:

- Securing the server itself
- Auditing
- Domain controller security
- Infrastructure server role
- File server role
- Print server role
- Web server role
- AIS server role
- Certificate Services server role
- Bastian host role

I can't stress enough the role that our earlier process plays in developing a secure environment. Because our servers are the central focal point for so many other endpoints, we need to ensure that the process we use for developing them is as secure as we can make it and that our process documents our decisions and actions.

CLOSING THE LOOP

This is where the standard Windows tools will no longer suffice. We're going to need some help because the basic premise is that the system will check its own integrity prior to talking with the network. We need to ensure that the system meets our stated level of trust prior to unleashing it on the rest of the network.

As we discussed in Chapter 4, we need a basic proportional control mechanism for controlling how we introduce risk onto the network. From a technology perspective, we have three choices:

- **NAC.** Network Admission Control, sponsored by the Trusted Computing Group (TCG) and a consortium of vendors.
- **CNAC.** Cisco Network Admission Control, a proprietary solution sponsored by Cisco. CNAC is supposed to be compatible with Microsoft NAP, but details haven't been released.
- **NAP.** Network Access Protection, the proprietary solution that comes with the new Microsoft Vista operating system.

For those of you who have been following the admission control argument, the main purpose of 802.1x is to address the identity management issue. Through the extension of standardized protocols, as in the case of NAC, or through the use of proprietary solutions, as is the case with CNAC and NAP, the authentication process has been extended to include the endpoint itself. By adding an integrity check of the system to the authentication of the user, you now have enough information to decide whether the endpoint meets your minimum security policy requirements.

Because this chapter has been about Microsoft, I would have liked to have finished this section with a Microsoft-only solution. However, the present offering from Microsoft, Network Access Quarantine Control, offered in Windows Server 2003, is not capable of closing the loop in the way we need. Consider this quote from the Microsoft Windows Server 2003 Network Access Quarantine Control guide:[17]

---

[17] http://www.microsoft.com/technet/itsolutions/network/vpn/quarantine.mspx

Network Access Quarantine Control is not a security solution. It is designed to help prevent computers with unsafe configurations from connecting to a private network; not to protect a private network from malicious users who have obtained a valid set of credentials.

Seeing this gap in Microsoft security support, other companies, such as Symantec, Funk (Juniper), Foundry Networks, and Mirage Networks, have rushed to fill the void. Juniper (through their Funk acquisition) and Symantec (through their Sygate acquisition) have expanded the capability of the 802.1x supplicant beyond simple authentication, and this is where we begin to see the foundation for a real proportional control standard that truly closes the loop today.

Foundry and Funk have embraced the standards from the infrastructure side and with the addition of a suitable agent, such as Symantec's Enterprise Protection, go beyond basic 802.1x and Extensible Authentication Protocol (EAP) authentication and check the endpoint to ensure that system-level policy issues have been complied with prior to allowing IP connectivity. In addition, remediation of the endpoint to ensure compliance has been addressed through inherent functionality and integrated with other remediation vendors such as Patchlink.

TOOLS AND VENDORS

In all my research, I came to the conclusion that although numerous sites discussed Windows vulnerabilities, the best site to find out how to harden Windows is really at Microsoft. Yes, there were lots of hardening templates, but each of those templates was addressing that particular enterprise's need and *didn't explain* in detail why certain decisions were being made the way they were. In the end, I used the Microsoft documents as the core of my reference material:

- www.microsoft.com/technet/security/topics/serversecurity/tcg/tcgch00.mspx
- www.microsoft.com/technet/prodtechnol/winxppro/maintain/rstrplcy.mspx
- Windows Server 2003 Security: A Technical Reference
  www.awprofessional.com/title/0321305019

This isn't for the faint of heart, because we know that Microsoft documentation will always default in the verbose mode more often than not. It also pays to verify things at other locations because you will pick up some interesting tidbits here and there.

Another great site that I found was www.windowsecurity.com. There are articles, tutorials, blogs, and RSS feeds. You name it, it's there. It's really a great place to start a search.

The following is a list of tools native to every Windows system that can be run from the command line:

- **Attrib.** Displays, sets, or removes the file attributes read-only, archive, system, and hidden
- **Dir.** Shows you what files and directories are listed
- **Getmac.** Shows you the MAC address of the system
- **Ipconfig.** Shows you the IP related information for specified or all network interfaces
- **Mmc.** Launches the Microsoft Management Console
- **Mode.** Displays or sets information about com and parallel ports
- **Nbstat.** Shows you NetBIOS over TCP/IP protocol statistics
- **Netstat.** Powerful tool for displaying route and TCP/UDP connection information and network processes
- **Ping.** ICMP echo request client; great for testing network connectivity
- **Route.** Displays or modifies the network routing table
- **Systeminfo.** Dumps information regarding hardware, software, and hotfixes (very useful)
- **Tasklist.** From the console, will show you all tasks running on the system
- **Tracert.** Displays the path that your packets are taking to reach a destination

There are a number of lists on the Internet, but you can find the complete and authoritative list at www.microsoft.com/resources/documentation/windows/xp/all/proddocs/en-us/ntcmds.mspx?mfr=true.

A small number of vendors support NAC and remediation:

- www.symantec.com/Products/enterprise?c=prodinfo&refId=1303
  Symantec Enterprise Protection, remediation, 802.1x and DHCP enforcement
- www.trustedcomputinggroup.org/specs/TNC
  Information on Trusted Network Connect
- www.funk.com/radius/enterprise/ea_radius.asp
  Juniper's NAC client
- www.mcafee.com/us/enterprise/products/network_access_control/index.html
  McAfee's Policy Enforcer

KEY POINTS

Windows is complex. There are many ways to compromise (and through built-in functionality, hide the compromise). An example of this is the use of ADS to hide malware. However, if you start with a known good build, have a documented process for evaluating security settings, and use some third-party software, you can ensure that endpoints that connect to your network meet your minimum level of trust.

START FRESH

It is best to start with a fresh, clean, secure build. When you can't, tools such as port scanners and system scanners can tell you with a fair degree of confidence if and how your system has been compromised. In some rare instances, the system can be repaired and brought back online with a high degree of confidence that the system is secure and free of malware.

ROOTKITS

Rootkits are sophisticated and complex tools designed to evade detection and can be problematic with regard to their removal. No one tool is really going to be able to detect how a system has been compromised when a rootkit is installed by a true expert. External views generated by port scanners can be compared to internal views of processes to generate a "difference" value that might identify a rogue port or service. With this information, a security administrator can sleuth the system in an attempt to uncover and remove the infestation. However, this is time-consuming and in the final analysis may not be sufficient in restoring confidence in the system's integrity. From an efficiency perspective, it is easier and faster to simply rebuild the system using a secure process.

THE SECURITY ARMS RACE

Although I used rootkits as the basic example, malware has a similar development cycle to the one that fires an arms race. The attackers devise new ways of subverting security and exploiting vulnerabilities as fast as defenders can add new layers and plug discovered holes. It is a constant cycle that, if treated as if it were a series of individual and unique events, will consume your time and energy in constant recovery activity. Simply identifying how a Windows endpoint was compromised and repairing it is no longer enough.

You must have a process that incorporates new information into securing all of your endpoints.

WINDOWS CAN BE SECURE

Although Windows is complex, documented methods, procedures, and tools enable you to build a secure endpoint. Security can be enforced to such a level that rogue applications aren't allowed to run on the endpoint. But there is a warning. At this level of security, even Microsoft admits that the ease of use and the flexibility of the system have been sacrificed.

Windows security can be centrally managed through the tools provided by Microsoft. Group Policy allows the security administrator to craft and deploy security templates to the enterprise that enforce corporate security policies. This reduces the amount of administrative overhead associated with Windows security.

PROCESS IS CRITICAL

A large number of attributes must be set in a Windows endpoint to make it secure. For this reason, a process that evaluates security attributes and their effect on system usability and application reliability must be employed.

THE LOOP CAN BE CLOSED

Although there are ways to secure Windows, there is no internal mechanism for "closing the loop" or ensuring that each time the endpoint connects to the network that it represents a minimum level of compliance with corporate security policy. However, through the use of NAC, CNAC, or NAP, a basic proportional control can be employed that ensures compliance and provides for remediation of noncompliant endpoints.

Apple OS X

Some things you just have to share with others. When I start researching for something, the first thing I do is bring up a search engine and type in what I'm curious about. In this case, I was curious about Macintosh security and what documents had been written and what woes people had been suffering. When I entered "macintosh security" into Google, I was greeted by a long list of potential places to investigate. At the top of the list was a site called www.macintoshsecurity.com.

Great, I thought to myself. A site dedicated to the very subject I was investigating. Actually, I would have been more surprised had there not been a site called macintosh-security, but I was pleased nonetheless. What did surprise me, however, was the unexpected message that accompanied the URL. The home page had been modified by a group calling themselves the Sorcerer Bitches and contained a fairly rude message notifying the site owner that they had cracked their security. I can't repeat the full text of the message because I'm sure that it would make a rap singer blush; let's just say that these ladies noted that the site security was suboptimal.

Because I'm the curious sort, I did some digging (pun intended) to find out a little more. I wanted to know what these folks have been hacking and whether it was an Apple OS. I discovered that there were two other sites—www.americanreform.com and www.bluesfooty.com—that had a similar message posted regarding their questionable security posture. I tracked the IP addresses to the Internet service provider (ISP) and reviewed their hosting products. It seems our Sorcerer friends had been busy breaking into Windows-based servers that the ISPs provide in their standard hosting package. I naturally sent their security people a note telling them about the preceding chapter.

•

PRÉCIS

As we did with the chapter on Windows, we're going to start this chapter by examining some special bits of information that I found interesting regarding the Macintosh.

We're going to look at the Mac as a stand-alone system for the purposes of determining initial health. By going through the process of checking one system, you'll better understand how much effort is required to manage and secure an Apple-based enterprise. Thankfully, Apple does have a network management tool for administering Apple-based enterprises, and we'll spend some time examining it.

After we do the initial health check, we're going to look at what we can do to harden the Macintosh OS X operating system. Being a UNIX-like system, many of the rules and tools that we have learned and used in the past will come in handy now. It's interesting that we can continue to build on our UNIX knowledge even if it's 20 years old.

The next stop in our Macintosh odyssey is at the application layer. Present security issues on the Mac seem to focus on this aspect of the Mac and specifically target email and chat applications. We're going to go through some of the apps in an attempt to supply a thought template that you can use when you install new apps or consider buying new apps.

Moving down the stack, the next level is at the networking layer, where we'll examine some of the system settings that can be engaged to reduce your exposure to network-based threats.

We wrap up the chapter with a discussion of the must-have tools for securing and managing an enterprise filled with Macs and how the Mac fits into the closed-loop process control (CLPC) model.

SPECIAL POINTS OF INTEREST

Macs, and OS X, are not immune from security vulnerabilities and the resulting malware that takes advantage of them. On February 16, 2006, Sophos reported that OSX/Leap-A was infecting Macs via chat programs. This little gem tries to replicate by sending a file called latestpics.tgz via iChat. As you may recall from Chapter 7, "Threat Vectors," instant messaging (IM) clients are not to be trusted, and this proves that the operating system you've selected isn't enough to protect you.

OS X is really an amalgam of the open source UNIX-based kernel called Darwin and the proprietary windowing system called Aqua. Darwin has some pretty interesting roots that date back to 1985 when Steve Jobs started NeXT. The NeXT operating system, NEXTSTEP, was based on the Mach micro kernel developed at Carnegie Mellon

University between 1985 and 1994.[1] Essentially, OS X is the next instantiation of NeXT's NEXTSTEP operating system and consists of the Mach 3 micro kernel and BSD UNIX services. Apple adds to that Cocoa, an object-oriented developer framework, and Carbon, an application programming interface (API) for C and C++ programmers, and Java. OS X has development environments for all the major programming languages and is designed to be "developer friendly" according to Apple literature.

The Mac OS supports a number of file systems, but the native file system is HFS+ (Hierarchical File System) or, as it's referred to by Apple, Mac OS Extended. HFS+ uses 32-bit-length block addresses for larger files and disk volumes and B*-trees to store volume information. HFS+ also supports n-forked files (think alternate data streams [ADS] in Windows), but only the resource fork and the data fork are implemented. This can be a bit misleading because PowerPC binaries store the executable code in the data fork. It means that you can still hide things in the forks.

Since its release in March 2001, OS X has continued to evolve at the rate of one major release a year. Starting with OS X 10.0 (Cheetah), Apple has used the family Felidae as the inspiration for their naming convention:

- Puma (10.1)
- Jaguar (10.2)
- Panther (10.3)
- Tiger (10.4)

I thought it rather interesting that version 10.4 finally saw a move from the small cat subfamily Felinae to the subfamily Pantherinae for Tiger. A small note to the folks at Apple: A Jaguar is really a species *Panthera* (roaring cats), and a Panther is really from the species *Puma concolor* (cougar), subspecies (*puma concolor coryi*) or, as it's commonly known, the Florida panther. I suppose it's okay because they're all in the same family as long as the major release number remained at 10. I would have expected a new major release number when they moved to a different subfamily. At least they're staying consistent with the big cat theme by naming 10.5 Leopard. I'm rather hoping that Apple brings back the Newton. They could call the OS Tabby.

Another interesting secret about OS X is that it has always supported the x86 processor. Steve Jobs admitted at the 2005 keynote address of the Apple Worldwide Developers Conference that OS X supported the x86 for most of its development life. It's interesting to note that running **mach_kernel** through the strings command and looking for "i386"

---

[1] http://en.wikipedia.org/wiki/Mach_kernel

does produce some results. In a terminal window and from the root directory, enter the following:

```
strings mach_kernel | grep i386
```

As recently as April 2006, there were reports of a scripting vulnerability in Safari that allows JPG files to open the terminal application.[2] The exploit uses how OS X stores execution information to take advantage of a Safari function called "Open safe files after downloading," thus tricking it into opening the terminal application. The Mac associates files with applications through the use of creator codes, which are stored in HFS+ meta data, by their file extension, or finally, by an "Open With" or, as it's known in the Mac world, the "usro" designation. The usro function allows the user to assign a file type to an application. The order of precedence is as follows:

1. Open With (usro)
2. Creator code
3. File extension

What is being called the heise.jpg exploit uses these resource designations to the detriment of "Open safe."[3] The JPG doesn't have a creator code, but it does have a usro resource that associates the heise.jpg file with the terminal application. The fix? Use a different browser such as Firefox that doesn't support the "open safe files after downloading."

Recently, Apple released their new Intel Duo-based Macintoshes. Apple continues to support the older PowerPC-based Macs, and the new Intel-based Macs will support older software through the use of an emulator called Rosetta. With this new release came the news that some creative folks had actually gotten Windows XP to run natively on the new Apple hardware.[4] I'm not sure of the security implications at this point of running OS X on an Intel chip, so the future remains to be seen.

INITIAL HEALTH CHECK

As we did with our Windows system, the first thing we're going to do is check to see whether our system has been compromised. If the system has been hacked, let's find out

---

[2]   www.heise.de/english/newsticker/news/69862

[3]   http://daringfireball.net/2006/02/safari_shell_script_exploit

[4]   http://onmac.net/

before we go any further. We have a few things that we can check that will tell us whether anything obvious has been done to our endpoint.

A system scan will tell us whether we're offering any services or ports to the rest of the network that we shouldn't be offering. We can also use this information when we do our rootkit analysis.

We'll check to make sure that we still actually control the system and look to see that a rootkit hasn't been loaded onto our system. Then, we'll look at our system files to see whether any of them have been corrupted. Next, we'll check into our running processes and examine our network resources to see whether there is anything that doesn't look secure. Finally, we'll look for spyware and cruise through the various logs that OS X creates for some nuggets of wisdom in the river of data.

SYSTEM SCAN

From an external machine on the same subnet, we're going to run our port scanner against our target machine. This will tell us whether our Mac is offering any services that we don't want it to offer on the network. In much the same way we scanned our Windows endpoint, we're going to use a tool such as nmap to examine our system.

A user endpoint should return an empty scan result. In other words, your firewall should prevent nmap from seeing anything meaningful. Figure 9-1 shows an nmap scan against a Mac on my network with the firewall on.

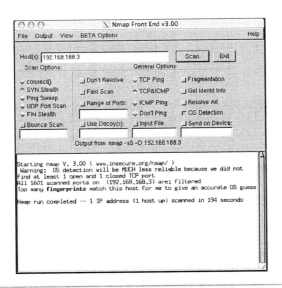

Figure 9-1 An nmap scan of a system with a firewall.

Notice that nmap reports that the ports are "filtered," which means that it knows that a firewall was intercepting the packets that nmap was sending. If there had not been a firewall and there were no services running, nmap would have reported that the ports were closed, as shown in Figure 9-2.

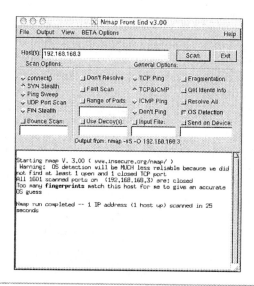

Figure 9-2   An nmap scan of a system with the firewall turned off and no services being offered.

Another major difference between having a firewall and not having a firewall can be seen in how long it takes to scan the endpoint. With the firewall on, it took 194 seconds to scan the endpoint versus 25 seconds without the firewall. The firewall throttles the responses to keep the endpoint from being overloaded.

For comparison purposes, I turned the firewall off and started some services on our target Mac so that we would have something to look at. Our target Mac is now providing the following:

- Apple File Sharing (Personal File Sharing)
- Windows Sharing
- Remote Login
- FTP Service
- Apple Remote Desktop

Figure 9-3 shows that there is quite a difference in the response. As you can see, our target Mac is now "target rich!" An attacker can try to FTP to the endpoint, or the attacker can try to actually log in to it. Add to that that it is exporting part of the file system, and you have a system that is ready to get broken into.

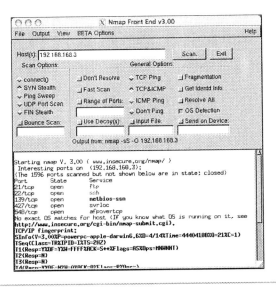

Figure 9-3 An nmap scan of a system with no firewall that is offering network services.

Netinfo Manager can be used to check on users, groups, and network associations. Instead of modifying etc/hosts by hand to add an entry, you can use Netinfo Manager to make the change for you. You can edit user and group information as well.

> **WARNING**
>
> You should have a deep knowledge of UNIX system administration before you start mucking about, changing things with Netinfo Manager. Because it is a tool to make a sysadmin's life easier by making it easier to make changes, you can screw things up at warp speed if you don't know what you're doing!

With some skill, you can effectively use Netinfo Manager to browse users, groups, networks, and aliases. For example, you can use it to verify group membership, and you can use it to check up on users. Although there is a nice GUI, this is a manual process with no reporting capability. Although it's almost easier to check the configuration files that

Netinfo Manager uses, it does present the information rather nicely. In Figure 9-4, you can see how one of my antivirus (AV) tools generated a user.

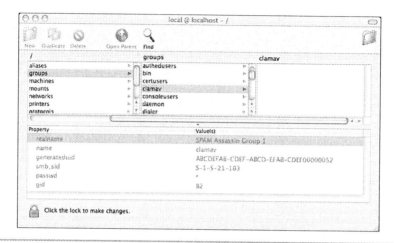

Figure 9-4   Netinfo Manager controls and displays user, group, and machine information.

System Profiler is another tool that reads various configuration files and presents them to you in a nice GUI. System Profiler goes a bit further by collecting information about the hardware as well as the software. System Profiler can present information about what type of graphic display and what kind of device is connected to your USB. Unlike Netinfo Manager, System Profiler is a read-only tool. We're going to use it later to check for malware.

FINDING ROOTKITS

You can use the same techniques that we discussed in Chapter 8, "Microsoft Windows," comparing the services and ports you see on the inside versus the services and ports you can see from the outside; or you can use a tool specifically designed to identify rootkits. The manual process is fairly time consuming and can take a major bite out of an otherwise productive day, so I opted for the tool-based method.

Keep in mind that as of this writing there weren't that many rootkits available aimed specifically at the Mac, and the ones that were available (opener) required the root password for them to be installed. Having said that, rootkits are available for most variants of UNIX and the UNIX clones, and the Mac OS is a variant of FreeBSD and is therefore vulnerable to them.

I ran rkhunter (www.rootkit.nl), a General Public License (GPL) project written by Michael Boelen. Outside of two vulnerable applications that I don't run, my Mac running OS X 10.4.6 received a clean bill of health. Just to be clear, it was the ownership of the application configuration files of an old version of gpg and Apache that rkhunter squawked about.

Figure 9-5 shows a sample output of the following command:

```
rkhunter -c
```

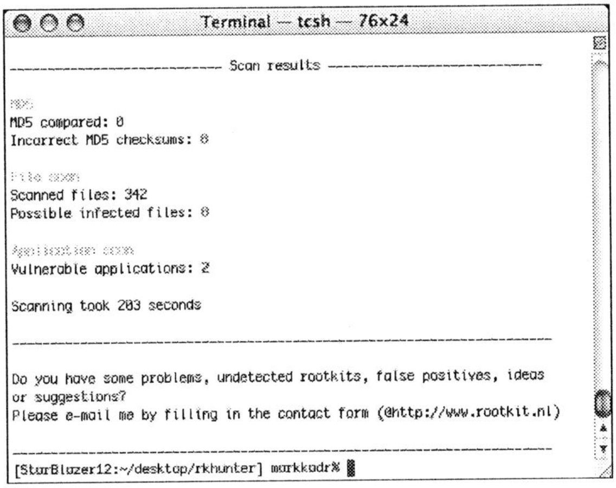

```
● ○ ○              Terminal — tcsh — 76x24

---------------------- Scan results ----------------------

MD5
MD5 compared: 0
Incorrect MD5 checksums: 0

File scan
Scanned files: 342
Possible infected files: 0

Application scan
Vulnerable applications: 2

Scanning took 203 seconds

_____

Do you have some problems, undetected rootkits, false positives, ideas
or suggestions?
Please e-mail me by filling in the contact form (@http://www.rootkit.nl)

_____
[StarBlazer12:~/desktop/rkhunter] markkadr% █
```

Figure 9-5 Output from rkhunter reveals there are no rootkits on this machine.

As I said before, if you do find something, save your data and reinstall a clean operating system.

SYSTEM FILES

The Mac comes with an application called Disk Utility that will assist you with some basic functions such as turning on journaling or unmounting the disk. Disk Utility will also perform some basic security functions such as verifying disk permissions. However, when you have nearly half a million files, the output can be pretty verbose.

The unfortunate result is that there is nothing in the OS to generate a baseline snapshot of the Mac OS and the critical files that it uses. However, there is a tool that is based on the open source version of Tripwire that provides this function. Tripwire tells you when a file is added, removed, or modified. Pretty handy if you're trying to keep track of how your file system is changing. Now the bad news: It has no GUI, and all the commands must be implemented via a shell and a command line. In addition, the reports must also be generated via the command line. If you have some OS X servers, it may be worthwhile to invest the time and effort required to install Tripwire and to generate and interpret the reports. Tripwire for the Mac is available at www.macguru.net/~frodo/Tripwire-osx.html.

PROCESSING YOUR PROCESSES

Because the Macintosh is essentially a UNIX machine, there are a number of ways to look at what's running on it. The simple way is to open a terminal window and enter **ps.** The results aren't very interesting, as you can see in Figure 9-6, because all this command will tell you is that your shell is running.

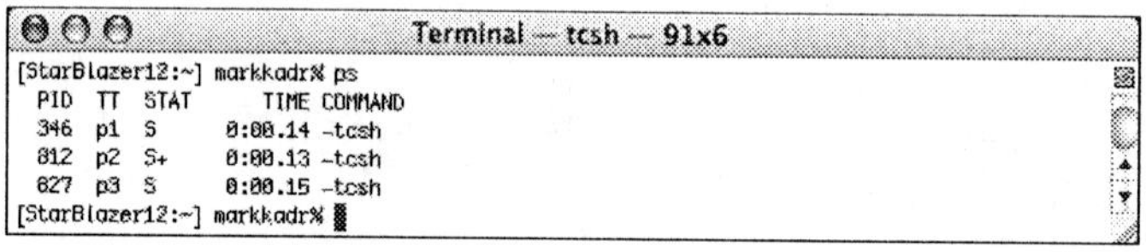

```
[StarBlazer12:~] markkadr% ps
 PID TT STAT      TIME COMMAND
 346 p1  S      0:00.14 -tcsh
 812 p2  S+     0:00.13 -tcsh
 827 p3  S      0:00.15 -tcsh
[StarBlazer12:~] markkadr%
```

Figure 9-6   A simple response from the **ps** command doesn't produce a lot of information.

To really get an idea of what's really running, you have to tell **ps** to list all the processes, including those that don't belong to you. The way to do that is by issuing the **ps** command with some switches that ask for more detail. I personally like this:

```
ps -ax
```

This tells **ps** to show all the processes, even those of other users (**a**), and to show processes that don't have a controlling terminal (**x**). This is a fairly long list on most machines, 82 processes on my Mac, but Figure 9-7 shows a bit of what this command returns.

As you can see in Figure 9-8, it's quite a difference in what processes are listed. You can add a **-u** to the **ps** command and will essentially spill its guts regarding USER, %CPU, %MEM, VSZ, RSS, TT, and when the process was started. The definitions for USER, %CPU, and %MEM are pretty self-evident, telling you who owns the process and how much of the CPU and memory is being used. The rest of them aren't as intuitive. VSZ is the total size in kilobytes of the process in virtual memory. RSS is the resident set size in kilobytes of the process and refers to the amount of nonswapped physical memory that a process is using. TT refers to the control terminal name associated with the process.

```
Terminal — tcsh — 184x46
[StarBlazer12:~] markkadrX ps -ax
  PID  TT  STAT   TIME COMMAND
    1  ??  Ss    0:00.91 /sbin/launchd
   26  ??  Ss    0:00.15 /sbin/dynamic_pager -F /private/var/vm/swapfile
   32  ??  Ss    0:03.75 kextd
   36  ??  Ss    0:00.83 /usr/sbin/KernelEventAgent
   37  ??  Ss    0:04.16 /usr/sbin/mDNSResponder -launchdaemon
   38  ??  Ss    0:06.11 /usr/sbin/netinfod -s local
   39  ??  Ss    0:02.83 /usr/sbin/syslogd
   40  ??  Ss    0:00.37 /usr/sbin/cron
   41  ??  Ss    0:00.03 xinetd -dontfork -stayalive -inetd_compat -pidfile /var/run/xinetd.pid
   42  ??  Ss    0:10.09 /usr/sbin/configd
   43  ??  Ss    0:00.47 /usr/sbin/coreaudiod
   44  ??  Ss    0:01.46 /usr/sbin/diskarbitrationd
   45  ??  Ss    0:00.18 /usr/sbin/memberd -x
   46  ??  Ss    0:01.02 /usr/sbin/securityd
   47  ??  Ss    0:01.22 /usr/sbin/notifyd
   52  ??  Ss    2:01.29 /usr/sbin/update
   56  ??  Ss    0:01.96 /usr/sbin/distnoted
   57  ??  Ss    0:04.11 /usr/sbin/DirectoryService
   59  ??  S     0:05.53 /usr/sbin/blued
   67  ??  Ss  100:09.76 /System/Library/Frameworks/ApplicationServices.framework/Frameworks/CoreGraphics.framework/Resources/WindowServer -daemon
   70  ??  Ss    0:06.43 /System/Library/CoreServices/coreservicesd
   72  ??  Ss    0:23.29 /System/Library/Frameworks/ApplicationServices.framework/Frameworks/ATS.framework/Support/ATSServer
   73  ??  Ss    0:07.29 /System/Library/CoreServices/loginwindow.app/Contents/MacOS/loginwindow console
   74  ??  S<    0:00.30 afax -v -v chevmoinrxtf -d/dev/tty.modem -iZ -18FE86D257x120 -i6C0 -iM1L0 -o1 -i 406-238-6456 -kZ -g -e -j58=4 -v -s -r XwXdXHxMbS
   84  ??  S     0:00.02 aodmod
  107  ??  Ss    0:00.00 /usr/libexec/crashreporterd
  147  ??  Ss    0:04.75 /Library/StartupItems/SygateAgent/sylinkd
  148  ??  S     6:53.91 /Library/StartupItems/SygateAgent/sylinkd
  149  ??  S     0:00.01 /bin/sh /Library/StartupItems/DigiTunnelStartup/DigiTunnelStartup daemon
  151  ??  S     0:00.17 /Library/StartupItems/DigiTunnelStartup/DigiTunnel-Daemon
  152  ??  Ss    0:01.07 /usr/sbin/cupsd
  153  ??  Ss    2:24.90 /System/Library/Frameworks/CoreServices.framework/Frameworks/Metadata.framework/Versions/A/Support/mds
  161  ??  S     0:24.47 /Library/Intego/integod
  164  ??  S     0:16.77 /usr/sbin/lookupd
  177  ??  Ss    0:00.64 /System/Library/CoreServices/pbs
  187  ??  Ss    0:15.06 ntpd -f /var/run/ntp.drift -p /var/run/ntpd.pid
  203  ??  Ss    0:00.00 nfsiod -n 4
  207  ??  S     0:17.54 /System/Library/CoreServices/Dock.app/Contents/MacOS/Dock -psn_0_524289
  213  ??  Ss    0:00.08 rpc.lockd -w
  216  ??  Ss    0:01.21 /usr/sbin/automount -f -m /Network -nsl -mnt /private/var/automount
  220  ??  Ss    0:00.06 /usr/sbin/automount -f -m /automount/Servers -fstab -mnt /private/Network/Servers -m /automount/static -static -mnt /private/var/automount
  222  ??  S     0:54.04 /System/Library/CoreServices/SystemUIServer.app/Contents/MacOS/SystemUIServer -psn_0_655361
  225  ??  S     0:13.73 /System/Library/CoreServices/Finder.app/Contents/MacOS/Finder -psn_0_786433
  237  ??  S     0:00.41 /System/Library/Extensions/IOSerialFamily.kext/Contents/Plugins/InternalModemSupport.kext/Contents/Resources/AppleModemOnHold.app/Contents/MacOS/AppleModemOnH
```

Figure 9-7 The command **ps -ax** produces information about all the processes, including those of other users and those without controlling terminals.

```
Terminal — tcsh — 184x46
[StarBlazer12:~] markkadrX ps -aux
USER      PID  %CPU %MEM    VSZ    RSS  TT  STAT STARTED      TIME COMMAND
root      882  27.8  0.2  27584   1748  p1  S+   2:17PM  197:10.59 top -f
markkadr  375  23.1 11.9 1627132  93512  ??  R    Sun11AM  446:34.69 /Applications/Firefox.app/Contents/MacOS/firefox-bin -psn_0_4849665
markkadr  343  14.7  4.1 178364  32312  ??  S    Sun11AM  10:09.63 /Applications/Utilities/Terminal.app/Contents/MacOS/Terminal -psn_0_3081009
windowse   67  10.6  7.5 240136  59308  ??  Ss   Sat09PM  155:12.52 /System/Library/Frameworks/ApplicationServices.framework/Frameworks/CoreGraphics.framework/Resources/WindowServer
markkadr  243   2.6  1.5 146624  11700  ??  S    Sat09PM  78:54.05 /Library/Application Support/radioSHARK/radioSHARKServer.app/Contents/MacOS/radioSHARKServer -psn_0_1572665
markkadr  301   1.4  7.0 485072  55336  ??  S    Sun12PM  90:02.17 /Applications/Microsoft Office 2004/Microsoft Word /Applications/Microsoft Office 2004/Microsoft Word -psn_0_52428
root     1810   0.6  0.1  27320    428  p2  R+   12:37PM   0:00.00 ps -aux
markkadr  350   0.5  3.4 269676  27024  ??  S    Sun11AM  71:03.67 /Applications/Microsoft Office 2004/Microsoft Entourage /Applications/Microsoft Office 2004/Microsoft Entourage -p
root       38   0.4  0.1  27584   1100  ??  Ss   Sat09PM   0:09.62 /usr/sbin/netinfod -s local
markkadr  812   0.4  0.1  31032    960  p2  S    2:38PM    0:00.14 -tcsh
markkadr  249   0.3  1.3 173380  10304  ??  S    Sat09PM  17:22.17 /Applications/Pop-Up Zapper.app/Contents/MacOS/Pop-Up Zapper -psn_0_2220225
root      148   0.2  0.1  31304   1012  ??  S    Sat09PM  10:55.76 /Library/StartupItems/SygateAgent/sylinkd
root       46   0.0  0.4  29848   3304  ??  Ss   Sat09PM   0:01.29 /usr/sbin/securityd
root       47   0.0  0.1  27056    856  ??  Ss   Sat09PM   0:01.05 /usr/sbin/notifyd
root       52   0.0  0.1  27240    800  ??  Ss   Sat09PM   3:17.63 /usr/sbin/update
root       56   0.0  0.1  27664    816  ??  Ss   Sat09PM   0:02.78 /usr/sbin/distnoted
root       57   0.0  0.7  33220   5192  ??  Ss   Sat09PM   0:19.58 /usr/sbin/DirectoryService
root       59   0.0  0.2  30832   1500  ??  S    Sat09PM   0:06.43 /usr/sbin/blued
root       70   0.0  0.9  52440   7036  ??  Ss   Sat09PM   0:07.15 /System/Library/CoreServices/coreservicesd
markkadr   72   0.0  0.4  81116   3136  ??  Ss   Sat09PM   0:25.58 /System/Library/Frameworks/ApplicationServices.framework/Frameworks/ATS.framework/Support/ATSServer
markkadr   73   0.0  0.6 134072   4504  ??  Ss   Sat09PM   0:08.07 /System/Library/CoreServices/loginwindow.app/Contents/MacOS/loginwindow console
markkadr   74   0.0  0.2  27932   1600  ??  S<   Sat09PM   0:00.30 afax -v -v chevmoinrxtf -d/dev/tty.modem -iZ -18FE86D257x120 -i6C0 -iM1L0 -o1 -i 406-238-6456 -kZ -g -e -j58=4
root       84   0.0  0.0  27632    312  ??  S    Sat09PM   0:00.02 aodmod
root      107   0.0  0.0  27244     84  ??  Ss   Sat09PM   0:00.00 /usr/libexec/crashreporterd
root      147   0.0  0.0  29268    108  ??  Ss   Sat09PM   0:07.40 /Library/StartupItems/SygateAgent/sylinkd
root      149   0.0  0.0  27604    284  ??  S    Sat09PM   0:00.01 /bin/sh /Library/StartupItems/DigiTunnelStartup/DigiTunnelStartup daemon
root      151   0.0  0.1  38232    992  ??  S    Sat09PM   0:00.17 /Library/StartupItems/DigiTunnelStartup/DigiTunnel-Daemon
root      152   0.0  0.1  26520    768  ??  Ss   Sat09PM   0:02.12 /usr/sbin/cupsd
root      153   0.0  0.5  46284   4000  ??  Ss   Sat09PM   3:37.13 /System/Library/Frameworks/CoreServices.framework/Frameworks/Metadata.framework/Versions/A/Support/mds
root      161   0.0  0.2  29416   1212  ??  S    Sat09PM   0:37.65 /Library/Intego/integod
root      164   0.0  0.1  29724    920  ??  S    Sat09PM   0:26.18 /usr/sbin/lookupd
markkadr  177   0.0  0.6  55684   4704  ??  Ss   Sat09PM   0:00.66 /System/Library/CoreServices/pbs
root      187   0.0  0.0  27580    244  ??  Ss   Sat09PM   0:13.15 ntpd -f /var/run/ntp.drift -p /var/run/ntpd.pid
root      203   0.0  0.0  29300     60  ??  Ss   Sat09PM   0:00.00 nfsiod -n 4
markkadr  207   0.0  1.2 137836   9712  ??  S    Sat09PM   0:10.51 /System/Library/CoreServices/Dock.app/Contents/MacOS/Dock -psn_0_524289
root      213   0.0  0.1  27300     76  ??  Ss   Sat09PM   0:00.00 rpc.lockd -w
root      216   0.0  0.1  30972   1092  ??  Ss   Sat09PM   0:00.35 /usr/sbin/automount -f -m /Network -nsl -mnt /private/var/automount
root      220   0.0  0.1  29412    652  ??  Ss   Sat09PM   0:00.06 /usr/sbin/automount -f -m /automount/Servers -fstab -mnt /private/Network/Servers -m /automount/static -static -mn
markkadr  222   0.0  1.8 172136  14016  ??  S    Sat09PM   1:18.95 /System/Library/CoreServices/SystemUIServer.app/Contents/MacOS/SystemUIServer -psn_0_655361
markkadr  225   0.0  2.1 179872  16420  ??  S    Sat09PM   0:18.97 /System/Library/CoreServices/Finder.app/Contents/MacOS/Finder -psn_0_786433
markkadr  237   0.0  1.1 139324   8816  ??  S    Sat09PM   0:00.44 /System/Library/Extensions/IOSerialFamily.kext/Contents/Plugins/InternalModemSupport.kext/Contents/Resources/Apple
markkadr  240   0.0  1.0 134840   8106  ??  S    Sat09PM   0:00.40 /System/Library/Frameworks/ApplicationServices.framework/Versions/A/Frameworks/SpeechSynthesis.framework/Versions/
markkadr  241   0.0  1.2 142808   9564  ??  S    Sat09PM   0:11.86 /System/Library/CoreServices/System Events.app/Contents/MacOS/System Events -psn_0_1310721
markkadr  242   0.0  0.7 129172   5752  ??  S    Sat09PM   0:00.19 /Applications/iTunes.app/Contents/Resources/iTunesHelper.app/Contents/MacOS/iTunesHelper -psn_0_1441793
```

Figure 9-8 Adding the **-u** to the **ps** command tells it to include statistics about the running programs.

Another interesting command-line tool is **top.** The **top** command lists in order of usage the processes loaded on your system and shows you in near real time who is the busiest. The nice thing about **top** is that it tells you the following:

- Processes
  - Total
  - Running
  - Sleeping
- Load average
- CPU usage
  - User
  - System
  - Idle time
- Shared libraries
  - Loaded
  - Resident as code
  - Resident as data
- Memory regions
  - Num
  - Resident
  - Shared
- Physical memory
- Wired (can't be used for paging)
  - Active
  - Inactive
  - Used
  - Free
- VM (virtual memory)
  - Total
  - Pageins
  - Pageouts

If you're thinking that this is quite a bit of information, you are quite correct. As Figure 9-9 shows, I can reduce the amount of information being displayed by using the following command:

```
top -ocpu
```

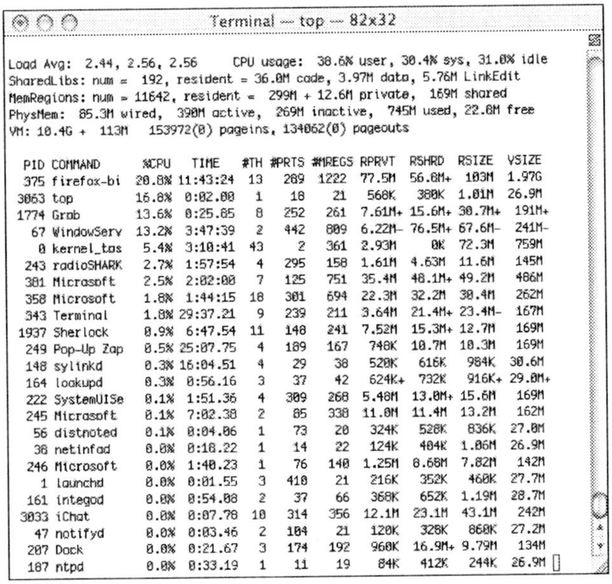

```
Terminal — top — 82x32

Load Avg:  2.44, 2.56, 2.56     CPU usage:  38.6% user, 30.4% sys, 31.0% idle
SharedLibs: num =  192, resident = 36.0M code, 3.97M data, 5.76M LinkEdit
MemRegions: num = 11642, resident =  299M + 12.6M private,  169M shared
PhysMem:  85.3M wired,  390M active,  269M inactive,  745M used, 22.0M free
VM: 10.4G +  113M   153972(0) pageins, 134062(0) pageouts

  PID COMMAND      %CPU    TIME   #TH #PRTS #MREGS RPRVT  RSHRD  RSIZE  VSIZE
  375 firefox-bi  20.8% 11:43:24  13   289  1222  77.5M  56.0M+  103M  1.97G
 3063 top         16.8%  0:02.00   1    18    21   568K   380K  1.01M  26.9M
 1774 Grab        13.6%  0:25.85   8   252   261  7.61M+ 15.6M+ 30.7M+  191M+
   67 WindowServ  13.2%  3:47:39   2   442   809  6.22M- 76.5M+ 67.6M-  241M-
    0 kernel_tas   5.4%  3:10:41  43     2   361  2.93M     0K  72.3M   759M
  243 radioSHARK   2.7%  1:57:54   4   295   158  1.61M  4.63M  11.6M   145M
  301 Microsoft    2.5%  2:02:00   7   125   751  35.4M  48.1M+ 49.2M   486M
  358 Microsoft    1.8%  1:44:15  18   301   694  22.3M  32.2M  30.4M   262M
  343 Terminal     1.8% 29:37.21   9   239   211  3.64M  21.4M+ 23.4M-  167M
 1937 Sherlock     0.9%  6:47.54  11   148   241  7.52M  15.3M+ 12.7M   169M
  249 Pop-Up Zap   0.5% 25:07.75   4   189   167   748K  10.7M  10.3M   169M
  148 sylinkd      0.3% 16:04.51   4    29    38   520K   616K   984K  30.6M
  164 lookupd      0.3%  0:56.16   3    37    42   624K+  732K   916K+ 29.0M+
  222 SystemUISe   0.1%  1:51.36   4   309   268  5.48M  13.0M+ 15.6M   169M
  245 Microsoft    0.1%  7:02.38   2    85   338  11.0M  11.4M  13.2M   162M
   56 distnoted    0.1%  0:04.06   1    73    20   324K   528K   836K  27.0M
   36 netinfod     0.0%  0:18.22   1    14    22   124K   404K  1.06M  26.9M
  246 Microsoft    0.0%  1:40.23   1    76   140  1.25M  8.68M  7.82M   142M
    1 launchd      0.0%  0:01.55   3   418    21   216K   352K   460K  27.7M
  161 integod      0.0%  0:54.08   2    37    66   368K   652K  1.19M  28.7M
 3033 iChat        0.0%  0:07.78  10   314   356  12.1M  23.1M  43.1M   242M
   47 notifyd      0.0%  0:03.46   2   104    21   120K   328K   860K  27.2M
  207 Dock         0.0%  0:21.67   3   174   192   960K  16.9M+ 9.79M   134M
  187 ntpd         0.0%  0:33.19   1    11    19    84K   412K   244K  26.9M
```

Figure 9-9 The **top** command shows you processes and their activity.

Another benefit of this form of the **top** command is that it lists things in the same order as the **ps** command, with the busy processes at the top.

Now that we have a list of the processes, we need to figure out which ones are good and which ones are evil. The ones with obvious names such as Terminal, Sherlock, and Pop-Up Zap are pretty easily eliminated as suspects, but what about launchd, netinfod, and integod? Integod sounds pretty suspicious to me! After some sleuthing on the Internet, I learned that the integod process is my aftermarket security software.

Launchd looked suspicious but is actually the new version of inetd. Inetd was responsible for listening to the ports and launching the appropriate process to handle it. Launchd combines inetd and a number of other functions into one program.

A fairly complete listing of Mac processes can be found at http://www.westwind.com/reference/OS-X/background-processes.html.

Another interesting tool for monitoring things in real time on a Mac is called **fs_usage**. This is a real-time process display tool and it is *extremely* verbose. I issued the following command and was rewarded with more than 177KB in less than 2 seconds:

```
sudo fs_usage > fs_dump
```

I tried watching it as it scrolled by on the screen at first and thought that I could capture the results in a file and then examine it at my leisure. I've found that the **uniq** command can help filter out some of the repetition:

```
uniq -f 4 fs_dump > dump
```

The preceding command will at least reduce the number of lines that you have to examine to something a little more manageable.

What's on the Network?

The first thing we're going to do here is to check and see whether anyone has diverted your traffic by checking the hosts file. On a Mac, the hosts file is located in the /etc directory and should look similar to what is displayed in Figure 9-10. Once again, and I'm sure that this will bite me later, I'm assuming that you know and understand enough about a Mac to open a terminal window. When you're in the /etc directory, the following command will produce results similar to those in Figure 9-10:

```
more hosts
```

Notice that there's not much there.

This is as it should be, and if you find anything that you haven't put here, you may have a problem. The interesting thing about the hosts file is that you can put your bank and its corresponding IP address as an entry, and you'll be guaranteed that you're getting the same site all the time. The following entry in your hosts file ensures that you will always return to the Wells Fargo Web site at this IP address:

```
151.151.88.133 www.wellsfargo.com
```

On the other hand, a bogus entry in your hosts file may indicate that your system has been compromised. As in the preceding bank example, if the IP address weren't owned by Wells Fargo, and you didn't make the entry in the hosts file, it could be a hacker trying to get you to enter your banking information in a phishing site.

Another interesting thing to do with the hosts file is to point all the evil Web sites to the localhost. Localhost (also known as the loopback) is the IP address that the system uses for internal communications. Directing things such as adserver.adtech.de to 127.0.0.1 ensures that any data sent to that URL never reaches the Internet.

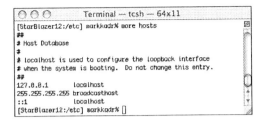

```
○ ○ ○          Terminal — tcsh — 64x11
[StarBlazer12:/etc] markkadr% more hosts
##
# Host Database
#
# localhost is used to configure the loopback interface
# when the system is booting.  Do not change this entry.
##
127.0.0.1       localhost
255.255.255.255 broadcasthost
::1             localhost
[StarBlazer12:/etc] markkadr% []
```

Figure 9-10 The hosts file can be used to assign IP addresses to URLs. In this file, the IP address 127.0.0.1 is assigned to the URL local host.

There is a great tool called netstat that can tell you things about your network connections. Netstat will tell you about the following:

- Active sockets
- Local addresses
- Remote addresses
- Send queue
- Receive queues
- Protocol
- Internal state of the protocol

Like any UNIX command-line tool, netstat does have some switches that make the output a bit more targeted for what you're trying to learn. For example, the following command produces the results shown in Figure 9-11:

```
netstat -A
```

As you can see, I have a connection to my POP server and some internal connections to the localhost. I have some connections to the Network Time Protocol (NTP). The services that don't seem absolutely intuitive will have to be investigated.

- 5353 is Multicast DNS.
- *.rockwell-csp2 is really port 2222, the Microsoft tattletale port for MS Office. When an Office product starts, it tries to find out whether anyone else has the same product ID. I verified that it was in fact Word by killing it and checking with netstat to verify that port 2222 had disappeared.

A simple tool for telling you about what your network interfaces are doing is ifconfig. For example, the following command will produce results similar to those in Figure 9-12:

```
ifconfig -a
```

```
○ ○ ○                        Terminal — tcsh — 100x39
[StarBlazer12:~] markkadr% netstat -A
Active Internet connections
Socket   Proto Recv-Q Send-Q  Local Address        Foreign Address      (state)
      0 tcp4       0      0  192.168.168.2.4922   pop-sbc-v1.m.pop3    ESTABLISHED
      0 tcp4       0      0  localhost.netinfo-   localhost.1015       ESTABLISHED
      0 tcp4       0      0  localhost.1015       localhost.netinfo-   ESTABLISHED
      0 tcp4       0      0  localhost.netinfo-   localhost.1017       ESTABLISHED
      0 tcp4       0      0  localhost.1017       localhost.netinfo-   ESTABLISHED
      0 tcp4       0      0  localhost.netinfo-   localhost.1021       ESTABLISHED
      0 tcp4       0      0  localhost.1021       localhost.netinfo-   ESTABLISHED
 18fa5f0 udp4       0      0  *.rockwell-csp2      *.*
 18fa300 udp4       0      0  192.168.168.2.4915   *.*
 18fa790 udp4       0      0  *.mdns               *.*
 18fa000 udp6       0      0  *.5353               *.*
 18fa930 udp4       0      0  localhost.49158      localhost.1022
 18f9680 udp4       0      0  localhost.49157      localhost.1022
 18fa2b0 udp4       0      0  localhost.1022       *.*
 18f9b60 udp4       0      0  localhost.49156      localhost.1023
 18f9800 udp4       0      0  localhost.1023       *.*
 18f9ea0 udp4       0      0  192.168.168..ntp     *.*
 18f9f70 udp4       0      0  localhost.ntp        *.*
 18fa040 udp4       0      0  *.ntp                *.*
 18fa860 udp4       0      0  *.ipp                *.*
 18faad0 udp6       0      0  *.5353               *.*
 18faba0 udp4       0      0  *.mdns               *.*
 18fac70 udp4       0      0  *.*                  *.*
 18fae10 udp4       0      0  localhost.netinfo-   *.*
Active LOCAL (UNIX) domain sockets
Address  Type   Recv-Q Send-Q   Inode     Conn      Refs  Nextref Addr
21b5880 stream      0      0        0        0         0        0
21b5900 stream      0      0        0        0         0        0
21b5a00 stream      0      0        0   21b5a18         0        0
21b5a18 stream      0      0        0   21b5aa0         0        0
21b5c38 stream      0      0  24876b4        0         0        0 /tmp/.modemOnHold
19cc110 stream      0      0        0   19cc198         0        0 /var/run/pppconfd
19cc198 stream      0      0        0   19cc110         0        0
21b5e58 stream      0      0        0   21b5ee0         0        0
21b5ee0 stream      0      0        0   21b5e58         0        0
19cc000 stream      0      0  21c98c4        0         0        0 /private/var/run/cupsd
```

Figure 9-11   Netstat can provide a great deal of information about the connections to your endpoint.

```
○ ○ ○                        Terminal — tcsh — 118x24
[StarBlazer12:~/desktop/rkhunter] markkadr% ifconfig -a
lo0: flags=8049<UP,LOOPBACK,RUNNING,MULTICAST> mtu 16384
        inet 127.0.0.1 netmask 0xff000000
        inet6 ::1 prefixlen 128
        inet6 fe80::1%lo0 prefixlen 64 scopeid 0x1
gif0: flags=8010<POINTOPOINT,MULTICAST> mtu 1280
stf0: flags=0<> mtu 1280
en0: flags=8863<UP,BROADCAST,SMART,RUNNING,SIMPLEX,MULTICAST> mtu 1500
        ether 00:0a:95:68:38:0e
        media: autoselect (none) status: inactive
        supported media: none autoselect 10baseT/UTP <half-duplex> 10baseT/UTP <full-duplex> 10baseT/UTP <full-duplex,
hw-loopback> 100baseTX <half-duplex> 100baseTX <full-duplex> 100baseTX <full-duplex,hw-loopback> 1000baseT <full-duple
x> 1000baseT <full-duplex,hw-loopback> 1000baseT <full-duplex,flow-control> 1000baseT <full-duplex,flow-control,hw-loo
pback>
en1: flags=8863<UP,BROADCAST,SMART,RUNNING,SIMPLEX,MULTICAST> mtu 1500
        inet 192.168.168.2 netmask 0xffffff00 broadcast 192.168.168.255
        ether 00:30:65:8b:89:ed
        media: autoselect status: active
        supported media: autoselect
fw0: flags=8863<UP,BROADCAST,SMART,RUNNING,SIMPLEX,MULTICAST> mtu 2030
        lladdr 00:0a:95:ff:fe:68:38:0e
        media: autoselect <full-duplex> status: inactive
        supported media: autoselect <full-duplex>
[StarBlazer12:~/desktop/rkhunter] markkadr% []
```

Figure 9-12   Ifconfig is a great way to find out how your network interfaces are configured and what their names are.

SPYWARE AND OTHER MALWARE

There are at least four known threats at the time of this publication, and each spreads in a slightly different way. I'm highlighting these because they've been observed in the wild and aren't just theory or speculation.

OSX.Inqtana.A[5] is a proof-of-concept exploit that takes advantage of an input validation error[6] in OS X Bluetooth. A remote Bluetooth attacker can take advantage of this as a directory traversal vulnerability and access files outside of the default directory. Apple has released security updates for this, and if you're up-to-date with regard to OS X updates, you're not vulnerable.

OSX.Leap.A[7] is a worm that spreads via iChat in the form of an incoming file transfer. I classify this as a "stupid user trick" because persons at the other end of the connection must click Save File, open the archive, and then execute the code by double-clicking what they think is a JPG. This is quite a bit of work to infect yourself! Surprisingly enough, the reports say that it won't propagate on the Intel-based Macs.

From our rootkit class of threats—SH.Renepo.A/SH.Renepo.B—AKA Opener is a rootkit that has the potential to allow an attacker to disable the software firewall, steal intellectual property, and destroy data. Because Opener can replicate itself by copying itself to other systems via shared volumes or mounted drives, some vendors such as Symantec consider it a virus. What's interesting about Opener is that it uses a shell called Bash to execute scripts that use the Mac's onboard tools as part of the exploit.

Last but not least is the Sony-based digital rights management (DRM) "solution" that hid the copy protection software from the user. I use the past tense here because Sony has suspended using their DRM for the time being. However, there are still plenty of CDs with this stuff on them.

This is a good news–bad news kind of situation, because if you haven't popped any Sony CDs into your Mac and accessed the enhanced content, you don't have a problem. If you have, well, there's a good chance that you have something that looks and smells very much like a rootkit loaded on your system. The tool, based on software supplied by SunnComm[8] called MediaMax, operates deep in the OS by adding two kernel extensions: PhoenixNub1.kext and PhoenixNub2.kext. The DRM hides any software with sys prepended to the name. Sounds like we should be looking for something called sysopener pretty soon.

---

[5] http://securityresponse.symantec.com/avcenter/venc/data/osx.inqtana.a.html

[6] www.securityfocus.com/bid/13491

[7] http://securityresponse.symantec.com/avcenter/venc/data/osx.leap.a.html

[8] www.sunncomm.com/Brochure/

Now that we know what we're looking for, we can make some decisions about what we can do. The virus stuff is going to require us to install some AV before we can find out whether we've been infected.

Like our Windows system, some malware installs itself so that it starts when the system starts up. System Profiler is a great tool for finding out what is starting when you start your Macintosh. Click the blue Apple icon in the upper-left side of the screen, and then select About This Mac. You should see the About This Mac window pop up, as shown in Figure 9-13.

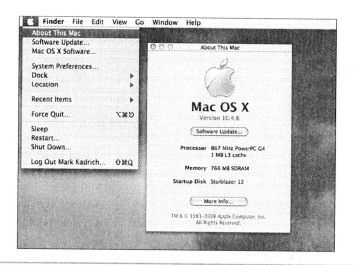

Figure 9-13 The built-in application that tells you everything about the Mac is About This Mac.

Click the More Info button, and the System Profiler window will appear. Click Software > Startup Items, and System Profiler should look as depicted in Figure 9-14.

What you should be looking at is another list of things for you to check. None of the services in this list is especially dangerous except for the possibility of Apache, but we are only using it to support our Common UNIX Printing System (CUPS) printing services.

Now we're ready to check for spyware. Yes, you can get spyware on a Mac. I use a tool called MacScan.[9] I recently downloaded the 2.0 version and gave it a spin. I was quite happy with the results, which you can see in Figure 9-15. Nothing like a clean bill of health from a chunk of software to give you that warm and fuzzy feeling of false security!

---

[9] http://macscan.securemac.com

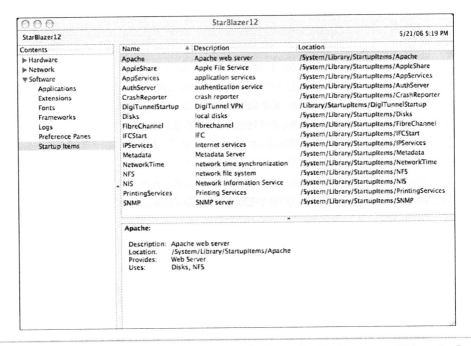

Figure 9-14 Clicking the More Info button brings up the System Profiler. You can run SP from the Finder, too.

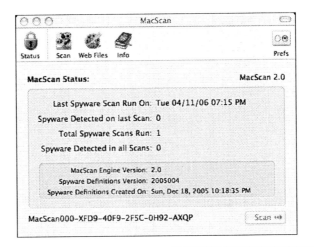

Figure 9-15 MacScan looks for spyware on the Mac. I tested the latest version, 2.0.

LOOKING AT THE LOGS

The first thing that a smart hacker will do is to kill logging and flush the logs. Thank goodness that not all hackers are smart.

Unlike the Windows machines, the Mac is full of log files. (Okay, that was a cheap shot, because Windows uses a unified Event Log.) You can check on the status of the system, users, and applications. Not only are there lots of logs to look at, but there are multiple ways of looking at them! You can use the System Profiler, or you can use command lines. You can always use the native application that produced the logs in some cases. In the case of logs such as wtmp, you must use a system command-line tool to view them.

The bottom line here is that the logs may tell you things about your computer that you're unaware of. For example, if you think that you have FTP turned off, and there are entries in your FTP log, you may want to check your startup configuration.

There are 10 logs that between them contain the entire state of the Mac:

- /var/log
  - Windowserver.log (information about the actual windows that are displayed in the user interface)
  - Wtmp (login and logout information about users)
  - System.log (information about what process start, stop, crash)
  - Secure.log (information about processes and users that require authentication or privileges)
  - Ppp.log (point-to-point connection log)
  - Netinfo.log
  - Monthy.out
  - ftp.log
  - ipfw.log
  - lpr.log
- /Library/Logs/
  - console
  - Software Update

You can use a couple of interesting commands from the command line to access the wtmp logs:

```
last - last users, ttys in use, reboots, shutdowns, and hosts
```

and

```
ac - accumulated connect times for all users (ac -p shows individual numbers)
```

If you execute the command **last** from a command-line shell, it will access the wtmp log file and display information similar to that in Figure 9-16. If you see someone other than yourself logged in to your system, you may want to start digging deeper!

```
Terminal — tcsh — 80x24
Last login: Mon Dec 11 21:53:30 on ttyp1
Welcome to Darwin!
[StarBlazer12:~] markkadr% last
markkadr  ttyp2                          Mon Dec 11 22:24   still logged in
markkadr  ttyp2                          Mon Dec 11 22:24 - 22:24  (00:00)
markkadr  ttyp1                          Mon Dec 11 21:53   still logged in
markkadr  ttyp1                          Mon Dec 11 21:53 - 21:53  (00:00)
markkadr  ttyp1                          Mon Dec 11 18:12 - 21:53  (03:41)
markkadr  ttyp1                          Mon Dec 11 18:12 - 18:12  (00:00)
markkadr  console  StarBlazer12.loc Tue Dec  5 19:12   still logged in
reboot    ~                              Tue Dec  5 19:11
shutdown  ~                              Tue Dec  5 18:22
markkadr  console  StarBlazer12.loc Mon Dec  4 18:02 - 18:22 (1+00:20)
reboot    ~                              Mon Dec  4 18:01
shutdown  ~                              Mon Dec  4 17:58
markkadr  console  StarBlazer12.loc Fri Dec  1 12:45 - 17:58 (3+05:13)
reboot    ~                              Fri Dec  1 12:44
shutdown  ~                              Fri Dec  1 12:05

wtmp begins Fri Dec  1 12:05
[StarBlazer12:~] markkadr%
```

Figure 9-16   The **last** command shows you who is logged in to your system and gives you a brief history of shutdowns and restarts.

HARDENING THE OPERATING SYSTEM

One of the nice things about hardening a UNIX-based operating system is that it's fairly simple if you consider that by reducing the number of contact points with the operating system you can reduce the potential for compromise. What's even better about the Mac is that it's shipped in a default secure configuration. None of the native services are turned on, so nothing is sticking out in the network packet breeze. The bad part of that is that you have to turn on those services that you want to use. Okay, maybe not so bad after all.

We'll start with the admonition that you must start with a fully patched system that came to life in a secure environment if you want to ensure a secure system. In the Apple world, that means, as of this writing, OS X 10.4.6. You can start with a different OS version, just make sure that you have the latest patches and there isn't a vulnerability the size of a truck that would force you to upgrade until you're ready.

You can do some basic things to make it harder for an attacker to gain access to your system:

- Disable automatic login.
- Required a password to unlock each secure system preference.
- Log out after *xx* minutes of inactivity.
- Use secure virtual memory.

To get to the screen that allows these configuration changes, click the Apple logo in the upper left of the screen and select System Preferences, as shown in Figure 9-17.

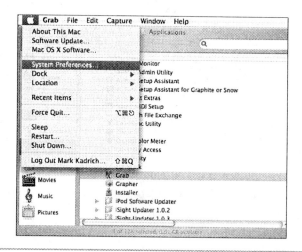

Figure 9-17   You can launch System Preferences from the Apple menu or the dock. In this example, we used the Apple menu.

You will be presented with the System Preferences screen shown in Figure 9-18. You need to click the icon in the top row that looks like a house and is labeled Security.

You'll have a screen pop up that looks just like the one in Figure 9-19.

I recommend checking all the boxes and, if you enabled secure virtual memory, resetting your computer so that the settings take effect. You may have to fiddle with the logout time a bit, however. I had it set to 10 minutes when I first started, thinking that it was a good time limit.

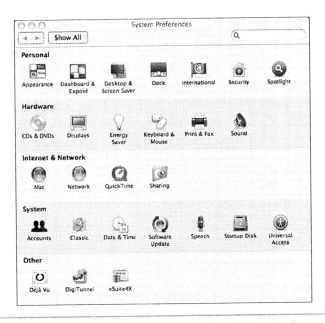

Figure 9-18 Virtually every aspect of the Mac OS can be configured from the System Preferences window. Some applications add their configuration widget to the Other pane.

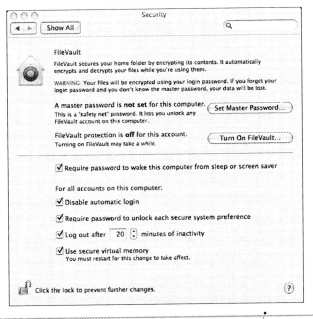

Figure 9-19 The Security window provides the interface that you need to turn on Master Password protection and the FileVault.

APPLICATIONS

As it turns out, the real vulnerabilities that the Mac has to deal with are in the applications. The most recent vulnerability used iChat to propagate through the network and mounted disk volumes and shares. The unfortunate side is that the only thing you can do to protect the applications is to harden the OS and networking.

The Macintosh has some built-in functionality called Bonjour that works with iChat. Bonjour enables you to chat and share music, pictures, and files with other endpoints on your buddy list over the wireless connection. I suppose that it's Apple's attempt at bringing networking applications to the house. It's a sort of ad hoc network connection that allows you to instantly connect with other Macs near you.

I turned it off.

I put this in the "Applications" section because this is what most people are going to try to protect. FileVault is the Apple answer to disk encryption. By locking things up on your disk, you can prevent the bad people from stealing your information. Unfortunately, if they break into your account while you're still in it, the encryption is pretty useless. You can turn on FileVault from the Security menu screen.

Any application that uses macros and creates and exchanges files is a potential threat; and if you're using Microsoft products, the threat is real. This is going to sound strange in a chapter on Macintoshes, but Microsoft Office allows you to seamlessly generate and exchange documents in their most popular applications with their PC counterparts. Fortunately, these applications have a security feature that allows you to receive a warning prior to opening a file with embedded macros. For example, as you can see in Figure 9-20, Word allows you to turn on a warning before opening a file with macros.

All the other Microsoft applications have this capability built in to them, including Excel and PowerPoint.

Email – warn before allowing other applications access to the address book. I think that it's probably safe to keep this notice turned on. You'll see this as a check box in the Microsoft Entourage Security preferences pane.

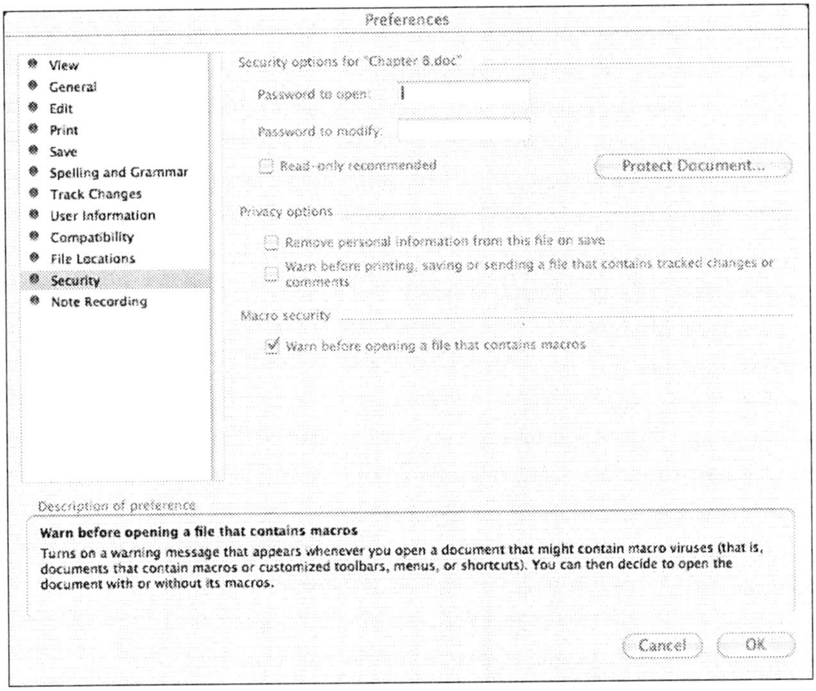

Figure 9-20 Most applications have a "security" preferences window that allows you to control the behavior of the application. This example is from the Microsoft Word application.

NETWORKING

From a networking perspective, the Mac is better suited to protect itself than most off-the-shelf endpoints because of its built-in firewall. The Mac comes with the firewall enabled and all services turned off, so you have to intentionally turn on things such as Apache or file sharing.

The Mac firewall is easy to use and quite effective. You can get to the firewall settings through the System Preferences panel. Now, being the king of intuitive interfaces, you would think that to turn on the firewall you would go to the Network icon, but you would be dead wrong. To get to the firewall interface, you must bring up the system preferences and click the icon that resembles a folder (labeled Sharing). Once there, click the Firewall button. If you've done everything properly, you should have a screen similar to the one in Figure 9-21.

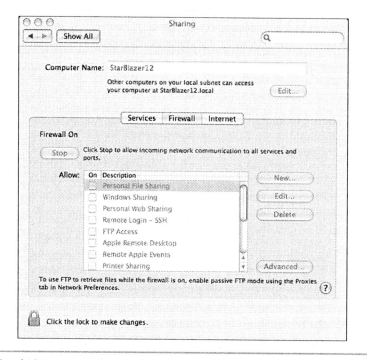

Figure 9-21   In a fairly unintuitive location, the built-in firewall allows you to control what the network sees of your Apple endpoint.

Notice that in our example the firewall is on, and there are no extemporaneous services running that could expose our Mac to attack.

Clicking the Internet button displays the screen that controls Internet sharing. Internet sharing should be "off" by default, and unless you have a pressing, gee I'm going to make a zillion dollars reason, I'd keep it off. I played with Internet sharing, and about all you can really do with it is rip off hotels that charge extra for the second connection. Come to think of it, if you share over the built-in Ethernet, you could manage to save $9.95 a day and still be secure. Of course, that means that you're connecting to the hotel over the air.

Because I mentioned it, the Mac, and OS X, does support wireless networking out of the box. You can set it up so that an administrator password is required prior to changing wireless networks, but everything else is pretty much automatic. OS X supports the following:

- WEP (Wired Equivalent Privacy in 40/128-bit ASCII or hex)
- LEAP (Lightweight Extensible Authentication Protocol)

- WPA (WiFi Protected Access)
- WPA2

Before I get a storm of letters, just because these wireless protocols are running on a Mac doesn't make them any more secure.

TOOLS AND VENDORS

Although the Macintosh comes with a number of great tools and some very well thought-out features, it still needs some additional tools to make it enterprise ready.

APPLE REMOTE DESKTOP

The big argument that Windows people make against Apple is that Macs can't be managed in large enterprises. Well, Apple Remote Desktop (ARD 3.0) is a tool that has similar functionality to that enjoyed by Windows network-based administrators. It enables you to configure and manage a large population of Apples without it seeming like you're tipping the apple cart every time you have to make a security change.

Apple administrators can remotely install packages, control encryption, configure users, and manipulate the file system. If necessary, ARD allows a remote administrator to do a hard restart of the endpoint. Using the remote Spotlight feature, an administrator can do a networkwide search for forbidden files and applications. ARD also provides reports that keep track of application usage!

Other interesting features include the following:

- Bandwidth throttling
- Software distribution
- Task Server

The combination of these three features is worth their weight in gold to a system administrator because they can reduce impact to the network when distributions are large and complex. Distributions can be scheduled for specific download times and installed according to the schedule in the Task Server.

Another feature, although not intended to be security related, is the asset management capability offered by ARD 3. This feature enables administrators to report on virtually any aspect of the system. From a security perspective, you can track application usage, both authorized and unauthorized, identifying those users who are skirting the edges of your policy.

Administrators can now keep tabs on how many of those valuable concurrent licenses are really being used. In some enterprises, the savings realized by merely paying for those copies of the application that are actually being used could save enough money to pay for ARD in short order.

If you're worried about someone intercepting your packets, worry not; your packets will be encrypted using Advanced Encryption Standard (AES) and a 128-bit key. The UNIX commands that you can send will be completely protected from those prying hacker eyes!

ARD does require an agent, but thankfully that agent is built in to every 10.3 and later OS. I wonder if we'll be thanking Apple for this in three years.

LITTLE SNITCH

Little Snitch is exactly what its name implies: a tattletale widget. When you install and run Little Snitch, it hooks into the kernel and runs in the background, alerting you to programs that attempt to make outbound network connections. As you can see in Figure 9-22, the presentation is much the same as a firewall rule-set.

Figure 9-22   Little Snitch is a great application if you're interested in what applications are trying to communicate with the Internet without your permission.

I'm giving the newest beta version a bit of exercise, and so far it hasn't puked or given me any indication that there are unhappy interactions with the OS.

The downside of this little tool is that it seems to be aimed at the individual user and subsequently doesn't possess any network reporting features. It would be nice if Little Snitch kept a log or sent alerts to a central console somewhere.

ANTIVIRUS

I can hear so many of you say, "There's hardly any viruses for the Mac, so why should I waste my money?" I really love this reasoning, and it's driven the industry for so many years that it's no wonder that so many people suspect that the AV vendors create the very viruses that they detect. Well people, a long time ago in the land that time forgot, the early Macintoshes were the targets, and people bought IBMs because they didn't have the same vulnerabilities to viruses that the Macs did. Granted, there aren't that many Mac-specific viruses, but many of the applications that run on the Mac support macros.

Those who don't watch the series the first time around are doomed to watching reruns in syndication.

Because what I'm going to talk about in the next few paragraphs is about vendor-supported products, I'm only going to present some facts and let you decide. I've run all the products, and none of them found a virus. Obviously a testament to my pristine Web browsing habits.

SYMANTEC

Symantec does have an AV product for the Macintosh called Norton AV 10.1 that has won awards from Macworld. One interesting feature is that it scans for PC and Mac viruses. When I first learned about this, I said to myself, "What a waste of processor cycles." I happened to mention this to a doctor friend of mine, and he nodded and made a noise that I've learned means "good." This got my attention, so I asked him why he thought that scanning for PC viruses on a Mac was a good idea. My friend went on to tell me that one of the reasons that we inoculate people is that some of us can become carriers—people who spread disease without contracting symptoms. He reasoned that just because a Mac can't be infected with a PC virus, there's no reason that a Mac could-n't be a carrier and spreader of malware. By identifying them and eliminating them on the Mac, Symantec has removed the Mac as an infection vector.

LiveUpdate automatically checks with the Symantec servers to see whether there are new virus signatures, thus keeping you up-to-date on the latest threats. There's even a widget that tells you what your virus posture is with respect to the rest of the world.

For comparison purposes, Version Tracker gave this latest version 4.5 out of 5 stars.[10]

Virex

McAfee has a solution that promises to find unknown viruses through the use of heuristic and generic detection technology. Virex examines files searching for code that has virus-like behavior patterns, and when it finds one it attempts to disinfect it.

Mounted volumes are automatically scanned, and all files are scanned when they are copied, created, or renamed. Of course, an automatic update feature ensures that you have the latest virus definitions.

Like Symantec, Virex has a central management console called ePolicy Orchestrator (ePO) that enables the administrator to generate a policy configuration and ship it out to all the Macs on your network. I haven't used the management function, so I can't comment on how easy or hard it is to use.

The folks who contribute to Version Tracker weren't as impressed with this particular version, giving it only 1 out of 5 stars. Ouch.

ClamXav

Springing from the open source community, ClamXav uses the open source and "very popular" (their words, not mine) ClamAV antivirus engine.[11]

The ClamAV project is stable at release 0.88.2.[12] A recent test posted on the project Web site claims that ClamAV is able to accurately detect W32.Polipos.A, which is a fairly nasty little thing that deletes checksum databases and replicates in all your EXE and SCR files. What makes this virus difficult is that it's polymorphic—it can change how it looks to evade detection.

The folks who rated ClamXav were very kind in their ratings, giving it 5 out of 5 stars. Me, I have to wonder about a claim that states, "ClamXav Sentry now thread-safe meaning fewer crashes and zombies." Fewer is good, but none is better.

---

[10] www.versiontracker.com

[11] www.macupdate.com/info.php/id/15850

[12] www.clamav.net/

CLOSING THE LOOP

Although the Mac does have an enterprise-worthy management solution, I found no evidence that there was a tool that would provide anything beyond basic 802.1x support for connecting to the network. Before the Symantec acquisition of Sygate, Sygate was working on an integrity product that would have provided the trust component that CLPC requires. Some companies have hinted at Mac support, such as Lockdown Networks,[13] through an enforcer type of architecture and the use of a client. However, digging into their Web site indicated that although they were partnering with Foundry Networks, Enearasys, and Microsoft, no mention was made of Apple.

KEY POINTS

There are many differences between Windows and OS X, but one of them isn't complexity. OS X is just as complex and sophisticated an operating system as Microsoft's flagship Windows. The Apple OS X operating system seems to have a similar number of patches and updates regarding security as Windows does, so let's not allow ourselves the warm and fuzzy feeling of security and smugness that some Apple owners seem to use as a security blanket.

NETWORKING

Configuring both wired and wireless networking on a Mac is fairly straightforward and easy to do. There are a few ways to check networking configurations thanks to the availability of the command line. You can use the GUI to set things, or you can issue commands through a shell.

Checking the status of networking applications is also easy thanks to the large number of available tools. Once again, you can check on things from the command line, or you can use the tools included with Aqua.

APPLICATIONS

Applications that can execute macros can carry and propagate malware. Chat applications have also demonstrated that stupid user tricks work on the Mac as well as they do on a Windows platform.

---

[13] www.lockdownnetworks.com

To secure applications on the Mac, you must go through each application one by one and set security settings appropriately. Setting Mozilla not to allow cookies doesn't mean that Safari won't accept cookies. These settings can usually be found under the Application drop-down menu under Preferences. You might have to hunt for the security-related settings, or they might have a nice tab that says Security.

ROOTKITS

Rootkits are as much a threat on the Mac as they are on a Windows system. They are a bit harder to install on a Mac, but once there, they are difficult to detect. You can use the same differential method of comparing external scans with internal scans to determine whether a rootkit is running, but then comes the difficult task of finding it.

Some tools are available that will attempt to detect and remove a rootkit, but if you suspect that you've been rooted, just rebuild the system. You'll never be able to trust it otherwise.

DATA PROTECTION

The Mac OS enables users to use the rich file access control afforded to them through the UNIX-like file system. You can control access based on user ID or group membership, thus reducing the exposure to your critical files.

The Mac also supports file system encryption through the use of FileVault. FileVault is built in to the Mac OS and provides an administrative key in the event the user forgets his or the user is no longer able to access the system.

CHECK THE LOGS

Logs on the Mac are rich and plentiful. Unfortunately, if you've been rooted, it's possible that the logs are also lying to you. At any rate, it's a good idea to check the logs for irregularities from time to time.

HOST INTEGRITY

Although the Mac can talk to an 802.1x-enabled network, it's not possible to link a host integrity check with network access at this time. Therefore, the loop really can't be closed through a Mac. An infected or poorly configured system can still gain access to the network.

SECURITY TOOLS

A number of third-party tools enhance the posture or better report on the posture of the Macintosh. Tools are available that check the file system, look for viruses, and check and notify you of the type of traffic leaving your computer.

Antivirus tools are highly recommended because the industry is beginning to see more Mac-specific viruses. Remember that Macs can act as a carrier of Windows viruses, and because they do possess this "Typhoid Mary" capability, they should be inoculated against it.

CLOSING THE LOOP

Although the Mac is an enterprise-capable endpoint environment, no tools are available for it that allow it to close the process control loop as described in a CLPC solution.

10
Linux

This chapter is going to look suspiciously like the preceding chapter because Linux is just another variant of UNIX, and the Mac is just a variant of FreeBSD, which is essentially UNIX. I know that I've started another argument, but the reality is that Linus Torvalds was dirt broke and couldn't afford UNIX, so in 1991 he started writing something that worked like UNIX.[1] Starting with a task switcher and posting the results to comp.os.minux, Torvalds commented that it was really just a hobby.[2] However, the support that he received and the involvement of others spurred him on to continue with his project. We know the results of that project as the Linux kernel.

The pure will say that Linux and BSD differ, and they are correct. However, the basic ideas and constructs are the same. Many of the same commands have the same result. The idea of the shell has moved from operating system to operating system and has the same functionality in MS-DOS as it does in Linux—only in Linux you're probably going to use bash, the Bourn Again Shell, rather than the limited and clunky DOS shell. There, I've started another argument.

The "pure" are also probably saying that there are different versions of Linux and they should be treated differently. To them I say: "Enjoy your pain—one kernel, different distributions." Ferret out the minute differences between how ps works in Red Hat versus Xandros versus Mandriva versus Debian versus SuSE. If you're really a deep geek, I'll

---

[1] SFGate.com, Rebecca Eisenberg, 8/2/98

[2] http://en.wikipedia.org/wiki/Linux_kernel

throw in Slackware. In the end, it's not the details that I'm going to discuss with respect to Linux but the similarities that allow them to work with the network securely.

Now, I'm sure that this next statement is going to cause some folks to go "hum…." For the purposes of this chapter, I selected Xandros Professional and Fedora Core. Now, for the people who just went "hum…," let me explain why.

My reasons can be grouped into two basic areas:

- Xandros is a commercially available version of Linux, and they can be sued; Red Hat is free, and they can't be sued.
- Xandros runs Crossover Office, and Red Hat runs OpenOffice.

Not that you would sue them, but knowing that there is a neck that you can get your hands around makes some finance and legal departments rest easy at night if you're a money-making enterprise. Well, even if you're a money-losing enterprise it's nice to have a neck to wring. Oh, and Red Hat does have a commercial offering of their product, but the purpose isn't to review Red Hat, it's to determine some fundamental basics regarding Linux as an endpoint security closed-loop control process (CLPC) platform.

Running an operating system in an enterprise is really about three things: support, enterprise management, and the applications. I wanted to see what the difference was between these three areas. How was support? Was it there when you needed it? Were the answers you received correct? How was the system supported in the enterprise? Was it easy to manage, or was the solution so arcane that you are never going to be sure that all the systems are properly configured and patched? Is there a difference in security between Crossover and OpenOffice?

PRÉCIS

So here we are, applying the same methodology to analyze the Linux system that we did to analyze the Macintosh. Note that I've said that word again, only in somewhat of a disguise: methodology. Methodology is a process in itself. It is something that one can repeat and learn from.

We follow the same process that we followed in the other chapters:

1. We do an initial health check.
2. We check out the operating system and harden it.
3. The applications receive some consideration.
4. Finally, we examine the networking features and exposure.

After we have an idea of what we're looking at, we'll discuss some tools that are available to make our lives easier.

SPECIAL POINTS OF INTEREST

Because Linux is a completely different environment when compared to Windows, many things about it are truly special. Things that differ are support, the applications, support applications, and of course, what you can do to investigate flaws and what you can say about what you've discovered.

Another interesting difference is that there are a number of efforts afoot to run Windows programs on the Linux platform. This actually makes a great deal of sense if you face the reality that Microsoft owns the office desktop. Applications such as Word and PowerPoint make the business go round, and without the ability to seamlessly share information and collaborate, we wouldn't have the flexibility that we enjoy today. So, thank you, Microsoft.

SUPPORT

The Linux community is as close to a rebel army as I've ever seen taking on the "empire" that is Microsoft. There is such an incredible amount of support for Linux that anyone who says that it's not a credible operating system doesn't know what he's talking about. The nice thing about this kind of support is that you can get just about any viewpoint on something because someone has probably already had the problem.

When you have to exist in a world that isn't monolithic, you tend to run into a much more diverse set of issues.

APPLICATIONS

I bought my Mac a few years ago, and the reason that I did was because I was tired of trying to get my documents to work for my Windows colleagues. Although close, there were just enough differences in file formats to make it annoying. The Mac had the promise of no compatibility issues because it was using Office X, a Mac-specific version of the Microsoft Office suite. Because all of my colleagues were using Windows (yes, I am quite the rebel), it fell on me to ensure compatibility. Office X allowed me to do that from the comfort of my Macintosh environment.

Flash forward three years, and now we have some very capable tools that enable us to work in a non-Microsoft environment yet exchange (no pun intended) documents with

Microsoft applications without the painful problems associated with picking a common, often less-capable, file format. We delve into detail on these environments later, but here's a list of the major applications as I see them:

- OASIS project (XML-based file format for office applications)[3]
- OpenOffice (http://openoffice.org)
- Star Office (www.sun.com/software/star/staroffice/index.jsp)
- KDE KOffice (https://www.koffice.org)
- The Gnome Office (www.gnome.org/knome_office)
- CrossOver Office (www.codeweavers.com)

All of these, except for one, run native applications on the Linux platform. CrossOver Office is a different story, however. CrossOver Office is an outgrowth of the Wine Project,[4] which is essentially an implementation of the Windows API over X and Linux. The Wine Project is probably talked about in hushed tones at Microsoft because it allows non-Windows machines to run Windows applications without any Microsoft license fees. Think of it as an execution layer between Linux and the Windows applications. Although I haven't played much with CrossOver Office, the people I've talked to swear by it.

FEDORA

The following quotation is from the Fedora Web site, http://fedoraproject.org/wiki/:

Fedora Core is an operating system and platform, based on Linux, that is always free for anyone to use, modify and distribute, now and forever. It is developed by a large community of people who strive to provide and maintain the very best in free, open source software and standards. Fedora Core is part of the Fedora Project, sponsored by Red Hat, Inc.

The advantage is that Fedora is free. It is driven by a dedicated group of people who are striving to make the best operating system and desktop that they can. They release updates, patches, and feature improvements. Fedora has even published a product roadmap.

---

[3] www.oasis-open.org/committees/tc_home.php?wg_abbrev=office

[4] www.winehq.com

The scrutiny afforded an open product suite such as Fedora can't be overstated. I like the idea that there is a large network of people working to solve a problem because they want to see a solution.

XANDROS

On the other hand, Xandros is not free. This quotation is from their website, www.xandros.com/about/corporatebackground.html:

> *Founded in May 2001, Xandros is the leading developer of a cost-effective, installation-friendly, complete Linux-based operating environment offering Windows compatibility and unparalleled technical support. Xandros is specifically designed to meet the computing needs of both professional and consumer users alike. Based on the former Corel Linux OS, Xandros marks the first true collaboration of ease of use philosophy and ground breaking technology aimed at the creation of the first true "Complete Linux Desktop Solution."*

The advantage is that Xandros costs money. I know this seems counterintuitive, but sometimes people place a higher value on things that they have to pay for. They trust them more. Maybe it's because they expect to have someone listen when they complain about something.

Profit is also a good motivator. When you have a good team of people and they're motivated to make a superior product to help their company succeed, there is a huge upside for profit. For this reason, you set up processes and procedures that work toward making a quality product through good coding practices and good customer support.

SUPPORT APPLICATIONS

The real test of an operating system is its capability to support, well, the enterprise. Until recently, Linux was classed as one of those operating systems that was cool for the geeks to play with, but if you wanted to support your enterprise, you'd have to use Microsoft. Well, thankfully, this is changing. Diversity of choice is important because it offers the customers more choices and forces the price point on commodity applications down. Well, it *should* force the price of commodity applications down. I suppose that this remains to be seen.

Returning back to the basic issue of the enterprise, I suppose that the basic issue could be classified as "management." How do you deploy, configure, and support an operating system without having to employ an army of support engineers? If you can't, you really can't think about deploying it as a solution in today's networks. That was always the argument against Linux: You can't use it in the enterprise because you can't centrally manage it.

To take on that challenge and make Linux a true enterprise platform, a number of vendors have taken up the banner. The most surprising among them is Novell. Rising up like the proverbial Phoenix, Novell is nesting in the Linux space with their ZENworks Linux management product.

Both of the Linux versions that I've selected for this chapter, Xandros and Fedora, offer some form of enterprise management bundled into the operating system build and installation. The interesting question for security people regards how the enterprise support function either increases or decreases the overall security of the network. Sometimes we must make a choice that pits ease of use against security.

Free Speech

Okay, maybe this is a bit of a soapbox, and maybe *free speech* isn't the most genuine term for this, but it does encapsulate the emotion as well as the meaning.

If you discover a vulnerability in a Microsoft product and you publish it without going through the proper channels, you can be labeled a hacker. If you try to go through the proper channels by contacting Microsoft and working with their people, you can wind up being frustrated. In the Linux world, if you discover a vulnerability, and you're a nice person, you send the information to the coder or the project, and someone will generate a lawyer-free fix.

Fit and Finish

Although this isn't a review of the installation process, I think some comments are in order. It's kind of like buying a car. Your first impression pretty much sets the tone for the test drive. If you see things that you don't like when you first see the car—such as edges that don't line up or wrinkles in the paint—you're going to be more suspicious during the test drive. "Hey, what's that rattle?" will forever cloud your thoughts if you ignore that little voice in your head that nagged you on the lot the day you bought the car.

Well, that's what happened here. The more I drove one system, the more questions I had about the other system. I even went as far as to reinstall both systems side by side so that I could compare the baseline configuration because I found myself asking, "Did I select to install the firewall?" Normally, this would be a no-brainer, but I wanted to be sure. Also, when I started this, I was only going to use one version of Linux; so when I decided to use two versions, I had to go back to the drawing board, so to speak.

Both implementations are high quality. However, it seems to me that the Xandros version has a few more configuration widgets that might make it easier to manage in an enterprise. Sort of. Firewall configuration in the Xandros is not intuitive, and it doesn't come up by default.

On the other hand, Fedora's firewall was up out of the box. One of the few questions that I was asked was "turn on firewall?" This can be the difference if you're installing in a dynamic and unmanaged environment.

No Endorsements!

Note that this is not an endorsement of either one of these operating systems. In the interest of fairness, I just want to make sure that Linux is properly represented. You can't get an open version of OS X, and neither can you get an open version of Windows. But you can get an open version of Linux as well as a commercial version. This gives us the unique opportunity to see whether there really is a difference between an open operating system and a corporate-driven flavor.

Initial Health Check

The initial health check looks very much like it did in the preceding chapter. We're going to look at the system from the outside using our nmap scanner, and then we're going to compare that to what we find on the system. Keep in mind that one of the things that we're looking for are rootkits, so doing this differential comparison is an important first step.

An interesting thing to note is that our health check starts during the installation process. Fedora asked whether I wanted to enable the firewall during the installation process.

System Scan

First off, we're going to turn to our nmap scanner again to get a hacker's eye view of our target operating system. We'll start with the Fedora box and then move to the Xandros endpoint.

Both systems are out-of-the-box installations, and both systems used the lazy installation choice to make it as fair as possible.

So let's start by seeing how our Fedora system stacks up from the network. An nmap scan against our system shows that the firewall is up and running. As you can see in Figure 10-1, we're not exposing anything, thanks to our firewall.

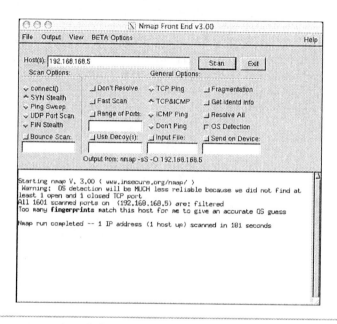

Figure 10-1 An nmap scan of our Fedora system shows that the endpoint isn't exposing any obvious services.

Sure, nmap saw that there was something there; it just wasn't offering any services. So, just to get an idea of how well our security is working, we're going to turn the firewall off and run the scans again. Figure 10-2 shows that even with the firewall off, we're only allowing Secure Shell (SSH) and SunRPC (Sun's Remote Procedure Call) through the firewall.

A quick check on our Fedora system and we discover that we're using OpenSSH version 3.6.1p2. Another quick check of SecurityFocus, CERT, and SANS, and I didn't find anything that made me nervous.

If we make the same initial check against our Xandros system, we discover some pretty interesting things. As you can see in Figure 10-3, we're running NetBIOS! It's actually Samba providing SMB/NetBIOS support, but because this was an out-of-the-box fast install, I was rather surprised to find this as a default configuration. However, upon further reflection—thinking about the enterprise market and who the Xandros potential customers are and what operating system they're presently running (Windows?)—I shouldn't be too shocked. The folks at Xandros are clearly aiming at replacing Windows in the enterprise.

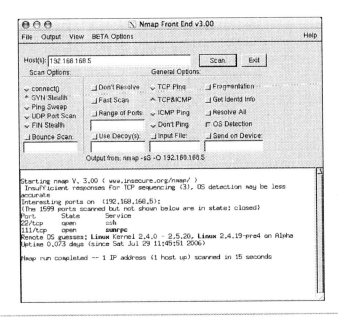

Figure 10-2 After we turn off the firewall on our Fedora system, another scan shows us that we're still not providing any obvious services other than SSH and SunRPC.

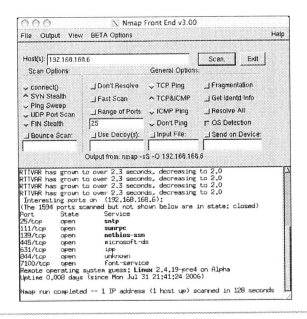

Figure 10-3 An nmap scan of our Xandros system immediately after installation shows that we're offering some risky services over the network.

I have to admit that it sure made getting the screenshots easy. From a security perspective, I have to say that this is a serious vulnerability that could easily be exploited on an untrusted network. I certainly wouldn't be attempting a Xandros install at DEFCON with this running on my default system.[5]

FINDING ROOTKITS

In some later sections, we compare the results of the externally observed scans with what we can see while we're on the system. We compare the services being offered with those that we've uncovered on the target systems. But, again, a quick check to see whether we really own the system is in order before we waste a great deal of time.

As we did with the Mac, we're going to load rkhunter (rootkit hunter) to tell us whether there's anything obvious from the inside.

I ran rkhunter on the Xandros and the Fedora system, with similar results coming back from both systems. As you can see in Figure 10-4, the results are pretty unexciting.

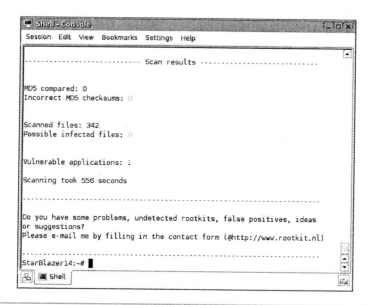

Figure 10-4   Rkhunter results from the Xandros system show only one vulnerable application, although it didn't check any MD5 hashes.

---

[5]   www.defcon.org (DEFCON is an annual hacker convention in Las Vegas, Nevada.)

Rkhunter whined about my version of OpenSSL (version 0.9.7e) on the Xandros system and complained that I was running older versions of Gnupg (version 1.2.4-2.1), OpenSSL (version 0.9.7a-35), and OpenSSH (version 3.6.1p2-34). One additional difference: Rkhunter didn't find any MD5 hashes on the Xandros system, whereas it did manage to check 49 MD5 hashes on the Fedora system.

We need to address the vulnerable files when we harden the system.

SYSTEM FILES

Now that we know what it looks like from the outside, let's take a look at what our file system looks like. If you did things right, you should be logged in as a regular user. This means that for some of the commands that we're going to use, you will have to **sudo** or **su** to get them to work.

The **sudo** command enables a user to execute a program with super user privileges. Think of it as saying "super user says do the following command." After the command is issued by the user, the system asks for the root password. It's a neat way of ensuring that regular, unprivileged users can't do privileged tasks. When the system goes off to execute the privileged command, the shell returns control to the unprivileged user so he can do other unprivileged things. This reduces the possibility of something breaking or getting broken while you're the root user.

On the other hand, Switch User (the **su** command) enables you to become any user, including the super user root. After you **su root,** it's as if you logged in as the root user, so it's not a recommended practice.

A major concern for security folks is the ability of attackers to create, modify, or delete files on the target endpoint. So, we're going to look for all the files that anyone can write to from anywhere on the system. We'll use the following command:

```
find / -type f \( -perm -2 -o -perm -20 \) -exec ls -lg {} \; > allwritable.txt
```

With this command, we're looking at all regular files (**-type f**), for all the files that are writable by the group and others \(**-perm -2 -o -perm -20** \ ), and we're using the **exec** command to get a detailed listing of each file. Using redirection, we're sending the output of the **ls** command into a file, allwritable.txt, which we can print and look at later. This is a handy command, and we use it later.

I looked at both the Xandros and the Fedora system and didn't find anything that looked out of place except that the Xandros antivirus (AV) log (update.log) was world writable. Besides that, there were a larger number of group-writable files in Xandros (98 files) than in Fedora (34 files).

Next, we're going to look for files that don't have an owner or group, because this could indicate that nefarious activity has occurred on your system. Many of the tools used to root your system are automated, and some may have been "tweaked" by those less talented than the original coder, so some mistakes, such as leaving off the owner, can occur. We'll again use the **find** command to do this, as follows:

```
find / -nouser -o -nogroup
```

The system starts to go through all the files on the disk, looking for files that don't have an owner or group assigned to them. The Fedora system came up clean on both counts, but as you can see in Figure 10-5, the terminal screen virtually exploded into life on the Xandros system. The offender? Skype!

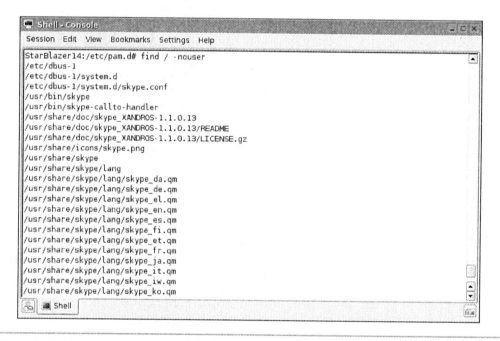

Figure 10-5   Skype turned up looking like it had no owner association on our Xandros system because the owner name was a number.

A quick check using the **ls** command and I learned that the reason Skype shows up isn't because it doesn't have an owner. Skype triggered our search because the owner is a number rather than text.

A great check is to look for hidden files, because they can be a leading indicator of nefarious actions by other individuals. Finding a hidden file doesn't mean you've been hacked, but you do need to know what's on your system, whether it's hidden or not. The **find** command is pretty good at churning through the file system, so we're going to use it here:

```
find / -name ".. " -print -xdev
```

Note that there is a space after the second period and the closing quote, so it should be dot, dot, space between the quotes.

PROCESSES

We're going to look at what's running on this system by issuing a **ps** command. The **ps** command will tell us what's running and who owns it. As we learned in the preceding chapter, the plain vanilla **ps** command doesn't provide any really useful details because it only reports on processes started by that user, so we'll have to attach some switches to it to get the system to spill its guts. To get some useful information from our Fedora system, I used the following command:

```
ps -Al
```

The switches **A** and **l** tell the **ps** command to provide a process list that selects all processes (**A** switch) and to provide the list in the long (**l** switch) format. Figure 10-6 provides an excerpt of the output. I didn't provide the entire list because it has 106 entries.

```
root@localhost:/mnt/usbflash/fedora                              _ □ x

File  Edit  View  Terminal  Tabs  Help
[root@localhost fedora]# ps -Al | more
F S   UID   PID  PPID  C PRI  NI ADDR SZ WCHAN  TTY          TIME CMD
4 S     0     1     0  0  76   0 -   680 -       ?        00:00:06 init
1 S     0     2     1  0  94  19 -     0 ksofti  ?        00:00:00 ksoftirqd/0
1 S     0     3     1  0  65 -10 -     0 worker  ?        00:00:00 events/0
1 S     0     4     3  0  65 -10 -     0 worker  ?        00:00:00 kblockd/0
1 S     0     6     3  0  66 -10 -     0 worker  ?        00:00:00 khelper
1 S     0     5     1  0  75   0 -     0 hub_th  ?        00:00:00 khubd
1 S     0     7     3  0  75   0 -     0 pdflus  ?        00:00:00 pdflush
1 S     0     8     3  0  75   0 -     0 pdflus  ?        00:00:00 pdflush
1 S     0    10     3  0  67 -10 -     0 worker  ?        00:00:00 aio/0
1 S     0     9     1  0  76   0 -     0 kswapd  ?        00:00:00 kswapd0
1 S     0   115     1  0  79   0 -     0 serio_  ?        00:00:00 kseriod
1 S     0   157     1  0  75   0 -     0 kjourn  ?        00:00:00 kjournald
1 S     0  1018     1  0  75   0 -     0 kjourn  ?        00:00:00 kjournald
5 S     0  1223     1  0  76   0 -   515 -       ?        00:00:00 cpuspeed
5 S     0  1413     1  0  76   0 -   709 -       ?        00:00:00 syslogd
5 S     0  1417     1  0  75   0 -   637 syslog  ?        00:00:00 klogd
5 S     0  1438     1  0  75   0 -   787 -       ?        00:00:00 portmap
5 S    32  1438     1  0  75   0 -   787 -       ?        00:00:00 portmap
5 S    29  1458     1  0  81   0 -   503 -       ?        00:00:00 rpc.statd
5 S     0  1485     1  0  76   0 -   682 -       ?        00:00:00 rpc.idmapd
1 S     0  1526     1  0  78   0 -     0 pccard  ?        00:00:00 pccardd
1 S     0  1532     1  0  75   0 -     0 pccard  ?        00:00:00 pccardd
--More--▮
```

Figure 10-6   An excerpt of the Fedora process list produced using the **ps** command.

We can also see the results of this command on our Xandros in Figure 10-7. You will see that because both systems are Linux kernel based, the results are very similar.

```
StarBlazer14:~# ps -Al
F S   UID   PID  PPID  C PRI  NI ADDR SZ WCHAN   TTY        TIME CMD
4 S     0     1     0  0  76   0 -   395 -       ?      00:00:01 init
1 S     0     2     1  0  94  19 -     0 ksofti  ?      00:00:00 ksoftirqd/0
1 S     0     3     1  0  70  -5 -     0 worker  ?      00:00:45 events/0
1 S     0     4     1  0  70  -5 -     0 worker  ?      00:00:00 khelper
1 S     0     9     1  0  70  -5 -     0 worker  ?      00:00:00 kthread
1 S     0    18     9  0  70  -5 -     0 worker  ?      00:00:00 kacpid
1 S     0    96     9  0  70  -5 -     0 worker  ?      00:00:00 kblockd/0
1 S     0   129     9  0  75   0 -     0 pdflus  ?      00:00:02 pdflush
1 S     0   130     9  0  75   0 -     0 pdflus  ?      00:00:19 pdflush
1 S     0   132     9  0  71  -5 -     0 worker  ?      00:00:00 aio/0
1 S     0   131     1  0  75   0 -     0 kswapd  ?      00:00:01 kswapd0
1 S     0   720     1  0  85   0 -     0 serio_  ?      00:00:00 kseriod
1 S     0   808     9  0  70  -5 -     0 worker  ?      00:00:02 reiserfs/0
0 S     0  1263     1  0  71  -4 -    42 -       ?      00:00:00 udevd
1 S     0  1702     1  0  79   0 -     0 pccard  ?      00:00:00 pccardd
1 S     0  1715     1  0  75   0 -     0 pccard  ?      00:00:00 pccardd
1 S     0  2496     1  0  75   0 -     0 hub_th  ?      00:00:00 khubd
5 S     1  2619     1  0  76   0 -   420 -       ?      00:00:00 portmap
1 S     0  2957     1  0  76   0 -  1692 -       ?      00:00:01 syslogd
1 S     0  2969     1  0  76   0 -   650 syslog  ?      00:00:00 klogd
1 S     0  3254     1  0  78   0 -   427 -       ?      00:00:00 acpid
5 S     0  3259     1  0  76   0 -  2129 -       ?      00:00:22 cupsd
5 S     0  3329     1  0  75   0 -   432 -       ?      00:00:00 cardmgr
4 S     0  3486     1  0  76   0 -   759 -       ?      00:00:00 master
4 S   100  3493  3486  0  77   0 -   769 -       ?      00:00:00 qmgr
5 S     0  3499     1  0  76   0 -  1681 -       ?      00:00:01 nmbd
5 S     0  3504     1  0  76   0 -  2265 -       ?      00:00:00 smbd
1 S     0  3515  3504  0  78   0 -  2265 pause   ?      00:00:00 smbd
1 S     0  3524     1  0  76   0 -   756 -       ?      00:00:00 xfs
1 S     0  3617     1  0  76   0 -   702 wait    ?      00:00:00 S20xprint
```

Figure 10-7 The **ps** command on the Xandros system returns similar results as those on the Fedora system because they are both Linux.

Another command that you can use to check on running processes on the Fedora endpoint is the **service** command. (Although this command exists on our Mac, it's not very useful, and I found no evidence of it on the Xandros system at all.) At the command line, enter the following:

```
service –status-all
```

You will be rewarded with a list of the installed services and their present status. The difference between the **ps** and **service** commands is that **ps** shows you what is running, whereas **service** shows you which services can possibly run and what their status is, as shown in Figure 10-8. You can use this list to verify that things such as TELNET and FTP haven't been enabled on your system.

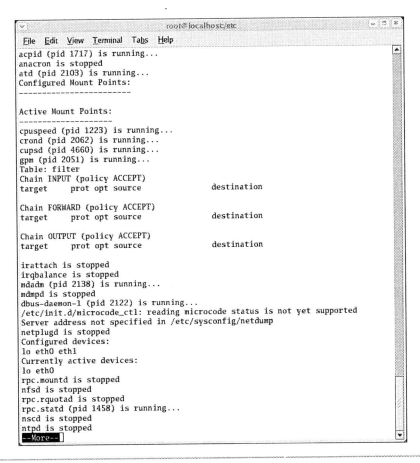

```
                          root@localhost:/etc
File  Edit  View  Terminal  Tabs  Help
acpid (pid 1717) is running...
anacron is stopped
atd (pid 2103) is running...
Configured Mount Points:
------------------------

Active Mount Points:
--------------------
cpuspeed (pid 1223) is running...
crond (pid 2062) is running...
cupsd (pid 4660) is running...
gpm (pid 2051) is running...
Table: filter
Chain INPUT (policy ACCEPT)
target     prot opt source              destination

Chain FORWARD (policy ACCEPT)
target     prot opt source              destination

Chain OUTPUT (policy ACCEPT)
target     prot opt source              destination

irattach is stopped
irqbalance is stopped
mdadm (pid 2138) is running...
mdmpd is stopped
dbus-daemon-1 (pid 2122) is running...
/etc/init.d/microcode_ctl: reading microcode status is not yet supported
Server address not specified in /etc/sysconfig/netdump
netplugd is stopped
Configured devices:
lo eth0 eth1
Currently active devices:
lo eth0
rpc.mountd is stopped
nfsd is stopped
rpc.rquotad is stopped
rpc.statd (pid 1458) is running...
nscd is stopped
ntpd is stopped
--More--
```

Figure 10-8   As we can see from this Fedora service list, both active and inactive services are listed.

Process accounting is a way of generating an audit trail that enables you to track which services have been run and by whom.

Another powerful tool in the Linux arsenal is the **lsof** command. The **lsof** command provides a list of all the open files, directories, and libraries. The **lsof** command has an interesting feature in that it can be told to provide output that can be parsed by other programs. This is useful because the basic amount of information that **lsof** provides can be quite large.

NETWORK

The first thing we're going to do with our network is to find out what network connections are running on our system. To do this, we'll issue the **ifconfig** command with suitable switches. The following command returns the output depicted in Figure 10-9:

```
ifconfig -a
```

We see the interface that connects us to the network, eth1, and it's using the IP address 192.168.168.5.

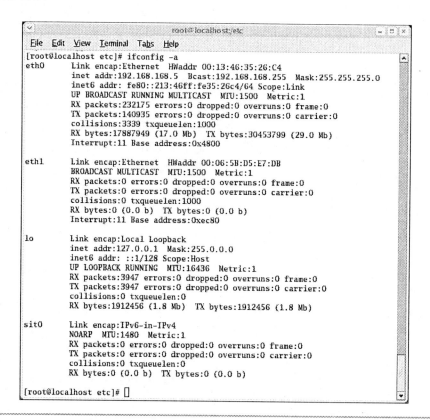

```
root@localhost:/etc                                    _ □ x
File  Edit  View  Terminal  Tabs  Help
[root@localhost etc]# ifconfig -a
eth0      Link encap:Ethernet  HWaddr 00:13:46:35:26:C4
          inet addr:192.168.168.5  Bcast:192.168.168.255  Mask:255.255.255.0
          inet6 addr: fe80::213:46ff:fe35:26c4/64 Scope:Link
          UP BROADCAST RUNNING MULTICAST  MTU:1500  Metric:1
          RX packets:232175 errors:0 dropped:0 overruns:0 frame:0
          TX packets:140935 errors:0 dropped:0 overruns:0 carrier:0
          collisions:3339 txqueuelen:1000
          RX bytes:17887949 (17.0 Mb)  TX bytes:30453799 (29.0 Mb)
          Interrupt:11 Base address:0x4800

eth1      Link encap:Ethernet  HWaddr 00:06:5B:D5:E7:DB
          BROADCAST MULTICAST  MTU:1500  Metric:1
          RX packets:0 errors:0 dropped:0 overruns:0 frame:0
          TX packets:0 errors:0 dropped:0 overruns:0 carrier:0
          collisions:0 txqueuelen:1000
          RX bytes:0 (0.0 b)  TX bytes:0 (0.0 b)
          Interrupt:11 Base address:0xec80

lo        Link encap:Local Loopback
          inet addr:127.0.0.1  Mask:255.0.0.0
          inet6 addr: ::1/128 Scope:Host
          UP LOOPBACK RUNNING  MTU:16436  Metric:1
          RX packets:3947 errors:0 dropped:0 overruns:0 frame:0
          TX packets:3947 errors:0 dropped:0 overruns:0 carrier:0
          collisions:0 txqueuelen:0
          RX bytes:1912456 (1.8 Mb)  TX bytes:1912456 (1.8 Mb)

sit0      Link encap:IPv6-in-IPv4
          NOARP  MTU:1480  Metric:1
          RX packets:0 errors:0 dropped:0 overruns:0 frame:0
          TX packets:0 errors:0 dropped:0 overruns:0 carrier:0
          collisions:0 txqueuelen:0
          RX bytes:0 (0.0 b)  TX bytes:0 (0.0 b)

[root@localhost etc]# []
```

Figure 10-9   The **ifconfig** command provides information on all the running network interfaces. The results also show that our Fedora system is tunneling IPv6 over IPv4 (sit0).

We also see our loopback address, or local host, at 127.0.0.1, and we see that we are tunneling IPv6 over IPv4 with our sit0 interface.

We can issue the same command on our Xandros system by opening up a terminal window and entering the same command. As you can see in Figure 10-10, the results are pretty similar except that we're using eth0 here.

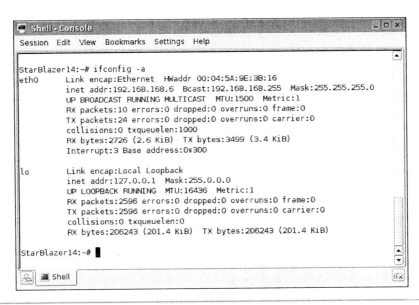

```
StarBlazer14:~# ifconfig -a
eth0      Link encap:Ethernet  HWaddr 00:04:5A:9E:3B:16
          inet addr:192.168.168.6  Bcast:192.168.168.255  Mask:255.255.255.0
          UP BROADCAST RUNNING MULTICAST  MTU:1500  Metric:1
          RX packets:10 errors:0 dropped:0 overruns:0 frame:0
          TX packets:24 errors:0 dropped:0 overruns:0 carrier:0
          collisions:0 txqueuelen:1000
          RX bytes:2726 (2.6 KiB)  TX bytes:3499 (3.4 KiB)
          Interrupt:3 Base address:0x300

lo        Link encap:Local Loopback
          inet addr:127.0.0.1  Mask:255.0.0.0
          UP LOOPBACK RUNNING  MTU:16436  Metric:1
          RX packets:2596 errors:0 dropped:0 overruns:0 frame:0
          TX packets:2596 errors:0 dropped:0 overruns:0 carrier:0
          collisions:0 txqueuelen:0
          RX bytes:206243 (201.4 KiB)  TX bytes:206243 (201.4 KiB)

StarBlazer14:~#
```

Figure 10-10 Network configuration information for the Xandros endpoint shows similar attributes to the Fedora system.

SPYWARE AND MALWARE

Linux is not without its problems, although spyware and malware don't seem to be one of the pressing issues. This doesn't mean that the problem should be completely ignored, however. To this point, Xandros claims that its browser will protect you from spyware.[6] Keep in mind that as a regular user, an attacker must compromise one of the system-owned services if it wants to propagate beyond your environment. The same holds true for other spyware and malware. This is an excellent, if not the most important, reason from a security perspective to not run as the root user and to keep the number of services offered to a minimum.

---

[6] Xandros Desktop OS Users Guide, page 193

Tools to find spyware in Linux are nonexistent at the present moment. There are AV tools, but except for ClamAV, they're only offered from the major AV vendors. (Some AV providers are mentioned in the section "Tools and Vendors" later in this chapter.)

LOOKING AT THE LOGS

I know that I've said this before, but the point can't be made enough times: Just because good hackers will change the log files doesn't mean that all hackers will. Some evidence may be buried somewhere in the log files, and it's just waiting for you to drag it out through the joyful and exciting process of log analysis. Yes, you might have to devote hours of time reading through megabytes of the same text, but just think of the feeling of elation that you'll get when you discover that you've indeed been hacked.

On another note: A way to increase the reliability of your logs is to send them to a central log host where you can centrally access them and back them up. Of course, this assumes that the log host hasn't been hacked. Be warned, however, that your logs will contain a large amount of information if you decide to use a syslog host, sometimes called a syslog server. You should take the time to plan the size of the system and the amount of effort required to process the data. Like other processes described in this book, it will take some time and effort, but the rewards are worth it in the long run.

HARDENING THE OPERATING SYSTEM

INSTALLATION

Although Xandros has a built-in AV, it doesn't have a default firewall loaded after installation. As we learned in the initial health check, a scan of our Xandros system immediately after the install (Figure 10-3) revealed that a number of services were leaking out of our system. You have to configure the firewall via a wizard before it's turned on after installation is complete.

On the other hand, Fedora installs a firewall by default if you select the option during installation but doesn't give you any AV protection. I want to stress this point: You must check the box Yes to install the firewall. If you click through the dialog boxes, you could miss it.

I think if I had my way, I'd rather have a firewall from the outset. Considering that Xandros is offering NetBIOS as a basic service, they might want to reconsider how the firewall is set up during the installation process.

REMOVING DUNSELWARE

For those of you who don't recognize the term, *dunsel* was a word first used in *Star Trek* to characterize Captain Kirk in the episode "The Ultimate Computer." The plotline was about a scientist, Doctor Richard Daystrom, who installs a computer that is designed to operate the *Enterprise* without the need of the crew. The new M5 computer would enable mankind to explore the galaxy without putting human life in danger. Without a crew, a captain is pretty useless, and at one point Kirk was referred to as Captain Dunsel. Of course, the computer went nuts and killed a bunch of people, so Kirk had to disconnect it from his ship to save the day so that they could continue to "go where no man has gone before." Outside of the obvious critical comments regarding society, one important thing survived from that episode: the word *dunsel*. Well, I'm using dunsel here to describe software or applications that don't need to be on your computer.

Because you don't have a crew, you don't need a captain (thus rendering Kirk obsolete or, as they say on *Star Trek,* dunsel).

So what we're looking for are files that don't serve a useful purpose on our system. Because good security starts with a minimalist approach, if it's not there, it can't be hacked or misused. We can delete files two ways: via the shell command line or via the handy GUI file browser. I will point out that it's easier to delete the files from a master build than to have to delete them from every system. You could write a script for most of the things we discuss here, but I think that managing from the build is a better way.

The first cut at eliminating dunselware on a user endpoint is to remove these "utilities":

- Anacron (You may want to keep this on notebooks.)
- Dosfstools (no need for them here)
- All games (sometimes in /usr/games)
- TELNET
- Sendmail
- FTP

The Fedora system uses **rpm** to manage the addition and removal of packages. For example:

```
rpm -q sendmail
```

will produce this response:

```
sendmail-8.12.11-4.6
```

Now you can enter the command that removes the package:

```
rpm -e sendmail
```

Keep in mind that **rpm** works in Red Hat. Each Linux variant has its own package man-ager—Debian uses dpkg, whereas Slackware uses pkgtool, for example. You can always do it by hand, but the package managers can check for dependencies so that you don't break other applications.

You can also look into what office tools you want to use because you may, if it's a stan-dard installation, have a couple of versions.

UPDATING AND PATCHES

At the core of any security implementation is the ability to identify vulnerabilities in the operating system and user applications and have the vendor fix them. Microsoft users have been doing it for years, and before them Sun system administrators did it at regular intervals. Without the ability to easily update the software, an endpoint becomes an unmanageable risk. We see this problem in embedded systems.

Thankfully, both Xandros and Fedora have built-in updating services that ensure that you have current images on your endpoints. An icon in the menu panel informs you that you have updates awaiting your disposition. If you're a stand-alone system, the decision to download and apply the updates is yours. If your system is managed via the enter-prise, the updates will be installed for you. After playing with both, I've come to some conclusions.

I will start by saying that the Xandros updater seems to be more invisible. I suspect that this comes from the product-marketing folks insisting that updates be as painless as possible. When I manually checked, I discovered that the updates had already been applied. The downside of this is that a downloaded update could adversely affect my application base. This issue is addressed a little later in the "Enterprise Management" section.

Fedora is a different story. Although I liked the big flashing globe with an exclamation point in the middle of it on the panel, the steps that you have to go through to get the updates installed are not trivial. The reason this is an issue is because if the process of updating the endpoint is difficult and time-consuming, users won't do it, and when a critical patch is needed, it won't be there to protect the system.

NETWORKING

In their default configuration, neither version of Linux allows remote root login. Attempts to **ssh** also failed with the message "Connection refused." This is due to the firewall being turned on. Step one in hardening a system: Make sure that the firewall is turned on and configured properly. I'm going to emphasize the last part because the firewall can be on but the configuration can be unsecure. Case in point, the Xandros system allows peer-to-peer (P2P) applications such as BitTorrent and Kazaa in the default configuration. You have to uncheck the P2P box. While you're at it, you may also want to disable inbound requests from the instant messaging bunch.

We need to check the hosts file to make sure that it hasn't been modified to your detriment. The hosts file is checked by the operating system every time you execute a network command that uses a host name. The hosts file is a static list of host names and IP addresses. A minimum hosts file will have only one line in it for the loopback network, and will look like this:

```
127.0.0.1      localhost
```

You may see an additional line for the broadcasthost:

```
255.255.255.255 broadcasthost
```

The automatic network configuration widgets in Xandros and Fedora handled entries in the hosts file a bit differently. Xandros added a line that bound the host name starblazer14 to the Dynamic Host Configuration Protocol (DHCP)-supplied Internet Protocol (IP) address. Fedora just added the host name starblazer15 to the loopback address line so that it looks like this:

```
127.0.0.1      localhost.localadmin   starblazer15   localhost
```

If you expect to use an IP printer, you're going to have to run CUPS (the Common UNIX Printing System).[7] CUPS uses a Web-based management system, and there have been some vulnerabilities reported, so make sure that the firewall is up and you have the latest stable release, which is 1.2.2. You can easily check to see whether CUPS is accessible from other systems by using your browser of choice and simply entering the following:

```
http://targetsystemIPaddress:631
```

It's pretty obvious if this works, because you get the CUPS management interface.

---

[7] www.cups.org

We also need to check to see what network services are going to be invoked, so we're going to check inetd.conf and xinetd.conf to see whether anything untoward is running that may bite us later. Inetd, and the more secure replacement for it, xinetd, are referred to as *super servers* and listen on all ports for incoming network traffic. Only one of them can run at a time. A more secure version of inetd, xinetd provides more security functionality due to the use of access control lists (ACLs), temporal filtering, and extensive logging capability. When you check inetd.conf, what you're looking for are pound signs in front of the undesired services, as shown in Figure 10-11.

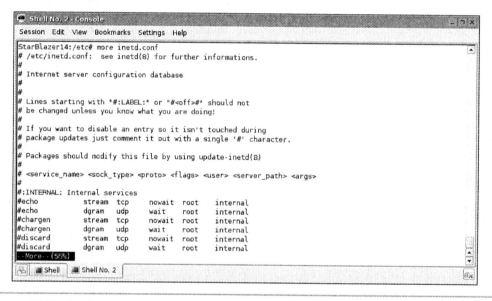

Figure 10-11 Services that are not to run are commented out in the inetd.conf file.

Another important difference between inetd and xinetd is that xinetd doesn't start up the service until it's requested. Inetd must have the requested service running for it to assign sockets, thereby increasing the potential attack surface (attackable programs) of the system. Xinetd can also use the host.allow and host.deny files, allowing you to specify which IP addresses are allowed or denied connections to your system. For those of us who have been around for a while, this is similar to how tcpwrappers operates.[8] The basic xinetd.conf file lives in the /etc/xinetd.d directory and looks similar to the file in Figure 10-12.

---

[8] www.vtcif.telstra.com.au/pub/docs/security/tcp_wrapper.txt (The original paper on TCP Wrapper, by Wietse Venema. Great read.)

```
root@Starblazer15:/etc
File  Edit  View  Terminal  Tabs  Help
[root@Starblazer15 etc]# more xinetd.conf
#
# Simple configuration file for xinetd
#
# Some defaults, and include /etc/xinetd.d/

defaults
{
        instances            = 60
        log_type             = SYSLOG authpriv
        log_on_success       = HOST PID
        log_on_failure       = HOST
        cps                  = 25 30
}

includedir /etc/xinetd.d

[root@Starblazer15 etc]#
```

Figure 10-12 Xinetd.conf from a Fedora Linux system.

The exports file tells the Network File System, or NFS, what file systems should be made available on the network. For most endpoints, this file should be empty except for the default comments.

The securetty file, located in /etc, is a list of which terminals root can log in from. Some securetty files have as many as 63 ttys that allow root access! Anything above tty1 is really not necessary. Besides, root shouldn't be logging in to anything. You should be using **su** or **sudo** if you need root-level access.

ACCESS CONTROL

Although access control is generally reserved for remote access, access control also means local access. Not just how users are connected to the system, but also, once connected, what resources can the user access (thus the term *access control*).

We can start with who has access to our system from the outside—our traditional definition of access control via the remote user.

Linux uses an authentication mechanism call Pluggable Authentication Modules (PAM). To be completely precise, it's Linux-PAM. The PAM architecture separates the authentication code from the application code and allows you to "plug in" authentication methods such as Kerberos, smart cards, DCE, and RSA. PAM is not something that you should approach without some knowledge, but there are a few things that you can do.

Start by checking /etc/security/access.conf. If all the lines start with a #, that means your system hasn't been tightened down yet. You can edit this file using a text editor such as vi, but I highly recommend that you review the Linux-PAM Administrator Guide before you start changing things. You can find a copy of this manual at www.kernel.org/pub/linux/libs/pam/Linux-PAM-html/old/pam.html#toc5.

You can also check the directory /etc/pam.d and look for configuration files for the following:

- su
- sudo
- login
- samba
- xserver
- passwd
- ppp
- ssh
- cron
- chfn
- chsh
- other

You probably noticed the last filename on the list is "other." This is the default file that PAM uses if it can't find a suitable configuration file. You can check this file to ensure that at least something is happening.

Make sure that you make copies of any file before you change it, and make sure that you have a session open as root when you're testing your changes.

WARNING

You can lock yourself out of the machine if you're not careful!

More than a few systems have been accessed via the guest account or other default accounts, so one thing we need to do is to remove all the dunsel default user accounts. This includes things such as the games user (Xandros) or the gopher (Fedora) user. You can do this from the command line by editing the passwd file, but this isn't for the uninitiated. An easier way is to use the GUI-based user managers that both Xandros and Fedora provide. You can activate, deactivate, and engage account encryption from these interfaces, so they are fairly effective and save you from having to use the shell commands.

Linux embraces a concept of proxy execution that allows a user to run an application with the same privileges as root. Called SUID (switch user ID) and SGID (set group ID). Over the years, hackers have learned how to exploit flaws in programs that switch a user's ownership of the program at runtime. For example, there used to be a vulnerability in the X Windows library that Linux used to display and manage the GUI.[9] By exploiting a buffer overflow, an attacker could get root access to the system. This was a pretty extreme case, but the potential does exist in all SUID/SGID programs. You can identify SUID and SGID programs with simple command-line syntax:

```
find / -type f -a -perm +6000
```

Add the **exec** command to grab some detail from the **ls** command, and the new command line looks like this:

```
find / -type f -a -perm +6000 -exec ls -al {} \;
```

You'll find that this command is generic enough to work on most versions of Linux. (Note that there is a space between the closing bracket (}) and the backslash (\).) What you'll also find is a fairly long list of programs, among them **su** and **sudo,** both of which can be pretty dangerous when in the wrong hands.

Another interesting comparison resulted when I looked at the number of SUID/SGID programs on Xandros and Fedora. Xandros has 65 versus Fedora's 37. An analysis of the two lists shown in Table 10-1 demonstrates just how different these two versions of Linux really are.

Table 10-1 Comparison of SGID Files from Fedora and Xandros (Both Indicate that Both SGID and SUID Bits Are Set)

Xandros	SGID	Fedora	SGID
/bin/su		/bin/su	
/bin/ping		/bin/ping	
/bin/login			
/bin/mount		/bin/mount	
/bin/ping6		/bin/ping6	

continues

---

[9] http://seclists.org/bugtraq/1997/May/0212.html

Table 10-1   Comparison of SGID Files from Fedora and Xandros (Both Indicate that Both SGID and SUID Bits Are Set) (Continued)

Xandros	SGID	Fedora	SGID
/bin/umount		/bin/umount	
		/bin/traceroute6	
/usr/bin/at		/usr/bin/at	
/usr/bin/apm			
/usr/bin/gpg			
/usr/bin/ksu			
/usr/bin/chfn		/usr/bin/chfn	
/usr/bin/chsh		/usr/bin/chsh	
/usr/bin/sudo		/usr/bin/sudo	
/usr/bin/wall	Yes	/usr/bin/wall	Yes
/usr/bin/crontab	Yes	/usr/bin/crontab	
/usr/bin/konnectwizard.bin			
/usr/bin/fileshareset			
/usr/bin/chage	Yes	/usr/bin/chage	
/usr/bin/log_clean	Yes		
/usr/bin/cdrecord.shm			
/usr/bin/setdate			
/usr/bin/ssh-agent	Yes		
/usr/bin/dotlockfile	Yes		
/usr/bin/cifsumount			
/usr/bin/hpoj_setup			
/usr/bin/eventview	Yes		
/usr/bin/cdrecord.mmap			
/usr/bin/cardinfo			

Xandros	SGID	Fedora	SGID
/usr/bin/XandrosSMA	Both		
/usr/bin/expiry	Yes		
/usr/bin/sperl5.8.4			
/usr/bin/konnectvpn			
/usr/bin/kgrantpty			
/usr/bin/autodetect_parport_printers			
/usr/bin/artswrapper			
/usr/bin/kdesud	Yes		
/usr/bin/newgrp		/usr/bin/newgrp	
/usr/bin/passwd		/usr/bin/passwd	
/usr/bin/gpasswd			
/usr/bin/readcd			
/usr/bin/cifsmount			
/usr/bin/smbmnt			
/usr/bin/smbumount			
/usr/bin/konnect.bin			
/usr/bin/cdda2wav			
/usr/bin/vtswitch			
/usr/bin/traceroute.lbl		/bin/traceroute	
/usr/bin/kcheckpass			
/usr/bin/autorun			
/usr/bin/cdrecord			
/usr/bin/bsd-write	Yes	/usr/bin/write	Yes
/usr/bin/kpac_dhcp_helper			
		/usr/bin/rlogin	

continues

Table 10-1   Comparison of SGID Files from Fedora and Xandros (Both Indicate that Both SGID and SUID Bits Are Set) (Continued)

Xandros	SGID	Fedora	SGID
		/usr/bin/lockfile	Yes
		/usr/bin/lppasswd	
		/usr/bin/gpasswd	
		/usr/bin/slocate	Yes
		/usr/bin/rcp	
		/usr/bin/rsh	
/usr/lib/XandrosAntivirus/sbin/ XAVUpdateDB			
/usr/lib/pt_chown			
/usr/lib/evolution/2.0/camel/ camel-lock-helper	Yes		
		/usr/lib/vte/ gnome-pty-helper	Yes
/usr/sbin/pppd			
/usr/sbin/pptp			
/usr/sbin/pppoe			
/usr/sbin/postdrop	Yes		
/usr/sbin/postqueue	Yes		
		/usr/sbin/utempter	Yes
		/usr/sbin/ sendmail.sendmail	Yes
		/usr/sbin/lockdev	Yes
		/usr/sbin/userisdnctl	
		/usr/sbin/usernetctl	
		/usr/sbin/userhelper	

Xandros	SGID	Fedora	SGID
/usr/X11R6/bin/X	Both	/usr/X11R6/bin/Xorg	
/usr/X11R6/bin/xterm	Yes		
		/usr/libexec/openssh/ ssh-keysign	
/sbin/unix_chkpwd			
/sbin/hibernate			
/sbin/cardctl			
		/sbin/pam_ timestamp_check	
		/sbin/netreport	Yes
		/sbin/unix_chkpwd	
		/sbin/pwdb_chkpwd	

The moral of this story is that you will have to change your system and then test it to ensure that all your management applications and your office tools work properly. Industry best practices dictate that any unnecessary SUID or GUID (both in the case of Xandros) should be eliminated. The command to do this is **chmod**. Now before we run off and **chmod** the snot out of our file system, let's look at some of the files that can't or shouldn't be changed. Users need the ability to change their password, so we can't change passwd because it has to access the password database. On the other hand, I don't think I want my users being able to **su** or **sudo,** so they're high on the list. Add to that anything that allows the user to poke around the network, and the minimum list begins to look like this:

- chage
- gpasswd
- wall
- chfn
- chsh
- newgrp
- write
- usernetctl

- ping
- ping6
- mount
- umount
- netreport
- traceroute
- traceroute6

Getting back to our **chmod** command, we can use the following form:

```
chmod a-s /path/filename
```

For example, when we change the permissions on wall, the complete command will look like this:

```
chmod a-s /usr/bin/wall
```

APPLICATIONS

Many of us hear the word *applications* and we think of word processing or spreadsheets. But in our world, the word *applications* also applies to the bits of code that help us manage our endpoints and provide security (and office functionality). What good is a management solution if it makes all your endpoints vulnerable to attack?

Applications are also all about data protection and reliability. More and more tools are being generated that ensure that the documents that you generate don't get into the "wrong hands." From an endpoint security perspective, this is the point where you can make decisions regarding how the document is going to be protected.

READING, WRITING, AND 'RITHMETIC

In the recent past, if you wanted to write a document, generate a spreadsheet, or wow folks with a presentation, you needed Microsoft tools. However, unlike a few years ago, when all you really had was Microsoft, we now have some choices in what office software we want to saddle our users with. The first choice we have to make is whether we want to use the Microsoft suite of office products. You may have a group of users who don't want to change, or you might have some existing license agreements that make it attractive to stay with Microsoft Office. If this is the case and the answer to the question is "yes," Wine and CrossOver are the only real choices.

Wine is an open source project that implements the Microsoft application programming interface (API) in original code for Linux. Their goal is to get Linux on the desktop, and the good folks at Wine believe that the only way to do that is to get Office applications to work reliably on the Linux desktop. I agree that without the ability to share Microsoft Office documents, Linux will have a tough time getting into corporate America.

Using Wine, CrossOver allows you (maybe not the best choice of words) to install the Microsoft Office suite on your Linux operating system.[10] Like Xandros, CrossOver is the commercial version of Wine. The Xandros system comes with CrossOver as the basic Office-support mechanism.

What this means to endpoint security is that the vulnerabilities that Microsoft Office carries with it get transferred to the Linux environment. Visual Basic and macro viruses and vulnerabilities are now a concern in a non-Windows operating system.

Another concern is how security applications, such as those that provide intellectual property management or identity management, work with this kind of solution. That's a fair concern. They would have to exist within the framework provided by Wine, I suspect.

The other option is to use an application that was written from the ground up to provide Microsoft Office-like functionality. Our first example is OpenOffice.[11] Like Wine, OpenOffice is an open source multiplatform office suite that is free to anyone who wants to use it. OpenOffice is compatible with Microsoft Office documents up to Office 2000 and can produce PDF files. The OpenOffice default is to store documents in the OASIS OpenDocument format, an open XML standard for documents.

OpenOffice also supports digital signatures for documents via W3C DSIG,[12] another open standard. Digital signatures allow you to ensure that the document that you're looking at is an unaltered and trusted version. Open is good.

The ying to OpenOffice's yang is StarOffice, a commercially available implementation of OpenOffice from the good people at Sun. It has the same capabilities as OpenOffice, with the support of a major vendor in Sun.

Putting my paranoid security hat back on, we discover that OpenOffice and StarOffice are not free of vulnerabilities. In June 2006, it was discovered that three major vulnerabilities allow a hacker to gain access to full system resources by using Java applets or

---

[10] www.winehq.org

[11] www.openoffice.org

[12] www.w3.org (World Wide Web Consortium)

macro code. The last vulnerability is a minor one and only crashes the system. InfoWorld reported that versions 1.1.x and 2.0.x are vulnerable.[13]

A significant security issue that may have the CISO clutching at his or her heart is what's not in OpenOffice or StarOffice. In the age of paranoia swirling around intellectual property, neither of these office applications support digital rights management (DRM). This can be a problem in a world obsessed with controlling intellectual property and who has it. It can be a worse problem if you're using Microsoft DRM capability and decide to migrate to an open standard, because you won't be able to open DRM-enabled documents.

REMOTE MANAGEMENT

Both systems can be remotely managed via an enterprise management tool or via Virtual Network Computing (VNC), a remote control tool that gives the administrator complete control over the keyboard, mouse, and display. Using this capability, administrators can install, remove, or fix the computer as if they were sitting right in front of it. Pretty handy for the good guys. Unfortunately, this remote control function can be pretty handy for the bad guys, too.

In my mind, and hopefully other minds, there is a difference between remote management and enterprise management, and that difference is based on the management objective. The purpose of remote management is to troubleshoot a specific issue or to assist the user with a specific task. It is a one-to-one administrator-to-user ratio, whereas enterprise management is a one-to-many administrator-to-user ratio.

Although both systems support VNC, each does it a bit differently. The Fedora system makes the assumption that you really don't want to run VNC, so the commands to get it going are buried in the system. Using the "service" application, you can indeed start the VNC server, but before you do, you must modify some configuration files if you want a remote desktop.

Xandros has a cool application that allows you to enable access via VNC either as a one-time action (fix my broken app, please) or to a specific user, such as the administrator, at any time. The user can set up an "invitation" that gets sent to the person who is going to access the system remotely. The invitation has things such as the port that is supporting the connection and the password that is protecting it. This invitation can be mailed to the invitee if you so choose.

The passwords that protect the system are generated if you're using Xandros, but you have to set them if you're using Fedora. The Xandros system picks some pretty complex

---

[13] www.infoworld.com/article/06/07/05/HNopenofficewarns_1.html

and hard-to-guess passwords. For example, when I generated an invitation, the Xandros system gave me the password SPFd-55p to pass on to the person I wanted to connect to my system. Subsequent requests generated passwords that didn't seem, to my off-the-cuff analysis, to be any more similar than the four characters, a dash, and three last characters. When I selected my Fedora password, I just used the letter *a*, and Fedora seemed to be fine with it.

Clearly the only real way to protect the connection and the session is via Secure Sockets Layer (SSL). The documentation says that if you want security, you need to use an encrypted connection. This will add more complexity to the solution, but it will allow you to manage remotely and securely.

NETWORKING

NETBIOS WOES

Xandros comes wired for a Microsoft network. From my test machine, I issued the following command:

```
net lookup starblazer14
```

The system responded with the correct IP address of starblazer14, which means that my Xandros system is indeed speaking NetBIOS, as we found in our scans. This doesn't mean that Xandros is vulnerable to all the exploit code that runs against NetBIOS. Quite the contrary. It means that Xandros has its own set of vulnerabilities waiting to be discovered and exploited!

WIRELESS

I think I've pretty much made my position on wireless pretty clear: It's evil. However, it is one of those delicious evils—like a trip to Hawaii right after you leave a painful job, or watching an adult movie after the kids have gone to sleep. Wireless makes our lives simpler, but at the cost of a possible loss of privacy and additional time that has to be taken to secure and manage the wireless connection.

Xandros makes the entire process of connecting to an encrypted network easier than Windows. As you can see in Figure 10-13, Xandros supports 40/64-bit and 128-bit WEP (Wired Equivalent Privacy) and 256-bit WPA (WiFi Protected Access) on up to 4 different keys. If I were configuring a wireless system, I wouldn't even consider any form of WEP, because attacking WEP has turned into a vocation for some people!

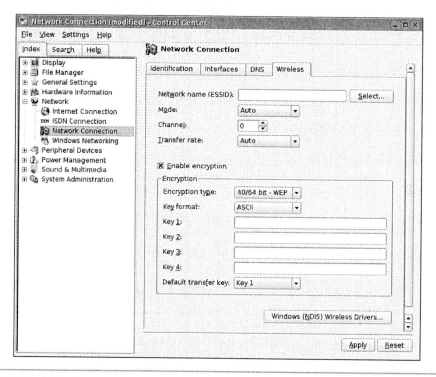

Figure 10-13   Although not great security, Xandros provides some wireless security via WEP and easy configuration.

NETWORK APPLICATIONS

Linux people have gotten used to having some basic network applications around that provide functionality at many levels. Most, if not all, have been cited for some security violation in the past. If you are using these applications, use caution; they can create security issues for you.

We'll start with BIND, the Berkeley Internet Name Domain service. BIND provides a mapping service between IP addresses and the domain names that are easier for us humans to remember. The problem is that BIND also provides some interesting problems because, as a server, everyone has access to it. It's a service that we can't live without, so we just need to be aware and make sure that we've eliminated any unnecessary risks.

Sendmail has been described as a vulnerability with some really cool features. Back in the old days, before processing speeds were measured in hundreds of megahertz, hacking sendmail was almost a religion. Well, things have changed, and the combination of maturity of code and better network security design has taken sendmail off of the hit list. However, like BIND, all sendmail installations should use known best practices regarding security. One of the major issues regarding sendmail that should be addressed is an MTA (mail transfer agent) acting as a mail relay. A mail relay allows A to send mail to C via B. Open relays have been used as spam broadcasters in the past, and if you are relaying spam, you can get "black holed" by network administrators.

NFS, the Network File System, is a way of sharing your files with other Linux systems, or for that matter, any other system on the network. You essentially "export" a designated portion of your file system over the network. Access can be controlled to a fairly high degree, but the configuration isn't easily managed by novice administrators.

File Transfer Protocol, or FTP, is a client/server tool that enables users to upload and download files to a server. Although you can specify or restrict users and hosts, FTP has a mode that allows anonymous users to log in and grab or drop files. There are two basic reasons that anonymous FTP is bad: attack and abuse. I differentiate between the two for a specific reason. There are those who want the service to operate so that they can transfer files, and those who want to attack the service for other nefarious means. Those who want the service to operate want it to distribute kiddy porn, pirated applications, hate literature, and so on. Those who want to attack the system want the service to break so that they can load a rootkit on it. Neither of these is generally good for the system owner. You know that your day isn't going to end well when the man at the door flashes a badge and says, "I want to talk to you about one of your servers."

OpenSSH is a secure suite of tools that are intended to replace TELNET, FTP, and RCP.

With OpenSSH, you can establish a session, transfer files, and remotely copy parts of the file system over an encrypted tunnel. Using public key technology, OpenSSH can verify the user and the system prior to allowing a secure connection. OpenSSH also allows port tunneling, which allows the user to use otherwise insecure protocols over the secure SSH tunnel. With OpenSSH, I can't think of any reason that an administrator would use TELNET, FTP, or RCP for administrative purposes.

Samba is a service that allows non-Windows systems to provide and access Microsoft Windows shared file systems. It also allows Windows-equipped endpoints to access other operating systems running a Samba server. An open source project, Samba has been providing file and print services to Server Message Block / Common Internet File System (SMB/CIFS) clients since 1992.

Apache is the other Web server. Apache is a full-featured HyperText Transfer Protocol (HTTP) Web server that is part of the Apache Software Foundation. Considered to be the most popular Web server on the Internet, Apache can trace its roots to the National Center for Supercomputing Applications (NCSA) HTTPd 1.3.

802.1x

I believe that the 802.1x protocol and some integrity widgets can serve as the basis for a good proportional control that can be the foundation for a trust-based architecture. The good news is that an 802.1x supplicant is available for Linux. The bad news is that it's not an easy thing to set up unless you're comfortable with command-line instructions and building code. As of this writing, there was really only one viable supplicant available, and it is only available from the open source community.

You can find the open source implementation of 802.1x, Open1x, can be found at http://open1x.sourceforge.net/.

From there, you can get the source distribution and a list of the past bugs. Make sure that the hash of the code matches the published hash code.

There is a good tutorial by Lars Strand on installing 802.1x at www.linux.org/docs/ldp/howto/8021X-HOWTO/index.html.

Another great article on installing Open1x was written by Matthew Gast for the *Linux Journal* in June 2005. It's a little more up-to-date because it addresses the kernel patches required to make the whole thing work. You can find this article at www.linuxjournal.com/article/8320.

The latest version of Open1x, as of this writing, was released in May 2006 with a revision number of 1.2.6. Version 1.2.6 fixed some nasty bugs, such as segment faulting on re-authentication, and is the latest stable version of Open1x.

ENTERPRISE MANAGEMENT

I spent considerable time thinking about where to put this discussion. I wasn't sure whether I should include this section or incorporate it as a subsection of the "Networking" section. I concluded that the ability to be managed from a central location is pretty key to any CLPC solution, because without it you have no way of establishing an auditable policy. If you don't have an auditable policy, you have no way of establishing a measurable level of trust. A key requirement is that you are in charge of how the update process works if you want to establish an enterprise policy that is auditable to your policy.

Once again, both the free and commercial versions of Linux have a management solution built in to them that allows for the centralized management of the operating system and applications. In the case of Xandros, it's called xDMS, for Xandros Desktop Management Server. You must have the Business Edition of Xandros to get the xDMS client. You must also have Xandros Server to get the management software. Oh, and a Lightweight Directory Access Protocol (LDAP) server. Updates to clients are provided via a central server rather than from the Internet. Therefore, Xandros can plug into a regression process that will ensure that the enterprise doesn't get hammered by the latest set of patches.

Fedora uses a program called up2date, or it uses the Red Hat Network (RHN). The up2date program uses the Red Hat Package Manager, commonly referred to as RPM, and the Yellow Dog Updater Modified, or yum. RPM works to manage the update packages, while yum does the work of unpacking and updating the selected package. Fedora has a cool icon in the panel that tells you that you need to upgrade. Although I was successful in upgrading the utilities and drivers, I was never able to get the kernel updated. I kept getting an error that the default server wasn't found. I had to resort to using yum from the command line to get the kernel updates.

From an enterprise endpoint security perspective, I have to say that there seems to be an advantage to paying some coin for the operating system. Although not nearly as developed as the Microsoft or Apple management solutions, the Xandros solution looks as if it will meet the requirements for enterprise-based control of policy.

Tools and Vendors

As mentioned earlier, lots of resources are available on the Web for Linux. I'm fairly sure that an entire book could be written on this subject alone. So for now, I'm just going to list some of the sites and built-in tools (at the bottom of the list) that helped me with this chapter:

- www.linuxinsider.com

  Lots of news and information on Linux and things that affect the Linux community.

- www.clamav.net

  ClamAV is an open source project for antivirus.

- http://sourceforge.net/projects/aide

  AIDE (Advance Intrusion Detection Environment) is available at this site. Similar to Tripwire, it generates a database about files on your system. When you run AIDE, it compares files to that database reporting changes.

- www.chkrootkit.org

  Chkrootkit. You have to build it yourself, however.

- www.gresecurity.net

  Gresecurity. Open source enhancements for Linux that add role-based access control (RBAC) and additional hardening, detection, and prevention features.

- pax.gresecurity.net

  PaX. Part of the gresecurity project, PaX brings Address Space Layout Randomization (ASLR) functionality to the Linux kernel, among other defense techniques.

- www.tripwire.com/products/enterprise/ost

  Tripwire. One of the first security tools ever written for UNIX.

- http://sourceforge.net/projects/aide

  Klaxon. Want to know if you're being scanned?

- www.insecure.org

  Nmap. My personal favorite! Nmap is the tool for poking around on the network.

- www.snort.org/dl/binaries/linux/

  Snort. Snort is a network-based intrusion detection system (NIDS). Snort turns your Linux box into a dedicated IDS. Lots of support and lots of happy users.

- www.sendmail.org

  Everything sendmail.

- www.samba.org

  Samba. Same thing here for SMB/CIFS.

- www.securityfocus.com

  Securityfocus. Because Symantec bought them, I'm not sure of their objectivity. With articles such as "Linux update becomes terminal pain"[14] and "The danger of 'free,'"[15] it begins to look a little self-serving to me. However, they do have some good vulnerability information.

- http://securitydot.net/

  News, information, vulnerabilities, and exploits.

- aplawrence.com/Unixart

  AP Lawrence. Articles and how-tos on many things Linux.

- www.linuxsecurity.com

- www.staroffice.org

  StarOffice users group.

---

[14] Robert Lemos, 8/24/06

[15] News Brief, 8/25/06

- Netstat. A great command to determine network activity and statistics. Various switches provide information on routes and connections.
- Lsof. Provides a listing of open files that can be parsed by other programs.
- FAM (File Alteration Monitor) can tell you when the file system changes. If you use a super server (such as xinetd) and the FAM API, your programs can be notified when changes are made to files or directories.

CLOSING THE LOOP

As much as firewalls, AV, and intrusion detection are part and parcel of our network security solutions, Linux is going to have to continue to live outside of the loop closure process for now.

Linux can continue to provide excellent platform services, such as IDS and firewalls, but without some method of verifying endpoint integrity prior to connecting to the network, and at regular intervals during a session, it's still part of the problem.

We've seen that 802.1x can provide one of the crucial building blocks needed in a CLPC solution, but 802.1x supplicants are still primitive and difficult to work with in the Linux world. Add the fact that there doesn't seem to be an integrity checker, and we have no way of determining whether the Linux system requesting access to our network resources is trustworthy.

One thing that Linux does have going for it is that the plain vanilla users (not the "I've been building code for years" type) aren't quite sure how to install new (read "rogue") software. The slow introduction of unknown software elements would tend to act as a derivative damper on the network security posture, and that's a good thing. A slow rate of change is a manageable thing.

Having said all this, it seems to me that there are enough tools to scratch out some sort of an integrity checker that could append the system status to a network access control (NAC) packet. PAM can provide authentication, FAM can check and monitor file system status, and **ps** could check the process list to make sure that the firewall is running and later poll the process list to see whether anything new popped up. All this information could be "glued" together, and a decision could be made about the status of the endpoint by a resident watchdog process. This status could be relayed to a policy server whose job it would be to determine whether the Linux endpoint met minimum trust requirements and answer the question "Should I trust this system with my enterprise data?" If the answer is "no," the switch gets told to drop the endpoint into a remediation, quarantine, or an Internet-only virtual local area network (VLAN). Figure 10-14 shows an example of such a system. You could easily use an encrypted policy file locally that could be updated via a management server and stored on a policy server.

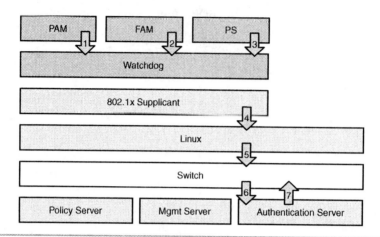

Figure 10-14   To perform an integrity check, PAM, FAM, and **ps** report to a watchdog (1,2,3). The watchdog then reports a combined status to the supplicant (4). Steps 5 through 7 are then the standard 802.1x authentication and NAC cycle.

Key Points

When I started this chapter, I wanted to come away with a better understanding of where Linux is and where it's going. I shouldn't be surprised at some of the conclusions that I reached, considering that it seems that the Linux community is courting the business user and not the consumer. However, it seems that in the quest to become a viable corporate desktop replacement for Microsoft, the Linux community is making some of the same compromises that Microsoft made.

Comparison of Two Extremes

This chapter was about understanding the various security issues associated with Linux. Like the next chapter on handheld devices, we have a large pool of candidates to examine. Unlike the handheld market, the versions of Linux are variants of each other and in many ways similar. One of the big differences in Linux offerings has to do with how they're brought to market. Is it a free version or is it a commercial version? The question seems out of place when we talk about Linux, but as it turns out, it is, in my opinion, the most important question because the answer has an impact on support and management.

The Xandros Business Desktop and the Red Hat Fedora Core operating systems are both Linux. Fedora is free, whereas Xandros is a commercial version of Linux. I have to admit that at some points I wasn't sure that I was really looking at the same basic operating system. For example, when we looked at SUID/SGID files, there was a pretty big difference between the two versions of Linux.

This chapter was a perfect example of the basic problem that security people struggle with every day: balancing security and ease of use. Out of the box, the Xandros system was easier to use, but the Fedora installation was more secure.

XANDROS RUNS NETBIOS

Xandros is a great example of a commercial version of an open operating system. It's obvious that a Herculean effort went into making the transition from Microsoft to Linux as painless as possible. Therein lies the basic problem: In an effort to make the operating system transition painless, the folks at Xandros lowered the security standard. Sure, it will make deploying Xandros easier on the enterprise, but I would have to say that a different build and provisioning process would have to be used than the one envisioned by Xandros.

Create a secure version of the build, and replicate it across your deployed systems. That won't be easy in large environments because it's not as simple as downloading an update.

Running NetBIOS without any protection tells me that the Xandros people believe that there isn't enough of a threat to worry about NetBIOS attacks during deployment. Granted, there might not be any at the moment, but that could change any day.

UPDATING FEDORA

Although you expect a certain amount of pain when you update a product, the number of decisions and steps that you have to endure will most likely have users just skipping the entire process, thereby opening their endpoint up to potential attack.

I wound up using the command-line version of the updater to get the kernel updated so that I could run rkhunter without it puking out reams of errors. This isn't something that I'd expect a plain vanilla user to be able to do. In light of that, you'd have to come up with a more effective plan for ensuring that the Fedora endpoints were current. I suppose that means spending the money for the commercial version of their product to get reliable automatic updates.

USERS ARE STILL THE PROBLEM

One of the nice things about Linux and the other UNIX variants is the separation between the administrator and the user. If you're not running as root, it becomes more difficult to subvert the entire system. This doesn't mean that you can't hose a single user, however. Depending on how applications are installed and permissioned, users can either be insulated from the problem, or it can become worse. Installing your office applications as root probably isn't a good idea because you'd need to give everybody access to it via SUID/GUID permissions, thereby exposing another part of the system to attack. There are other ways to solve the problem, such as installing it as office user, but then you run into data file problems. No matter how you slice it, however, the user still has the ability to butcher his or her own environment.

PLAN FOR SUCCESS

This chapter wasn't intended to be a complete treatment of Linux security. What this chapter does point out is that enough differences exist between the various versions of Linux for you to be successful in securing your network. However, you will need to keep the different versions of Linux to a minimum, and you will have to do some research on how to secure the version that you've selected.

LOOP-CLOSURE POSSIBILITIES

I mentioned that the tools needed to be in place to close the loop, and I'm certain that within the next year there will be commercial versions of software that will take advantage of a CLPC trust model. Until then, you either have to deal with Linux and an open-loop system or craft the solution from existing tools and some glueware.

PDAs and Smartphones

Our world has continued to provide newer and faster ways to connect us with our networks. Each day we pick up the newspaper, there's a new device that's supposed to be the hottest thing on the market. The end result to you as a professional is that you wind up having to support, and worry about, a million different threats to your network.

PRÉCIS

In this chapter, we explore the world of the mobile micro platforms supplied to us by the likes of Verizon and AT&T. Just like their big brethren, the market for these tiny marvels sports multiple operating systems just to keep life exciting. But, unlike the gravity-hampered notebooks, the fits-in-your-pocket market also supports different hardware. Yes, there is Apple in the notebook market, but not with the penetration that some of the non-Windows systems have demonstrated in the personal digital assistant (PDA) and smartphone (SP) market.

We'll start with a look at each of the operating systems, what their architectures look like, what some of their weaknesses are, and what we can do to mitigate any threats that presently exist.

POINTS OF INTEREST

For the purposes of this chapter, I'm not going to differentiate between a handheld organizer and a smartphone. The way I see it, the difference is in where the device started its evolution. Did it start the way the Palm and Windows did, as an organizer, or did it start like Symbian, as the heart of a cell phone? This is similar to the firewall argument that touts the benefits of a proxy-based firewall over those of a stateful packet inspection firewall. Each has its benefits, but in the end the market-driven forces of evolution have pushed each vendor to include some elements of each technology in their offering. So it is with PDAs and SPs. So, for the purposes of making the discussion easier, I refer to this entire class of devices as "handhelds," because you must hold them in your hands to use them.

Handheld devices are, for the most part, new additions to our networking environment. Until recently, most PDAs or cell phones were generally relegated to voice calls or synchronizing contact and calendar information over a serial port. Times have changed, however, and the handheld is now considered one of the great tools of our enterprise. They are also a great pain for the security group that protects your network.

Unfortunately, they have about the same maturity with respect to security that notebooks had five years ago. The operating systems claim to have security functionality, but malware continues to spread. Companies claim to have tools, but phones are still getting clobbered. In a strange "life imitates art" kind of event, let's look at what happened to Paris Hilton and her phone. Paris lost control of her address book, and although she didn't seem to have a serious problem with it, the folks who were on the list did. Apparently, some folks didn't want the world to know that they were on Paris Hilton's speed dial. In a nutshell, it was embarrassing for them in much the same way it was embarrassing for the Veterans Administration (VA) to lose millions of veterans' personal information. In case you're curious, I've already received my notice from the VA (because my name was on the list). I'm actually hoping that someone steals my identity. Maybe they can get my credit score above 350.

We need to come to grips with the fact that handheld endpoints are the single largest threat to our networks today. The multitude of connection methods multiplied by the number of operating systems means that security people are going to be very busy for the next few years trying to plug the holes in the dike. There might be some interesting tools, but they have to become a part of our architecture and philosophy for them to succeed.

A SERIOUS THREAT TODAY

Although we are beginning to see more malware aimed at PDAs and SPs, I think the biggest threat is really the loss of device and the resulting loss of data. Someone may steal your device, and if you don't protect it, that person will have access to the valuable data stored on it. In my chats with people, I've learned that people will put all kinds of data on their PDA because they don't associate the value of the data with the ease that the data could be lost.

It doesn't have to be a malicious attacker who gets your data. It could be just about anyone, and you could be the reason. On more than one occasion, I've seen the lone phone slide down the X-ray machine conveyer belt with no owner in sight to claim it. I've also listened to folks putting themselves back together after the trek through the metal detector start conversations with "I think you picked up my phone."

And, you don't just lose things at the airport. According to Hertz spokeswoman Paula Stifter,[1] cell phones and cell phone accessories are the items most often left behind in their rental cars. In this same article, De Lollis quoted Donna Maxi, the Transportation Security Administration's logistics manager at Los Angeles International, as saying that at least four notebooks and three to four cell phones are lost, *every day!* If you figure that number is probably an average for an airport of that size, you're looking at more than 30,000 endpoints missing in action every year.

INTERESTING SOLUTIONS

There are ways to protect against the threat posed by theft or loss, but it does mean using a couple of protection mechanisms in tandem in much the same way we use layered defense in our network environments.

One of the tools that I ran across would erase the device information if it decided that the device was being threatened. Of course, that means you need some serious password management tools to ensure that just fat fingering your password doesn't trigger a data meltdown. But the interesting conclusion is that you've lost physical control of the device and it must be destroyed! This is similar to the safeguards placed in military communications devices. If the enemy attempts to open the device, it "self-zeroizes" the contents, making the device useless to the enemy.[2]

---

[1] *USA Today*, 3/28/05, Barbara De Lollis, "Many travelers have tales of missing gadgets"

[2] FIPS 140-2 Level 3

CONNECTEDNESS

I can't help but think that a handheld endpoint is really today's version of a protocol bridge. As you can see in Figure 11-1, they communicate over serial, infrared (IrDA), Bluetooth, USB, and WiFi. With little effort, data could be passed from one protocol to the other.

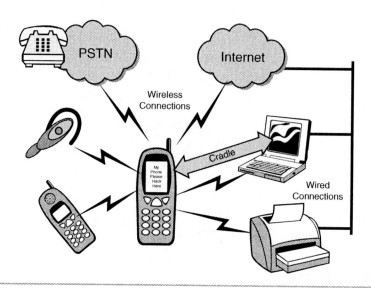

Figure 11-1   The handheld device has become a nexus for multiple communications protocols and technologies. IrDA, radio, cable media over serial and network protocols.

This means that these devices have two ways to synchronize: over the air (OTA), or through the host, which usually means a cradle. When syncing OTA, the device must be capable of protecting itself and engaging in a secure conversation with the data service. In most cases, this means an encrypted link back to an exchange server.

Using a host means that the handheld is synchronizing with the data on the host through USB, serial, or IrDA. Hopefully, the host has some security tools on it to reduce the exposure that the handheld has to viruses and worms.

NEW TERRITORY

One interesting thing that I discovered is that there's not a whole lot about handheld device hardening out there. This is clearly new territory, which means that there's going to be lots of mistakes made. As we learn more, we'll begin to classify those mistakes and begin to create a body of best practices knowledge to help us create templates and guidelines.

I suspect that the main reason that there's not much information is due to the diversity of operating systems and the lack of focus within the hacking community that this engenders. With Windows, you have a nice, well-defined target. Not so here.

OPERATING SYSTEMS

A number of mobile operating systems power the handheld endpoint market. Palm led the pack for a considerable time, but Symbian is the worldwide front-runner, with Windows Mobile and Linux slugging it out for second place. Of course, there would be no discussion of operating systems, no matter their size, without mentioning Linux and its fervent followers.

WINDOWS MOBILE

Windows Mobile is the name that Microsoft gives to its class of software that powers any number of endpoints that aren't chained to a desk. Debuting on PDAs starting in 1996,[3] it was the competition to the Palm operating system. If you were a geek, you were probably looking down on Windows CE as big, bloated, and slow. But that's changed. The newest version of this mobile operating system is sleeker, faster, and more capable than its predecessors.

But CE isn't alone in the Microsoft mobile computing stable. If you go to the MSDN page,[4] you'll find CE listed with XP Embedded, Windows Embedded for Point of Service, and NT Embedded. Quite a selection. We'll go over the Embedded class of software in Chapter 12, "Embedded Devices," but for this chapter we're going to look at Windows CE, because it's the operating system tucked inside of PDAs and SPs.

Keeping up with the marketing times and changing its name to Windows Mobile, Microsoft has been making inroads into the SP market. Depending on who you talk to, Windows Mobile is either as popular as Linux or more popular than Linux.

Any way you shape it, Microsoft is turning into a real player in the mobile market. I suppose you would have to have some faith in the operating system if you actually dumped your own operating system in favor of CE as Palm did by dropping Palm

---

[3] http://upload.wikimedia.org/wikipedia/commons/c/cb/Windows_CE_Timeline.png

[4] http://msdn.microsoft.com/library/default.asp?url=/library/en-us/wceintro5/html/wce50oriwelcometowindowsce.asp

Source. That faith translated into more than 50 percent growth last year, with revenue topping $74 million.[5]

The Mobile kernel is based on WinCE 5.1 and offers enhanced wireless multimedia extension (MMX) capability. I suppose that this is an admission that the world is going to be wireless and multimedia oriented—as far as Microsoft is concerned. I wonder what they're going to call it when all the media types are seamlessly integrated?

Windows CE is architected as a layered solution. As you can see in Figure 11-2, the four basic layers starting from the top are as follows:

1. Application

2. Operating System

3. OEM

4. Hardware

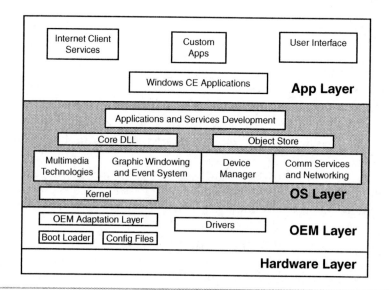

Figure 11-2   The Windows CE embedded operating system is a layered construct that employs an OEM layer that interfaces vendors' unique hardware with the Windows CE kernel.

---

5 www.brighthand.com/default.asp?newsID=9147

SYMBIAN OS

Symbian claims that they have licensed over 700 million copies of their operating system on 100 different phone models.[6] Founded in 1998, Symbian has more than 1,300 employees and is owned by Ericsson, Nokia, Panasonic, Samsung, Siemens, and Sony Ericsson. Symbian is essentially a company that creates and licenses their operating system to all the phone manufacturers. In Q1 of this year, their licensees shipped more than 11.7 million Symbian-powered phones.

Symbian also claims that it is based on open standards, runs in real time, and sports a multithreaded kernel that "provides the basis for a robust, power-efficient, and responsive phone."

The basic architecture of Symbian is based on an old concept called the Trusted Computing Base, or TCB. The idea behind the TCB is that it is small and well understood. Failure modes of the TCB are predictable and properly mitigated. Symbian builds on this model by surrounding the TCB with a semi-trusted layer called the Trusted Computing Environment. User processes then plug into the next layer, which is treated as untrusted. Figure 11-3 shows a diagram of how this works.

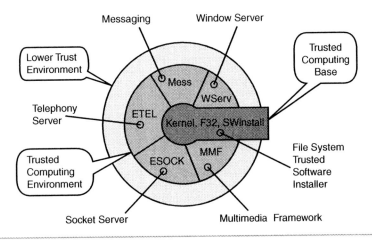

Figure 11-3 Symbian employs a TCB-based architecture that reduces the kernel's exposure to untrusted code.

Saying that you have a TCB doesn't imply that you have perfect code; it just implies that you have trust in how it operates and how it fails. It also doesn't imply that there won't be security flaws, because the TCB needs to operate within a particular security context.

---

[6] www.symbian.com

Symbian supports their security context through the use of something called *capabilities*. Why they chose this term to describe how their security context works is beyond me, but the best I can come to guessing why is that they consider specific actions, such as writing to memory, a capability. Sure, in the strictest sense, writing to memory is a capability, but I really think that something more security related, such as "permissible actions," would have worked better.

A capability allows an application to do things, and as you would expect, the further you get from the TCB, the fewer actions you're allowed to have.

Actions are communicated through an Inter Process Communication protocol that is mediated by the TCB. As applications request access to files and services, such as dialing a phone number, the TCB checks to see whether the application has the suitable capability. If it doesn't, the request is denied. An interesting extension of this also applies to code segments that the application loads to support its function. Any application that loads a dynamic link library (DLL) must check to ensure that the DLL has *at least* the same capabilities as the calling application. This makes it very difficult for a rogue application to take advantage of a Symbian native application, because it must have the same, if not greater, level of trust.

The architecture supports DLLs and plug-in software modules, making it extremely versatile. The most recent version is 9, and it does have some interesting security features:

- Applications are granted access based on signed certificates.
- Hardware-based memory protection.
- Applications can have private protected data stores.
- Certificate management.
- Full encryption.
- Secure protocols. HTTPS, SSL, and TLS.
- WIM framework.

As you can see from the list, Symbian understands certificates! Signed applications have a level of trust even if they operate in untrusted user space. The reason for that is to ensure that if malware does get loaded onto the system, it can't use the capabilities of a signed application to gain greater access.

All the design constraints associated with Symbian indicate a well thought-out security design, but like every well thought-out design, a weak spot exists. Symbian relies on a vetting process for applications prior to granting a signature. As long as the vetting process continues to work, things will be fine. However, it will only take one time, one missed hole, to destroy this trust.

BLACKBERRY

Research In Motion, or RIM, has been in the hardware business since 1984. Their premier product, the Blackberry, has evolved since its introduction as a two-way pager in the mid 1990s. Many of the mobile solutions today owe their success to the trials and tribulations that RIM endured as they pioneered this new market.

In 1999, the first Blackberry debuted as a wireless email device and quickly got the derogatory nickname "crackberry" because of the constant and habitual usage by Blackberry owners. Being able to get your email anywhere proved more addictive than anyone would have assumed.

The basic premise of the RIM solution involved the pushing of email to the handheld device. Mobile users could respond to emails as if they were sitting at their desk, although the common responses were generally as few words as possible.

To integrate the Blackberry into your corporate network requires the use of a product called the Blackberry Enterprise Server (BES). As shown in Figure 11-4, BES acts as a proxy or relay by scanning the inbox of your Exchange, Novell Groupwise, or Lotus Domino server and relaying the messages to RIM's network operations center (NOC). The NOC relays the messages to the wireless provider that is supporting your version of the Blackberry.

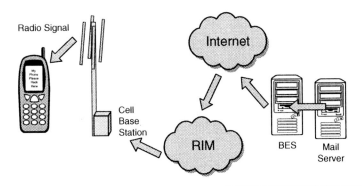

Figure 11-4   The Blackberry uses the BES to check for email on the corporate server, and a service at RIM to relay email messages.

RIM claims that the proprietary operating system is multitasking capable and has built-in connection encryption using Triple DES (3DES) and Advanced Encryption Standard (AES). The Blackberry also supports Java ME (Micro Edition). Being Internet Protocol (IP) capable, the Blackberry supports email protocols and Wireless Application Protocol (WAP), thus making it an effective solution for your mobile endpoints. There is some limited security functionality provided, because third-party applications must be signed if they want to use restricted functionality. However, this is not an attestation of application security but is merely an identification of authorship.

The Blackberry isn't without its fans. At Black Hat USA 2006, a presentation on analyzing complex systems featured the Blackberry and the supporting communications infrastructure.[7] The conclusion was that a back channel to the corporate network could be discovered and leveraged.

From a business perspective, with more than five million Blackberry users,[8] we must assume that this is going to be pervasive solution despite RIM having to pay NTP Inc. $612.5 million for the rights to the Blackberry technology.

PALM

It's hard to predict the future. After all, who would have thought that that Novell was staging a comeback? But I think it's pretty safe to say that unless the folks at Palm Source do something quick, it's only a matter of time before the Palm operating system becomes an interesting milestone in the handheld historical timeline.

Starting life as a PDA and evolving into what it is today, a very capable and connected handheld endpoint, the Palm has provided a similar marketing force as the one provided by RIM. Palm enhanced their PDA functionality and added the networking capability later in the product's evolution.

One nice add-in feature is Palm Security 5.0p. Palm Security 5.0p adds 128-bit data encryption in AES, RSA, or RC4. To address those who are constrained by regulation, Palm Security 5.0p is FIPS 140-2 certified when using AES.

Something that you would think would be a standard feature for all devices, failed password protection, is also part of this package.

MOBILE LINUX

The Open Software Development Lab, or OSDL, is pushing what they call a mobile Linux initiative. Their hope is that the open source people will help prepare Linux for use in the handheld mobile computing market.

---

[7] www.blackhat.com/html/bh-usa-06/bh-usa-06-speakers.html#FX, Analyzing Complex Systems: The Blackberry Case, FX, Phenoelit & SABRE Labs

[8] www.macworld.com/news/2006/04/07/blackberry/index.php

There are other users of Linux, such as MontaVista, who have shipped more than eight million phones in the last two years.[9] The downside of Linux is that it takes time and money to customize it so that it works on the handsets. It would seem that one of Linux's strengths, its flexibility, is going to be its biggest hurdle to acceptance in the handheld market.

But this is not to say that the mobile computing companies aren't working on Linux. As I said earlier, depending on who you listen to, Linux is at least as popular as CE. If you look at Japan, it's incredibly popular, and this region alone may account for the surge in the operating system's popularity. Panasonic and NTT DoCoMo have recently released the P902iS to run on their 3G network.

INITIAL HEALTH CHECK

This is the hard part for these systems: determining what the security state of the device is. All the security functionality seems to focus on prevention. No tools are available to check the health state of your device!

About the only thing you can do to check the security posture of your device is to turn it on and run some applications. If it runs, you're probably okay. At this point, I would only say that this is more an indication on the state of the malware "industry" than a testament to the security of handheld endpoints.

SECURING HANDHELDS

So flash back to before the time of Windows NT, when hardening your computer meant running antivirus (AV) software on it. That's pretty much where we are today with the present state of handheld devices. There are some third-party security tools that we'll discuss later, but for the most part they're signature-based AV or encryption tools.

It is my opinion that the present market isn't driven by security functionality, and the diverse nature and competitiveness of the operating system vendors is creating a huge security vacuum. Couple that with the hardware manufacturers' push to get new technology literally into the hands of more people, and the mobile endpoint community begins to look more like a ripe target of opportunity.

That said, you can do a few things to protect your handheld, but virtually all of them require you to add more software to your system.

---

[9] http://mobile.newsforge.com/article.pl?sid=05/12/13/174241&tid=97&tid=2

WINDOWS MOBILE

The first thing you should do is enable the PIN or password feature on your mobile end-point. It will ensure that in the event that your system is lost or stolen, nobody will be able to read those erotic stories you've been secretly writing. It will also prevent the loss of any personal information that you've put on it. I know folks who have their ATM PIN and their various passwords stored on their mobile toy of choice.

This strategy will slow down some digital attacks, too. When I was synchronizing my HP Jornada with my Mac, I actually had to disable the PIN feature on the HP to make it work. Suffice it to say that I sent the manufacturer, PocketMac, a note saying that this was unacceptable. I was assured that it would be addressed in future versions. However, PocketMac Pro 2.0 does not support password protection. Why is this important? Because it means that the PIN is used to authenticate the device prior to allowing access.

SYMBIAN OS

The Symbian operating system has numerous viruses and Trojan horses that are actually in the wild. For example, CommWarrior.a[10] will spread using Mobile Messaging Service (MMS), but will only infect Symbian-equipped phones. There is some good news here, however: For the moment, the code doesn't seem to be very well written. And if you consider that the threats all have a low risk of data loss, although they might hose your phone's operation, it's not too bad.

As for trying to determine whether the device has been successfully attacked, it would seem that the only way to determine that is to look at your device. If it's working, you're fine.

All of the security software seems to address the following:

- PIN locking
- File encryption
- Systems Management Server (SMS) security
- AV

---

[10] www.infosyncworld.com/news/n/5835.html

PALM

The first thing that you should do is password protect your Palm device. You can use the Security application to assign a password and to set the endpoint to automatically lock itself during idle periods.

You can also "hide" sensitive data from prying eyes. The Palm allows you to classify data as "private," and when you engage the security application, you can either hide or mask records. If you hide them, you can't see them, but the mask option leaves a gray bar in the file list. When you attempt to access files marked as private, you must enter the password before the record is accessed.

All other security is via third-party providers. You can get password managers, encryption tools, and some hacking tools if you dig hard enough. Because this is a practitioner's book, we do discuss tools later, but you'll have to find your own hacking tools.

BLACKBERRY

RIM touts the fact that the Blackberry has been "approved" by various governments for use with sensitive data. Canada, Australia, New Zealand, and the United Kingdom have approved the Blackberry for restricted and protected (protected B) type information. Protected information corresponds loosely to SBU (Sensitive But Unclassified) and is focused primarily on industrial security.

NATO has also approved the Blackberry for transmission and storage of data to the NATO "restricted" classification.

Just for clarification, the only level of classification lower than restricted is public, and depending on who you talk to, just about anything can be considered "restricted."

A certification that does carry some weight is FIPS 140-2. FIPS is a crypto certification that ensures that your crypto engine and the associated functions operate properly. The Blackberry 7290 has been approved to Assurance Level 3.[11] Without going into a complete breakdown of FIPS 140-2, I will say that this is fairly impressive, because it incorporates the following:

- **Level 1.** Basic security compliance and the use of approved algorithm, crypto module (CM) specification, CM ports and interfaces specification, finite state model, key management, electromagnetic interference / electromagnetic compatibility (EMI/EMC) testing, self-test (power on and on demand), design assurance document

- **Level 2.** Tamper evidence and role-based authentication for cryptographic module management and/or usage

---

[11] http://csrc.nist.gov/cryptval/140-1/1401val2005.htm#593

- **Level 3.** Tamper prevention and zeroization of critical security parameters (CSPs in FIPS lingo) and identity-based authentication

The documents required for FIPS certification easily outweigh a Blackberry.

Perusing the 7290 Users Guide isn't very useful if you're a security person. Basic security functions are as follows:

- Enter device password
- Lock/unlock keyboard
- Content protection

Although the device password and keyboard locking are fairly straightforward features, content protection isn't. Content protection is pretty general and can get in the way when your device is locked. I ran across a trouble ticket that says if content protection is enabled and the device is locked, names won't appear in the display when a call comes in. The ticket resolution was to disable content protection. So much for content protection.

There is an upside to the Blackberry security: You can't exchange files using Bluetooth.

SYNCHRONIZATION

For many people, the method of choice is still the "hot sync" process, whether it be through Bluetooth or a serial connection. This is still a connection, however, and as such, it is an infection and attack vector. However, as more handhelds become IP ready, their capability to synchronize via the network is growing.

The Mac seems to have standardized on a synchronization protocol that incorporates some standards, such as SyncML, but most of the sync routines are custom to the device being synchronized.

You should know that some synchronization tools require that you drill holes through your firewall for them to work. This begs the question of how much access is being provided to both the handheld and the host endpoint. For example, the instructions in PocketMac Pro 2.0 tell you to open the firewall to ports 990, 999, 5678, and 5679. Because there is no other identifier, we must assume that any device that attempts to access those ports will be presented with access.

This isn't only on the Mac. Active Sync behaves the same way on the PC and also adds NetBIOS to the mix of required ports.

Believe it or not, there is a standard for exchanging synchronization information, and it's called SyncML. Begun in 2000 as the SyncML Initiative, it is now supported by the

Open Mobile Alliance,[12] with the newest version of the specification referred to as OMA Data Synchronization V1.2. This is a candidate release based on the V1.1.2 Approved Enabler spec that increases the functionality of the service considerably. OMA uses Hypertext Markup Language (HTML) to encode data and incorporates data management facilities that allow you to sync with numerous devices. OMA Data Synchronization is supported by virtually all SP and PDA manufactures.

The nice thing about OMA is that it uses existing HyperText Transfer Protocol (HTTP) to exchange information. This is also a problem because it becomes difficult to differentiate between authorized synchronization activity and data theft. The good news is that OMA does use authentication, but the authentication protocol relies on HyperText Transfer Protocol Secure (HTTPS) to protect the credentials.

APPLICATIONS

I don't know about you, but my eyes are getting too old to look at the tiny type on the screens of these mobile devices. Truth be told, I'm starting to look real hard at going from a 17-inch to a 21-inch monitor just to get bigger print for the same amount of information displayed.

Aside from the size of the screen, most people I talk to tell me that they use their mobile devices for one of three things:

- Email
- Messaging
- Browsing

The next three sections discuss the security issues of these applications so that you will understand that these emerging problems require some thought. Each application does have its own set of security concerns, but the solution used is quite platform dependent, because each platform's capability to protect various aspects of the operating system differs.

EMAIL

The app that made the Blackberry famous! I've had people curse their widgets in the same breath that they've claimed that their pocket annoy-a-tron had saved not only their careers, but also the future of their company. All by being able to respond to a message when it came through.

---

[12] www.openmobilealliance.org/index.html

But the simple fact is that in their native state, email applications allow suspect content to be sent to your mobile endpoint, where it could be a potential threat to the data.

MESSAGING

Instant messaging (IM) is the fastest-growing medium for communication, but this also shows up in the fact that it's the fastest growing threat space. IM protocols work just like email, except that they're happening in real-time rather than store and forward.

So, let's take a message from the past here. IM and Internet Relay Chat (IRC) protocols are the method of choice for botnets, and if what we're seeing in the desktop and notebook world is any indication, the mobile handheld world is next on the list. Botnet owners act with impunity and show no sign of giving up. They are driven by profit, and as the handheld community grows, they are going to become a target for the botnet community.

BROWSING

As more networks allow for the downloading of complex multimedia content, the higher the probability that this content will be exploited to the detriment of the user. Many of the attacks that we've seen rely on the user browsing to sites that aren't what they purport to be, resulting in malware being downloaded and installed on the target system. Although this isn't widespread yet, neither is handheld browsing when compared to the mainstream habits of desktop- and notebook-based endpoints.

NETWORKING

If you look at the ways that handhelds get infected, it's by some form of networking. Physical access generally means that you've either lost the darn thing or someone has taken a spark plug and broken a side window of your car to steal your stuff.

There is a good news–bad news kind of ending here, however. The good news is that modern technology has made it easy for you to network your endpoint over any number of choices. You can wire, or you can go wireless. If you choose wireless, you have a few choices to pick from. More good news is that the handheld manufacturers have included all the popular methods of connecting your device to the countless masses who yearn to send you a message. You can use the good old cell phone protocols because they provide basic message exchange, photo (really just a file) exchange, and a connection to the Internet. Using 3G, or third generation cellular technology, you can have the Internet at your fingertips.

WiFi

Without doubt, 802.11 has its problems. From the early days of this wireless protocol to the current version of 802.11g, there has been a trail of hacked networks and lost data that demonstrates that the hackers are ahead of the designers.

Wireless is a textbook example of complexity versus ease of use. When you first turn it on, there is no security. From a product sales and customer satisfaction perspective, this is the kind of customer experience you want new customers to have. I turn it on, and it works! This wouldn't be the case if I had to connect a computer to the access point (AP) and tell it what computers to allow on to the network. I'd have to do a bunch of things prior to having that joyous experience that only doing a Google search from an SP can give! Okay, maybe not nirvana, but there have been a few times when I was glad that I didn't have to search for a network connection.

You can add "security" to a WiFi network in numerous ways. You can restrict the computers allowed to connect to your network by maintaining what is called a "while list" of authorized computers. The Media Access Control (MAC) address of the wireless endpoint is added to the AP's list of permissible devices. If your MAC address doesn't match with one in the list, the AP won't talk to you. Sounds simple enough, but it eliminates the flexibility that WiFi is supposed to provide. It also adds administrative complexity, because now you have to know how to find the MAC address on any endpoint that wants to connect to your network, and you have to manually update the list as endpoints are added and removed.

So, to accommodate our need to search from the comfort of the local Starbucks, handheld vendors are adding 802.11 protocols to the feature set of their devices. And thankfully, the good folks at Starbucks are using some security protections to keep your precious data secure. But, are they really? Let's examine how the process works.

WiFi is a physical medium, which means that it's at the lowest layer in the stack. For you to connect to a password-protected network, you need to know the password prior to connecting. I've actually been to some hotels where the password is written on a piece of paper at the front desk! WEP encryption works this way. Sure, it keeps the neighbors out for a little while, but you have to figure that eventually the password will get out. Some places have "solved" this problem by changing the password on a weekly, or should I say "weakly," basis, but the clear indication is that this simple method of restricting access isn't adequate.

Originally, WiFi security—well, I should correctly say "privacy"—was provided via the WEP protocol, but as more users came online, WEP came under enough scrutiny that multiple holes were discovered. To address these holes, new security protocols, such as WPA, were added to enhance WiFi security.

BLUETOOTH SECURITY

Bluetooth is wireless technology typically used to connect a headset to a cell phone, synchronize your calendar with your PC, connect to a printer, connect keyboards and mice to PCs, or to transfer photos or ring tones between cell phones. Note that all these uses expose the host device to some form of threat. In the case of the headset-to-cell phone connection, most allow the headset to issue commands to the cell phone, such as "take a picture." When you connect one piece of hardware to another, as is the case with printers, keyboards, and mice, you open the door to impersonation. The last "feature," sending photos and ring tones, is essentially a file transfer protocol, and that's just wrong over a weak public channel such as Bluetooth.

Technically, Bluetooth uses a 48-bit device identifier (which looks suspiciously like a MAC address) and frequency hopping over 79 channels coupled with low power to prevent misuse and confusion between devices. Although the protocol does provide the connectivity features quite effectively, the privacy aspects of Bluetooth leave quite a bit to be desired.

When BT made its debut, the security freaks were told "it's a short-range radio protocol, so don't worry." Two years ago at the Black Hat Briefings in Las Vegas, Adam Laurie and Martin Herfurt did a presentation outlining the many flaws of Bluetooth.[13] To make matters worse, or more interesting depending on your perspective, Bruce Potter and Brian Wotring, both members of the famed Shmoo Group,[14] did a presentation and demonstration called Tracking Prey in the Cyberforest during the Black Hat Briefings. During the conference, Bruce and Brian set up sensors designed to pick up and track Bluetooth devices. Dubbed "proximity-based Bluetooth tracking," Brian and Bruce successfully demonstrated that BT could be used for purposes other than those intended by the original designers. They tracked people as they migrated through the conference. So much for worry; now it's reality that we have to think about.

One feature of BT is the capability to "hide" the device in a way that is similar to how 802.11 hides, by not broadcasting a service set ID (SSID). Called nondiscoverable, it essentially hides your device by not broadcasting its ID. However, last year a paper was written by Wong and Stajano on discovering hidden Bluetooth devices through brute-force attacks.[15] It's slow, but it proves yet once again that security by obscurity isn't a good plan.

---

[13] Black Hat Briefings 2004, Bluesnarfing - The Risk From Digital Pickpockets

[14] www.schmoo.com

[15] Ford-Long Wong and Frank Stajano, University of Cambridge Comp Lab, "Location Privacy in Bluetooth"

Although some manufacturers are starting to become security-aware, authentication is not the default; and if it is, it's pretty weak. I hope that I'm not giving up any corporate security secrets, but take my Motorola E815. The default Bluetooth pin is 0000, and I haven't found a way to change it. At that point, why bother the user with entering a PIN at all? Maybe the designers think it makes us feel better. Like taking off our shoes at the security checkpoint at the airport.

To make matters worse, BT authentication isn't consistent across devices, and this inconsistency has been realized as the lowest common denominator in authentication implementations. Authentication usually occurs during the pairing process. As I brought up with my Motorola earlier, a PIN is exchanged that causes the generation of a link key. The link key is then used to authenticate with the aforementioned security mechanisms being used to protect the key.

One interesting thing about this networking protocol is that there is no logging! A search through the specification doesn't even generate a hit on the word *logging* (or *log*, for that matter).

I took the liberty of perusing the BT 2.0 specification titled "Specification of the Bluetooth System, Covered Core Package Version 2.0 + EDR." First, fascinating reading. I begin to see why there are so many interpretations of the standard. Second, much of the security is recommended. For example, if you wanted to launch a brute-force attack against the endpoint, the mechanism that prevents that is an ever-increasing time between allowed attempts. However, the spec says, "That is, after each failure, the waiting interval before a new attempt can be made, could be for example, twice as long as the waiting interval prior to the previous attempt." Note the use of the word *could*.

I'm not a cryptographer, but it seems that the cryptographic functions leave something to be desired. Keys are based on the PIN (which defaults to 0000 in the preceding example), the BD_ADDR (the device BT MAC address), and a random number. If we know the first two and we have a poor random number generation (RND) function, breaking the encryption seems trivial.

Although BT uses separate keys for authentication and encryption, the encryption key can range from as little as 8 bits to a maximum of 128 bits. Encryption keys are based on authentication keys, and because authentication keys don't change, and if you happen to break through the encryption used, you gain access to the authentication key.

One more interesting thing that I noticed was that all pairing activity is done in clear text. That is, it's not encrypted. Encryption is *optional*.

Linux has a BT configuration tool call hcitool that enables you to control the BT connection from the command line. It's convenient in that it allows very detailed control of remote devices. The following list of hcitool commands indicates that there is a rich set of commands that you can use to connect to a BT device, submit commands, or change configurations. Of particular note are the commands that enable you to enumerate other BT connections and delete them:

- **dev**   Display local devices.
- **inq**   Inquire remote devices. For each discovered device, Bluetooth device address, clock offset, and class are printed.
- **scan**   Inquire remote devices. For each discovered device, the device name is printed.
- **name <bdaddr>**   Print device name of remote device with Bluetooth address bdaddr.
- **info <bdaddr>**   Print device name, version, and supported features of remote device with Bluetooth address bdaddr.
- **cmd <ogf> <ocf> [parameters]**   Submit an arbitrary HCI command to local device. **ogf, ocf,** and **parameters** are hexadecimal bytes.
- **con**   Display active baseband connections.
- **cc [--role=m|s] [--pkt-type=<ptype>] <bdaddr>**   Create baseband connection to remote device with Bluetooth address bdaddr. Option **pkt-type** specifies a list of allowed packet types. **<ptype>** is a comma-separated list of packet types, where the possible packet types are DM1, DM3, DM5, DH1, DH3, DH5, HV1, HV2, and HV3. Default is to allow all packet types. Option **--role** can have value **m** (do not allow role switch, stay master) or **s** (allow role switch, become slave if the peer asks to become master). Default is **m**.
- **dc <bdaddr>**   Delete baseband connection from remote device with Bluetooth address bdaddr.
- **sr <bdaddr> <role>**   Switch role for the baseband connection from the remote device to master or slave.
- **cpt <bdaddr> <packet types>**   Change packet types for baseband connection to device with Bluetooth address bdaddr. **packet types** is a comma-separated list of packet types, where the possible packet types are DM1, DM3, DM5, DH1, DH3, DH5, HV1, HV2, and HV3.
- **rssi <bdaddr>**   Display received signal strength information for the connection to the device with Bluetooth address bdaddr.
- **lq <bdaddr>**   Display link quality for the connection to the device with Bluetooth address bdaddr.

- **tpl <bdaddr> [type]**   Display transmit power level for the connection to the device with Bluetooth address bdaddr. The type can be 0 for the current transmit power level (which is default) or 1 for the maximum transmit power level.

- **afh <bdaddr>**   Display AFH channel map for the connection to the device with Bluetooth address bdaddr.

- **lst <bdaddr> [value]**   With no value, displays link supervision timeout for the connection to the device with Bluetooth address bdaddr. If value is given, sets the link supervision timeout for that connection to value slots, or to infinite if value is 0.

- **auth <bdaddr>**   Request authentication for the device with Bluetooth address bdaddr.

- **enc <bdaddr> [encrypt enable]**   Enable or disable the encryption for the device with Bluetooth address bdaddr.

- **key <bdaddr>**   Change the connection link key for the device with Bluetooth address bdaddr.

- **clkoff <bdaddr>**   Read the clock offset for the device with Bluetooth address bdaddr.

- **clock <bdaddr> [which clock]**   Read the clock for the device with Bluetooth address bdaddr. The clock can be 0 for the local clock or 1 for the piconet clock (which is default).

Another tool, obexFTP,[16] enables you to transfer files to and from most BT-equipped phones. With these two tools and a script, it seems trivial to automate address book theft or SMS message fraud.

There is also a turnkey solution that you can buy if all you want to do is snarf BT packets. Frontline[17] has a device designed to help out in the BT development process by providing access to intercepted and decoded BT signals. It listens on all 79 channels and can report on packet error rates. Pairing is important!

CELL PROTOCOLS

As I said earlier, cell phones can bring the Internet to your fingertips. The downside of that is that now, the Internet is at your fingertips with little or no security. Sure, your calls are encrypted, but as I've often said before, an encrypted pipe is a great way for a hacker to hide his activities.

---

[16] http://linux.softpedia.com/get/Communications/Telephony/ObexFTP-9007.shtml#

[17] www.fte.com/blu07.asp

Modern 3G cell protocols, such as EDGE[18] (Enhanced Data rates for GSM Evolution) and EVDO[19] (1x Evolution-Data Optimized), allow for broadband network connections and the applications that chew up that bandwidth. Most users have no real security on their SPs and instead rely on the cellular company to provide security and privacy. This means that as you browse the network or engage in your IM conversations, you're leaving yourself open to attack.

Some cell phone protocols are now encrypted, thereby making it more difficult to intercept conversations; but when the channel is terminated at the other end of the radio, the communications channel is again unencrypted. As you can see in Figure 11-5, the encryption only protects the airborne portion of your call.

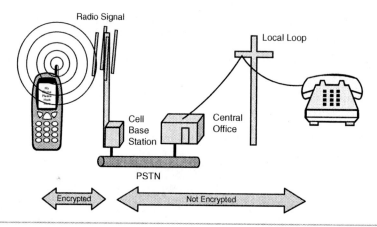

Figure 11-5   Your cell phone conversation is only encrypted to the cell base station. When your call is on the Public Switched Telephone Network (PSTN), it is no longer encrypted.

The EVDO folks are fond of saying that they can use AES to encrypt your cell conversations, and the cell phone industry has been using an algorithm called Cellular Authentication and Voice Encryption (CAVE). Through a fairly convoluted process, a 42-bit key called a *long code* is used to seed the CAVE algorithm. The output of that is then used as the key material for AES. Unfortunately, a paper titled "Cryptanalysis of the cellular authentication and voice encryption algorithm" suggests that CAVE is significantly flawed.[20]

---

[18] Technically, a 2.5 GSM bolt-on

[19] CDMA2000

[20] By William Millan and Praveen Gauravaram, IEICE 2004

This doesn't mean that GSM is any better. In a paper penned in 2003, it is suggested that the authentication algorithm COMP128 and the communications cipher A5/3 are vulnerable to various attacks, including a fairly trivial brute-force attack.

TOOLS AND VENDORS

"See a need, fill a need" seems to be the motto here. A number of vendors are adding varying forms of security to our mobile endpoints, but none of them seems to have learned from the mistakes that we've made in the past. From what I can tell, they're focusing on transport security and data-at-rest security. Each vendor seems to be staking out their portion of the market, thereby reducing their business risk. It also allows them to focus on their solution set. Yes, there is of course AV, but once again that is, in my opinion, just an extension of the existing commodity AV market.

One caveat: I have experience with the Good product line and not the others. This is not an endorsement of any vendor, because, like weapons development, marketing is about leap-frogging the competition. At one point, Good will be better than SMobile; and at some point, Mobile Armor will take the lead. When nobody is watching, Bluefire will surprise us all and start the process all over again. So, evaluate each vendor on their present product offering as it meets your needs. Although a good roadmap is important, buying on future features is a bad idea.

What follows is a description of the major vendors, their products, and the platforms that they operate on. So, having made all the required legal disclaimers, *caveat emptor.*

GOOD[21]

It seems that a major player in the handheld security market is Good.[22] We can have lots of fun at the expense of the good people at Good, but I'll let the wordplay die here.

Through internal development and some clever acquisitions, most notably the purchase of JP Mobile, Good has expanded their product line so that it addresses the problems of secure connectivity as well as endpoint protection.

Good tools integrate into either the Microsoft Exchange or the IBM Domino environments on the server side, and they support Palm OS, Windows Mobile, and Symbian OS on the handheld side.

---

[21] Good was purchased in November 2006 by Motorola.

[22] www.good.com

If you're an enterprise, you should consider the centralized management component that Good provides.

From a feature perspective, Good provides the following:

- **Password management.** The user is locked out after successive failed attempts; temporary administrative passwords are supported.

- **Feature control.** Controls which features the user can change or use.

- **Application lockdown.** Uses a white list of approved applications.

- **Encryption management.** Controls the encryption of native, storage card, and specific applications.

- **Data erase.** The Final Solution wipes data and applications from the handheld.

- **Secure messaging.** Secures SMS on Windows Mobile and Palm.

- **OTA management.** Over the air push technology that reduces the number of IT touches of the handheld.

- **Centralized management.** Provides for policy driven device management.

- **Compliance manager.** Ensures that systems comply with the minimum level of policy.

Good supports AES 256 and Blowfish 64-, 128-, and 512-bit flavors.

BLUEFIRE SECURITY TECHNOLOGIES

When you first go to the Bluefire Web site, the first thing you see is this message: "Bluefire provides a complete handheld security solution." If you click the Products tab, you're greeted with a cute wheel picture that shows all their products. There was no mincing of words or any indication that they're not focused on mobile handheld devices.

One thing that I found that none of the others were talking about was the fact that their firewall blocks traffic over 802.11, code division multiple access (CDMA), and General Packet Radio Service (GPRS). Another thing that they talked about was *logging and alerts.* Other features of the Bluefire Mobile Security Suite 3.6 product include the following:

- **Firewall.** Traditional rules-based type that does IP and port filtering
- **VPN.** Via Bluefire VPN 2.0
- **AV.** Bluefire bundles either McAfee VirusScan PDA Enterprise or Symantec AntiVirus Corporate Edition PDA

- **Real-time logging.** Password attempts, password resets, quarantine overrides, port scans, firewall security level changes, and integrity violations
- **Intrusion detection.** Almost intrusion prevention, because it blocks some attacks
- **Integrity management.** Alerts user and generates a log when violations occur (can also quarantine a device)
- **Authentication.** Enforces power on PIN or password requirements
- **Central management.** Essential for any enterprise-grade solution

I think the feature that intrigues me the most is the Integrity Manager, because it has the most potential to add a loop-closure mechanism to the handheld endpoint solution.

Another good thing is that their cryptographic module is certified under the FIPS CMVP (Cryptographic Module Validation Program). This is commonly referred to as FIPS 140-2. You can find a complete list of all vendors and their associated products at http://csrc.nist.gov/cryptval/140-1/1401val.htm.

This might be a simple thing (simple is good), but it means that the crypto module has been examined and compared to a published standard (FIPS 140-2) and has been found to comply with that standard. Having been through the FIPS process, I can tell you that it means that the crypto module has been well engineered and shouldn't be a vulnerability in and of itself. This does not mean that the algorithms are any good; it just means that they've been implemented properly.

Like Good, this is an enterprise-grade solution that you should consider if you're going to deploy handhelds. The only downside that I can see is that Bluefire Mobile Security is only available for Windows Mobile (Windows Mobile 2003 versions of Pocket PC and Phone Edition) and Palm OS (5.2 and 5.3). If you're running Symbian or Linux, you'll have to look elsewhere.

SMOBILE SYSTEMS

SMobile Systems,[23] formerly FB-4 Systems, does have an impressive list of supported handhelds and seems to be the only vendor serious about Blackberry AV. If you have a diverse environment, perhaps SMobile deserves a look. But coverage across devices isn't consistent, with the common denominator being AV protection. For Palm and Blackberry, you're pretty much constrained to AV products. When you move into the Windows Mobile platform, you can add SMS protection for the phone version. The good news is that if you're Symbian powered, you get AV, SMS Guard, and PIN Guard.

---

[23] www.smobilesystems.com

VirusGuard is pretty much an AV protection application, and although it seems misnamed, PIN Guard adds file encryption and provides some security but seems to be focused on file protection only. This is not an access control mechanism in the traditional sense. Entering the password decrypts the files only.

PointGuard can filter messages by blocking unwanted connections and can use either a white list or a black list to control how SMS and MMS messages are permitted to the handset. PointGuard sports a firewall that can filter data packets on the cellular and WiFi mediums and also has a feature I wish my cell phone had—it can filter incoming calls.

MOBILE ARMOR

Unlike Good and SMobile, Mobile Armor supports more than handheld endpoints. Based on your position, this can either be good or bad. It can be good if the company understands that they need to have a management solution that integrates policy in such a way that all mobile endpoints are addressed effectively and efficiently. It can be bad if the company treats every solution as a stand-alone silo, hoping that through the magic of the merger and acquisition process that a solution can be bought that solves their problem.

Although not listed on their Web site, Mobile Armor has sold a solution called Wireless Suite to the U. S. Secretary of Defense.[24] Wireless Suite combines a number of features into one centrally managed solution that provides the following:

- AV
- VPN
- Encryption
- Firewall
- Compliance and remediation
- OTA delivery and management
- Centralized management

Mobile Armor only support handhelds that sport Windows Mobile 2003, Windows 2005, or Palm with their MobileFirewall, VirusDefense, and RemoteNetwork products.

---

[24] www.eweek.com/article2/0,1895,1970784,00.asp

AV VENDORS

I was going to give each vendor their own section, but in the end I decided that they didn't deserve it. All they're offering is a knockoff of their standard AV product or something that they bought so that they could say that they have an AV product for handhelds.

The upside of using one of these "big players" is that you may already have an investment in their enterprise products, so they might just want to "throw in" some handheld AV the next time you negotiate a contract. I hasten to say that I'm not advocating this approach, but there are those who think a cheap product that shows that they were at least thinking about it is better than nothing at all. Then again, they're usually not the ones that have to spend the time to manage "yet another console" in the NOC.

Once again, I'm not going to rate AV products, because there are lots of articles that talk about AV products and how well they do their jobs. As a matter of fact, there's even a comparison of comparison articles![25] Surprisingly enough, there is little agreement about what is best, so I'm just going to list those vendors that have mobile AV products and the name and version of their product:

Company	Product	MS	Symbian	BB	Palm
F-Secure	Mobile Anti-virus for Business	X	X		
McAfee	VirusScan Mobile for Enterprise	?*	?*	?*	?*
Trend Micro	Mobile Security	X	X		
Symantec	Mobile Security	X	X		X

* Claimed that their solution was "designed for the phone operating system in which it is installed"

NONENTERPRISE USERS

I'm mostly focused on solutions that address the problems of the enterprise, but I would be remiss if I didn't spend a few words talking about single-user solutions. After all, they have the same problems that enterprise users do. Bad people are trying to break into their endpoints or just render them useless.

To start with, you need to enable PIN or password access to your system. If your endpoint has a privacy setting, turn it on. Finally, you should load some form of AV onto the

---

[25] www.consumersearch.com/www/software/antivirus-software/reviews.html

thing. All the major vendors offer some form of handheld AV product, but make sure that you check to ensure that they handle your operating system and hardware (because it can be pretty specific).

Depending on your operating system, you might look at the following:

- **BitDefender.** A Google search will turn up numerous sites for free software.
- **Symantec.** Palm and Windows Mobile.
- **Tucows.** Multiple solutions for various operating systems.
- **McAfee.** All operating systems as long as they're Windows Smartphone or Pocket PC.

WEB SITES

Thanks in part to the fact that if you put three people together you will get at least two religions and two political parties and a will to express it, numerous sites on the Internet provide a fountain of information about all the mobile endpoints discussed in this chapter. Be warned, however: Although the vendor sites tend to be complete and for the most part accurate, many "independent" sites don't spend as much time checking their solutions in multiple configurations, but they might have a solution that addresses your particular set of issues. Here is a short list of sites that might prove helpful:

- http://my-symbian.com/main/index.php
- www.simworks.biz/sav/AntiVirus.php?id=home
- www.symbiangear.com
- www.freewarepalm.com (pretty much speaks for itself)
- http://www.tranzoa.com/html/compete.htm (A pretty good list of Palm-focused security programs. It's humorous to see that they've listed a good number of password-protection programs, and listed close to the bottom is a selection of password-defeating programs. It reminds me of a comic I saw called the Wizard of Id. A salesman was trying to sell the knight some arrow-proof armor. When the knight told him that he already had some, the salesman asked, "So, do you want to buy some armor-piercing arrows, then?)
- www.jpmobile.com/default.asp

CLOSING THE LOOP

The good news here is that some vendors are actually looking at compliance as a security function in their products. However, it is the traditional compliance model based on a policy that only works with regard to the handheld and the vendor product suite. The network is essentially a packet carrier and nothing else.

A separation exists between the mobile device and the infrastructure that must support it. The network isn't aware of the device connecting to it, and the mobile device isn't aware of the network. Until mobile devices can add a basic proportional control to their trust model, we will have to deal with this separation, using other mitigation techniques such as severely limiting the platform choices allowed to connect to and use our enterprise networks.

KEY POINTS

The industry is still grappling with multiple platforms and therefore many multiples of issues. This is creating confusion and frustration for the folks who have to support mobile devices. Unlike the desktop, where a decision could be made to support only one operating system based on the cost associated with procurement and support, the mobile endpoint has a low enough price point and model-specific functionality that two systems are usually the norm.

THE INDUSTRY IS NOT MATURE

I would say that the handheld mobile world is where the desktop world was about five years ago. Convergence is occurring in the mobile security industry, but new features and functionality are appearing faster than enterprise security groups can integrate them. Exceptions to security policy that are required during the integration process, missing features, and poorly executed functionality are creating gaps in our security that an attacker can leverage.

HANDHELDS ARE THE NEXT TARGET

Handhelds have been left alone for the past few years for the same reason that Macintoshes have been left alone: There wasn't a large enough community of them with the requisite vulnerable application base to be interesting to the malware world. This is going to change.

NETWORKING WOES

The multiple methods of networking create multiple problems for protection. We rely on a series of encryption protocols that have demonstrated at least theoretical, if not real, vulnerabilities to protect our authentication and authorization information. Security has been made optional in most of our networking protocols, and when security is engaged, it's in a flawed and vulnerable manner.

SOLUTION AND SECURITY DIVERGENCE

Because each operating system came at the problem from a slightly different perspective, it stands to reason that each solution will have its own set of strengths and weaknesses. As an enterprise begins to address the issues of handheld endpoints, an effort will be made to reduce the number of different platforms supported. The worst-case scenario is to combine two solutions with divergent issues (for instance, Microsoft and Symbian), because the solutions will have to be individually managed.

ENFORCEMENT WILL COME

Future developments will take advantage of 802.1x simply because networks will evolve to the point where all network connections will be vetted prior to allowing access and it's cheaper to put the supplicant on the handheld than it is to enter an exception for each and every device. If your endpoint does both cellular protocols and WiFi, you need to have an enforcement point to prevent network bridging. If you think that spam is annoying, just wait until the spammers start going through your mobile endpoints with direct marketing campaigns!

NO CLPC YET

The unfortunate conclusion is that there is no way to close the loop on these devices, so the best we're going to get is reactive security. The closest we get to this is the Bluefire Mobile Security Suite product, but it still falls short of actual active loop closure, because it is not network aware.

Better PIN programs, some firewalls, AV, and secure communications protocols are all we can expect today. An agent that actively checks the mobile endpoint for compliance and engages in an active exchange of trust information with the network doesn't exist yet for handheld mobile devices. When we allow a mobile endpoint to connect to our networks, we're hoping that the reactive measures that we've taken are in place and working.

Because the mobile endpoint can properly generate a crypto tunnel, we assume that the device is secure. This is a mistake and is similar to the belief that end users are capable of ensuring the security of their systems.

Embedded Devices

We might not realize it, but we're surrounded by embedded computer systems. In this chapter, we take a look at what they are, where they are, why they can be a threat, and what we can do to mitigate the threat.

This brings an important point to mind that we should clarify at the beginning. Embedded systems permeate our lives, but not all of them are a threat. I doubt that you would consider your microwave oven a threat, but most modern microwaves have a microprocessor controlling them. It's only when we start connecting them to the network that we're going to start getting worried.

PRÉCIS

First, we're going to discuss what an embedded system is, where they're located, and why you should be worried. We'll then go through the initial health check to see what kind of exposure we have. We're going to use some tools that we've used before, namely nmap, to find the embedded systems that are on your network. Then we're going to go through a methodology that will help you identify what your exposure is through your embedded systems. We have some interesting examples to discuss.

We end the chapter with a discussion of the applications, networking issues, and some tools that may help us with the problem.

SPECIAL POINTS OF INTEREST

Embedded systems exist everywhere around us. They're in our peripherals, our appliances, our medical equipment, our avionics, and our vending machines. We literally can't turn around without running into an embedded system.

Embedded systems can be carriers and spreaders of digital disease and not even know it. Just as our desktop systems are networked, designers of embedded systems understand the benefit of networking them, and therein lies the foundation of the problem: The networks that make these systems easier to manage and more useful are the same networks used to attack us.

Although we might think of most embedded systems as outside of our sphere of worry, a direct link exists between industrial control systems and our data networks through Ethernet. This opens up a whole new world of exposure and an entire galaxy of threat agents that we've never considered.

WHAT IS AN EMBEDDED SYSTEM?

An embedded system can easily be defined as any purpose-built computing system. The first modern embedded system is generally agreed to have been the Apollo Guidance Computer (AGC) developed by the MIT Instrumentation Laboratory under the guidance of Charles Start Draper and Eldo C. Hall. All this little jewel had to do was take navigation information from various sensors and convert it into the outputs that controlled the thrusters on both the command module and the lunar modules that went to the moon. Using 4K of memory and a 1MHz clock, the AGC reliably sent men to the moon and returned them back without ingesting a virus or Trojan horse. However, that was way back in the late 1960s. Although state of the art in its day, that system wouldn't even qualify as a decent printer buffer today.

Generally, embedded systems are designed to operate for years without user intervention or maintenance. Many embedded systems have failure recovery built in to them so that in the event of a power outage or other type of failure, they can self-recover. Self-recovery proves pretty handy if the embedded system we're talking about is the one controlling an elevator or rail shuttle.

Another characteristic of embedded systems is that they're usually, and I say "usually," based on real-time operating systems such as QNX, a POSIX compliant real-time operating system.[1]

---

[1] http://en.wikipedia.org/wiki/Posix

WHERE ARE EMBEDDED SYSTEMS?

The first point of interest is that embedded systems are everywhere! We tend to identify with the computers that we see on our desk or on our laps because they offer an easy way to identify them: They have a display. However, we have an "out of sight, out of mind" kind of attitude regarding the other systems that don't have an obvious computer display. Because we don't "see" them, we tend to forget that they're even there. For example, the automated teller machine (ATM) is an example of an embedded system that you run across every day.

Another example of an embedded system is your printer, as shown in Figure 12-1. Your printer most likely has an embedded controller in it that manages data coming from the Ethernet, provides a Web-based interface, and manages the print engine. If your printer is a network printer, it does have an embedded controller because it will also have a Web interface on it for remote management. Checking your printers is easy; just try to browse to your printer's address! If you get a Web page, there's an embedded system in your printer.

Figure 12-1   A multifunction printer with a Web interface is a good example of an embedded system. This one happens to be the author's trusty HP OfficeJet 7130 that we pick on in this chapter.

A popular embedded system is the Apple iPod. Essentially an Advanced RISC Machine (ARM) processor with dedicated silicon for the audio encoders and the display, the iPod is a very capable system indeed. Yes, there's more packed into an iPod than some encoders and a display, and some folks are taking advantage of that by using iPods as bootable drives.[2] Some really enterprising folks are actually porting Linux[3] to the iPod!

Not all embedded systems are as easily recognizable. For example, the computer that controls the engine in your car is a purpose-built closed-loop process control computer (see Figure 12-2). It takes analog signals from various sensors, such as the oxygen sensor, and converts them into digital data that can be used to control the spark timing and fuel-to-oxygen ratio. The Engine Control Unit (ECU) also manages a communications bus that uses a standard called Controller-Area Networking (CAN). Information such as diagnostics is pumped through this bus so that the "auto technician" can troubleshoot engine problems.

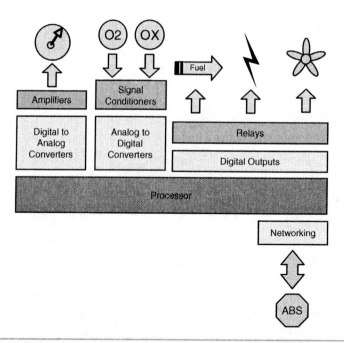

Figure 12-2 ECU block diagram showing analog output to cruise control, analog inputs for nitrous oxide and oxygen, and digital outputs to fuel injectors, spark plugs, and fan. ECU communicates over CAN to the antilock braking system.

---

2 http://features.engadget.com/2004/08/17/how-to-use-an-ipod-as-a-bootable-drive/

3 http://ipodlinux.org/Main_Page

This discussion takes us right into the area of industrial controls. CAN is a physical medium that allows for high-level protocols to ride on top of it in a way that is similar to how Ethernet works. In the industrial world, CAN is one of the physical mediums that supports the Common Industrial Protocol (CIP). A recent change to the industrial floor has been the introduction of CIP over Ethernet.[4] Yes, an industrial control protocol over our beloved Ethernet. Why? Because of the TCP/IP stack and the versatility and standardization that the TCP/IP stack brings to industrial control engineers. Ethernet is ubiquitous, and the physical interface chips are cheap. Let's not mention that CAN is a 500Kbps protocol and the Ethernet hardware is easily an order of magnitude faster. Instead of worrying about getting the message between systems, engineers can concentrate on enriching data structures and making systems more efficient.

WHY SHOULD I WORRY?

Because they are buried and you might not know where they are, and not knowing that something is out there waiting for you to make a mistake is very bad. Ask anyone who doesn't have a RADAR detector.

Another reason to be worried is called SCADA. Supervisory Control and Data Acquisition systems are the computers that watch the computers that control industrial robots, pumps in sewage-treatment plants, and control rods in nuclear reactors. For years, these systems talked to their programmable logic controllers (PLCs) and remote terminal units (RTUs) over serial lines such as RS-232 and phone lines. A communications protocol called IEC 60870-5 specifies how packets will be formulated in much the same way that Simple Mail Transport Protocol (SMTP) specifies how email is moved around. For example, in Figure 12-3, our control computers talk to the PLCs via a serial line. The PLCs talk to their sensors through a dedicated channel. Think of PLCs as big honking control computers. They do essentially the same thing that the ECU-type embedded systems do, except that they do it on rail systems, in power stations, and in chemical plants.

Getting back to why you should be worried, in the old days locomotive systems and the power grid were separated from other networks for two reasons:

1. Specialized control functions meant specialized protocols.
2. Serial connections didn't provide long-distance links.

---

[4] www.odva.org/

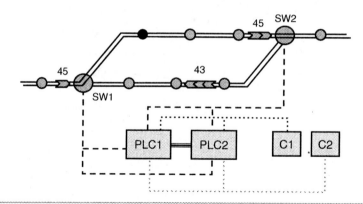

Figure 12-3 A SCADA display as one might see in a railway control room. Note the connection between C2 and PLC1 and that PLC2 is down (as is a rail sensor—black dot).

In today's control networks, it's possible to have the link between C1 and the PLCs *be* a network connection rather than a dedicated serial line or a modem connection. In that case, Figure 3 might not accurately indicate all the systems that have connectivity to the PLCs.

The problems of effective utilization of equipment, and in some cases reusing of old equipment, has forced SCADA implementers to turn to more effective communications protocols: in this case, Ethernet. A number of vendors provide bridges between Ethernet and RS-232, and these vendors are actually touting the capability of their products to be remotely managed via TELNET, HyperText Transfer Protocol (HTTP), and Simple Network Management Protocol (SNMP). One vendor, Data Comm for Business, is even bragging that their system can be used over Cellular Digital Packet Data (CDPD) networks![5]

So, just to sum up, we're linking serial and Ethernet and tossing in the cellular network, and at the end of these networks are endpoints that control critical infrastructure systems.

Another reason for concern is that embedded systems are showing up in places where you might not expect (such as medical equipment). Not that embedded systems in medical equipment are bad, but newer medical equipment is coming equipped with network interfaces, and that has the potential to be very bad.

None of this would be especially bad if the embedded industry kept up with the rest of the industry. The embedded industry is fairly entrenched and seems to be about five

---

[5] www.dcbnet.com/datasheet/ethergate.html

years behind the rest of us. They've recently added networking capability (and, as you'll see later, not in a secure way).

EMBEDDED THREATS

We've covered a number of threats in the Windows, Mac OS X, and handheld systems; now we're going to discuss a few of the vulnerabilities that afflict their embedded cousins.

QNX Software Systems' Neutrino RTOS (Real-Time Operating System) has, like all other operating systems, vulnerabilities posted by organizations such as iDefense.[6] Although discovered by an individual in 2004, iDefense reports that public disclosure occurred in February 2006. According to iDefense, the vulnerability is in how a program called phfont spawns another program called phfontf.[7] An attacker can replace phfontf with something evil, and because phfont spawns phfontf, the attacker can set UID root, giving the evil program root privileges. Just the kind of vulnerability I want in my nuclear reactor controller. The good news is that iDefense reports that QNX Software Systems hasn't even acknowledged that the vulnerability exists. I followed up with some checking and discovered that like other operating systems, QNX has a history of vulnerabilities that can be remotely exploited by a malicious attacker.

You can find a fairly complete list of current vulnerabilities at www.openqnx.com/index.php?name=News&file=article&sid=417.

The nine vulnerabilities on this list can result in root access. The only "fix" so far is to grant trusted users only access to the QNX-equipped systems.

Not enough? How about the fact that some Digital Subscriber Line (DSL) modems run embedded systems that allows a remote attacker to gain access via the Web server? I talk more about this in the following section.

There has been considerable talk in the recent past about how the JetSpeed 500, JetSpeed 520, and Allied Data Technologies CopperJet 811 RouterPlus DSL modems allow an attacker to gain access to these devices via the embedded Web server provided by Virata-EmWeb.[8] I did some digging and found that the same Web server, Virata-EmWeb/R6_0_3, might be responsible for a vulnerability in the 3Com SuperStack 3 NBX and 3Com NBX 100 network Voice over IP (VoIP) solutions[9] that can result in a denial-of-service attack.

---

[6] http://labs.idefense.com

[7] www.idefense.com/intelligence/vulnerabilities/display.php?id=383

[8] http://xforce.iss.net/xforce/xfdb/24304

[9] http://packetstorm.linuxsecurity.com/0405-advisories/3COMdos.txt

To make things a bit more personal, embedded systems are creeping into your house and on to your home network. These systems will allow an attacker to control the locks on your front door and your thermostat, all from the comfort of the Internet. Some folks are using Web cams to monitor their babies, not realizing that the device is a conduit for attack.

INITIAL HEALTH CHECK

Once again, the initial health check is more a case of being able to identify what your exposure is, because you're not going to be able to do much about it. There are two ways to approach this problem: blind scanning and pinpoint identification.

I've been through both processes, and any way you stack it, it means work. Asset management systems claim to be an answer, and although they will clearly help in situations in which some form of provisioning system exists, they rely on humans to enter the data and are therefore inaccurate. You must go through the scanning process to determine how much change there has been and what that change is.

Blind scanning is simple: Run a scanner such as nmap, pop in your IP address range, wait for the results, and pump them into a spreadsheet or database. You can then map that to your known list of desktops, servers, notebooks, routers, switches, printers, and other addressable bits that you have in your inventory. The things that you don't have on the list will stick out like a sore thumb. This will take some work, and you must write some scripts to make it work. Nmap has a feature that enables it to save machine-readable logs, thereby making this easier. If you have a large, distributed network, this is probably your only real choice, and it makes some pretty broad assumptions. First, it assumes that you have an inventory that you can compare things to. Second, it assumes that you have complete access to the entire network.

A word of warning on scanning, however: There has been some discussion about the inability of some SCADA systems to endure a network scan. Some systems are fragile and might need some attention. You might even have to hunt down dead systems.

The other method works for small shops and involves identifying potential target devices. The scenario runs something like this: You walk into a cube and see a new printer that wasn't there before. You can select through the printer's display menu to the network section. It doesn't make a difference what printer it is; most of them have fairly intuitive menus. When in the network section, look for the IP address section and copy that address down and return to your scanner.

I ran the scanner against my printer just to see what I could find out. As you can see in Figure 12-4, the printer is running and providing a complete TELNET interface to the network!

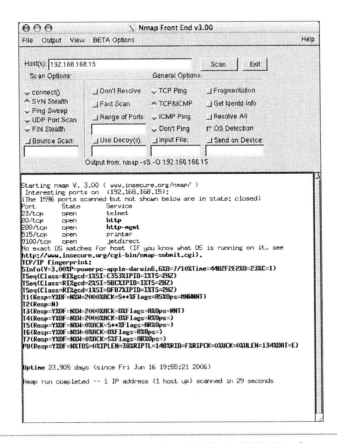

Figure 12-4 A screen capture of an nmap scan of an HP OfficeJet 7130 All-In-One printer, scanner, and fax. Note that port 23 is open and waiting for a TELNET connection.

Finding that TELNET was running on the printer, I did what any self-respecting geek would do: I started a session! Figure 12-5 shows the results. As you can see, a complete menu is offered over the network. You can manage which network protocols are offered, how the printer is configured, and get help. Who needs windows!?

I navigated through the TCP/IP settings to the Access Control screen, as shown in Figure 12-6. From this menu, you can configure how the printer responds over TCP/IP. You can set ports and print options, but the interesting selection is, of course, #4, "Access Control."

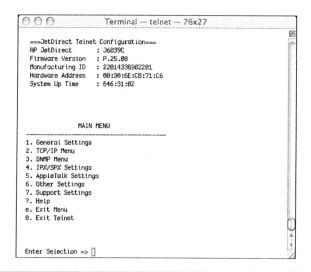

Figure 12-5   The menu provided to the network by the printer's management interface.

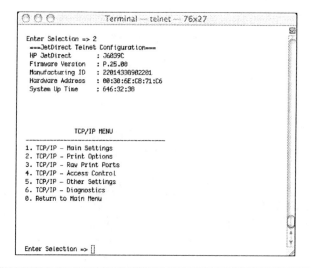

Figure 12-6   The TCP/IP settings menu allows the administrator, or a hacker, access to how the printer behaves on the network.

Entering 4 and pressing Return brought me to the screen in Figure 12-7. What this figure displays is that a primary security mechanism for this printer is IP address filtration. All I had to do was to manually enter the IP address that the filter allowed into another notebook, and I was allowed to access the printer.

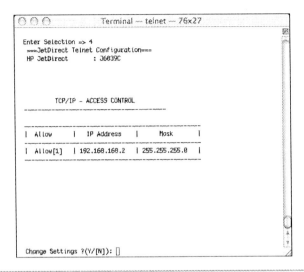

Figure 12-7 Simple IP address filters are the first line of defense in this embedded application.

If we explore the menus on this printer, we also discover that it supports SNMP. SNMP enables network administrators to query the printer for status or set specific parameters. The HP printer that we're looking at has SNMP enabled, as you can see in Figure 12-8.

Figure 12-8 An unset SNMP community string is inviting unwanted access. This endpoint allows SNMP read and write access by default.

With the Cmnty Name (short for community string) unspecified, this printer has the capability to write to other devices on the network to store things such as scanned images, pictures from cameras, or faxes. That means that if I can control the printer, and the printer has a trust relationship with other endpoints, I can write data to them at will.

Because the printer was accepting packets on port 80, I decided to try to TELNET to it to determine what Web server was running. I entered the command shown in Figure 12-9, but was greeted with only the standard escape character message, as shown. However, when I entered a bad request, the Web server puked, telling me that my request was bad (HTTP/1.1 400 Bad Request) and, to help me troubleshoot my error, the type and version of the Web server were provided. This is what put me down the path investigating the Virata-EmWeb vulnerability discussed earlier.

Figure 12-9 Error messages can reveal information about a target endpoint (in this case, what Web server is running on the embedded system).

None of this was rocket science. I think I invested about 15 minutes going through the entire process, and I didn't do anything special. All I did was this:

1. Scan the network

2. Probe some ports

3. TELNET to some open ports

4. Take control of the endpoint

Now in the interest of fairness I have to tell you that the printer can set a password. As you can see in Figure 12-10, it's almost a suggestion, and the default is no password.

When you set a password, there are no checks for minimum length. I set the password to "a," and the system was fine with that. When I did set a password, the system asked for a user name (stating that "root" or "admin" are acceptable user names). The truth is that any user name will work! When asked for a user name, I entered "blaa"; the system then asked for the password. I entered my super-secure password of "a," and I was back in.

The point is that if it's this easy to do, I'm not the only one doing it!

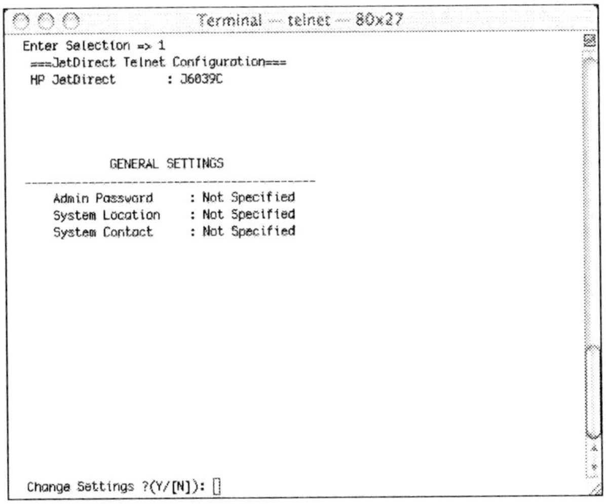

```
○ ○ ○                    Terminal — telnet — 80x27
Enter Selection => 1                                                    ⊠
   ===JetDirect Telnet Configuration===
   HP JetDirect       : J6039C



              GENERAL SETTINGS
   -----------------------------------------
   Admin Password     : Not Specified
   System Location    : Not Specified
   System Contact     : Not Specified






Change Settings ?(Y/[N]): []
```

Figure 12-10 Password protection on this embedded system is not enabled by default.

APPLICATIONS

Normally, when we think of applications, we think of chunks of code that enable us to generate documents, create presentations, or capture and store photos. Generally, anything that runs on our general-purpose computers is an "application." Some of them are utilities that enable us to configure widgets here and there, and some of them are full-blown suites that enable us to write an email to our significant others. Any way you look at them, they're specialized code running on a generalized architecture. This is not the case with embedded systems.

Embedded applications are really best described as the how the endpoint is used rather than what's running on it. In some cases, the embedded system is managing the power plant in your car, or in some really benign cases, managing the CD that's presently in the player. In the industrial applications, embedded systems are running the following:

- Assembly line robots (painting and welding)
- Locomotive systems (trains and tracks)
- Electrical power grid (load controllers)

Moving from the industrial to the medical, we'll find embedded controllers in the following:

- Patient care systems
- ECG/EKG (Electro CardioGraph)
- Ventilators

In your office or home, you'll find embedded controllers in these:

- Handheld devices
- Printers
- Scanners
- Vending machines
- VoIP handsets

Just to ram this point home, Samsung and LG have home network solutions that connect things such as your door locks, washing machine, and gas valves to control pads and your home PC. The Samsung page has this cute animated graphic that shows a path from the Internet to your gas valve![10] It gives new meaning to the notion of denial of service.

So, we need to change our idea of what a computer looks like, because it can, and has for some time, looked like something other than a PC.

NETWORKING

In an interesting fusion of technologies, I found an embedded controller being sold by a company called VDI Tele Assist. Called the CardioGSM, it records and transmits heart information to the hospital or patient care facility. If you thought that the GSM part looked familiar, you would be right. The CardioGSM uses the cellular network as a data conduit. The CardioGSM also functions as a cell phone so that patients can chat with the doctor while placing the 12 leads required to gather data on their bodies. I want to point out here that the cellular network is a full-duplex, bidirectional, *insecure* network. I think that my heart rate might elevate a bit if I were to attach such a device to my body!

---

[10] www.samsung.com/homenetwork/HomevitaSolutions/HomeControlling/ApplianceControlSolution.htm

As discussed earlier, Controller-Area Networking provides an internal type of communication medium that enables the actuators and sensors to share acquired information and control signals.

The IEC 60870-5 protocols are designed to allow the exchange of telecontrol messages between two systems and as such is really a circuit-based protocol in much the same way that DNP3 is.[11] DNP3 is designed to connect a SCADA master to RTUs that control devices such as PLCs and other "smart" control devices. The main reason that these protocols exist is to provide some level of interoperability between equipment in power system control solutions. These protocols become more interesting when they're transmitted over Ethernet and the IP protocol suite.

TOOLS AND VENDORS

This section is usually reserved for vendors and tools that can help you solve the problem discussed thus far in each chapter. Unfortunately, the only vendor that was doing security for embedded systems was a company called Sygate Technologies, and they were bought by Symantec in late 2005. The unfortunate aspect of any acquisition is the inevitable delays and cancellations that result from "realigning" and "integrating" the acquired company. It is unclear at this time what the future holds for Sygate's technology.

The remaining companies consider security to be the implementation of a virtual private network (VPN). SafeNet offers a product that is aimed at printer vendors and offers a fairly rich set of VPN tools, but that's pretty much it.

Certicom seems to have targeted VoIP, but it also supports traditional endpoint security products.

EMBEDDED SECURITY

That leaves us with the work that the TCG is doing. Specifically, the Trusted Platform Module (TPM) is a hardware device that must be embedded within the hardware architecture before it can provide any services.[12] You might be thinking "smart card," and you are close. The TPM is in itself a microcontroller that stores keys, certificates, and hash values in a tamper-resistant environment. Because it is a microcontroller, you can also use the TPM to generate keys dynamically. However, it must work in conjunction with a processor.

---

[11] Distributed Network Protocol IEE 1379-2000

[12] https://www.trustedcomputinggroup.org/groups/tpm/

Many of the TCG's specifications are based on the trust foundation provided by the TPM. However, the TPM can't work alone and must rely on external trust agents to provide checks. For example, when a system boots, part of the kernel checks the hash values of modules as they load. The kernel checks with the TPM to verify that the hash values are correct. The Trusted Network Connect (TNC) has been referenced in this book as being an open standard that a CLPC solution can be based on. Once again, I want to point out that the TPM alone will not accomplish the tasks required of a true CLPC solution. I also want to point out that there are many hurdles to implementing the TNC as envisioned by the TCG. Although the TNC specification does discuss obtaining some measure of integrity via the Integrity Measurement Controller (IF-IMC), the discussions are too high level to be of any real use.

It's interesting to note that all the major manufacturers of PCs have jumped on the TPM bandwagon. You can purchase a PC with an embedded TPM from the following:

- Lenovo (was IBM)
- HP
- Gateway
- Fujitsu
- Dell
- Toshiba
- NEC
- Sony

Missing from this list are embedded system designers such as Wurlitzer. Yes, Wurlitzer. Deutsche-Wurlitzer makes vending machines, and one of the options is a cashless payment system. In addition, Deutsche-Wurlitzer has been working with VendSMARTT through a partnership with SL-Tech[13] to create Healthy Vending at local schools. The vending machines are interfaced with the SL-Tech food service computing systems via the network, both wired and wireless.

CLOSING THE LOOP

Although embedded systems, PLCs, and SCADA systems are dedicated control-based devices and take advantage of many internal closed-loop processes, they are light years

---

[13] www.school-linktechnologies.com/news_healthyvending_hotbutton.asp

behind even the mobile development community. Network access control isn't even considered as part of the roadmap at this time.

Basic security functionality, such as vulnerability management and antivirus (AV), has to be addressed before we can begin to discuss the advanced concept of trust-based CLPC within the context of embedded systems. Combine that with the push to add network functionality to SCADA systems, and we have a recipe for disaster.

KEY POINTS

Embedded system are all around us, and for some reason we have ignored the security features that should be embedded within them. We have no real security policy that addresses them, nor do we seem to be pushing vendors to do anything about it.

WE'RE SURROUNDED

We are all quite literally surrounded by embedded systems, and the number is growing each and every day. Medical equipment, industrial controllers, and vending machines are all around us. Video cameras provide Web interfaces that make it easy to integrate them with your Web applications. Our traffic light system is essentially an embedded system, and we trust it with our *lives*. Have you ever given thought to what would happen if all the traffic lights were green at the same time?

In a very short time, most of the phones that we're going to rely on will be VoIP powered and therefore will all contain some form of embedded controller in them. I remember a time when I could pick up a phone in the middle of a power outage and still get a dial tone. Not so with the complicated answering machine/walkie-talkie/multiple-handset phones that we're buying now. When the power goes out, so does the phone. For personal security, I always keep a simple old analog phone connected so that in case the aliens come and nuke our power, I'll still be able to call someone to complain about it.

Medical equipment is relying on embedded controllers to acquire, store, and transmit patient care information. In some cases, our very lives are in the hands of embedded systems. When we drive our car, we're relying on numerous embedded systems, such as antilock brakes, to keep us safe. BMW even has a model with adaptive cruise control that keeps you from slamming into the car in front of you when the moron is only doing 55mph in a 65mph lane.

No Real Security

Unlike the tidy world of Internet security, there is no single vendor of embedded security solutions. Although the TCG does have the TPM, and it is a piece of hardware, it's not a piece of hardware that's making its way into our everyday home network controllers, such as those offered by Samsung and LG.

No standard says how embedded systems are to be tested or just what services should be offered. Although I whine about the fact that vendors have been driving our security solutions, the embedded industry has nobody driving the boat.

There's no concept of embedded firewalls unless you're talking about a DSL modem. Then a firewall is a "feature." Even our DSL modems are turning out to be vectors of attack, however, because of their embedded systems. Worse, with the multiple ways that we can connect to embedded systems and controllers, we're creating hidden paths that will allow an attacker to sneak into our networks not by outsmarting the security, but by going around the security.

TPM Isn't Helping Embedded Solutions

Embedded systems are the classic cost versus security problem. Why? Because one of the stated objectives of using an embedded system is to engineer it to be specific to the task that it is trying to accomplish. By being specific, you reduce cost and improve performance. We're in a world now in which we're talking about $100 per "seat" of security tools on every system on our network. Increases of $7 to $10 a seat receive minute scrutiny. I'll tell you right now that security isn't going to fly in a world where things have to cost less than $5 a piece to make. Adding TPM to your $5 solution just doubled the cost to $10.

Embedded systems are also at a different stage in their development as networking systems than our enterprises are. Embedded systems haven't had to endure the years of relentless attack that Windows, and our networks, have had to suffer through. As more embedded systems come online, however, that will change.

Closing the Loop

There is no easy way to say this. Embedded systems, PLCs, and SCADA systems represent the largest threat to our security that I've seen in a long time. Not only is the loop not closed, but in some places the loop isn't even being discussed. SCADA systems control critical infrastructure, and they do so with obsolete and vulnerable technology.

Basic security functionality must be added to these devices in the next generation of products if we are going consider CLPC security technology in the near future.

YOU CAN DO SOMETHING

We do have some tools that we can use to identify embedded systems on our network. After we identify an embedded system, we can examine it to ensure that it's as secure as we can make it, replace it if warranted, or remove it if need be. Most embedded systems are going to have similar security capabilities to our printer example (your DSL modem, for example), but it will take time to ferret them out and configure them properly. Then it becomes a matter of documenting what you've done so that when the time comes to change the embedded endpoint's configuration, you, or your replacement, can do so effectively and securely.

Case Studies of Endpoint Security Failures

As has been the case for many parts of this book, understanding some history is an important aspect of the learning process. All too often, we fail to learn from our mistakes, and it costs us dearly in the future. I hope this brief look into the past helps you understand how the proposed solution in this book can work to your advantage.

PRÉCIS

In this final chapter, we discuss some network environments that had to deal with some "issues" that caused the enterprise owners significant loss/embarrassment. We've all read in the newspapers about some of the high-profile attacks, but what about some of the failures that didn't make the papers? As a consultant and a security world insider, I get to learn of some pretty scary things. Because I learned of these failures in my capacity as a consultant, I'm really not at liberty to give out names, dates, or places. I think the circumstances, outcome, and analysis serve to make the important points. Besides, if it were you, would you want the world knowing about your failures?

Each section examines the failure mode, how the endpoint was involved, various impacts, the missing process control, and how the failure could have been avoided.

CASE STUDY 1

A large commercial manufacturer of computer products

FAILURE MODE: WHAT WENT WRONG

This company had the practice of giving all employees who inhabited a cube or office a computer and a stack of boxes that contained all the Microsoft Windows software packages. The thought was that by getting familiar with the process they would become familiar with the hardware, software, and the "customer experience." I suppose the idea was to feel the customer's pain and thereby become sensitive to it. As a business model, it did exactly that. Employees became familiar with all aspects of the computing "experience."

Any person could have a server or any service running that he or she wanted. All flavors of servers, desktops, and notebooks were running Web servers and FTP servers, sharing files, and, in general, using the snot out of the rich feature set that Microsoft provides. Essentially, the network was there to provide connectivity between systems and services.

Like most large companies, this company was managed as individual divisions, and each division had a great deal of autonomy to make decisions regarding resources. This meant that IT was there to make sure that each division stayed on the network. Customer interfaces, and a great deal of customer support, were hinged on the network being up. For this reason, no expense was spared when it came to deciding on network hardware. They weren't foolish, but they did have some heavy-duty iron running and slinging packets.

It was that heavy-duty iron that allowed the almost instantaneous spread of CodeRed.

HOW THE ENDPOINT WAS INVOLVED

In this instance, it was a pretty simple correlation between the unprotected endpoints and the spread of the virus.

THE IMPACT

In a matter of minutes, every system that could be infected was infected. The network was running at collision rates that had the data centers glowing red from the collision lights. Thankfully, the network being at overload helped slow down the spread.

Some estimates put the level of infection at higher than 90 percent, and they couldn't fix it. As they would bring a new system up, other systems would attack it. All totaled, they lost more than three days of productivity. Production stopped, shipping stopped, receiving stopped; and because the trouble ticket system was now dead, customer service was being handled over a private branch exchange (PBX) system that wasn't designed to handle the load. Customers didn't care that there was a problem; customers were only concerned with their individual problem. It's interesting to note that many of the customers were calling to complain that their systems had slowed down or crashed, and they wanted to know what to do.

MISSING PROCESS CONTROL

I could start by saying that from an endpoint security perspective that they did everything that you could possibly do wrong. But that would be unfair. Business is business. The reality of the situation was that they had no real process except a trouble ticket system.

There was no:

- Centralized build process
- Centralized patch management
- Enforcement of antivirus (AV) requirements

HOW IT COULD HAVE BEEN AVOIDED

The sad truth here is that until the corporate mind set changed, there wasn't going to be any real improvement in the situation. Management had to come to grips with the fact that handing a new employee a stack of cool technology and hoping that the employee could get it to work while learning something about the customer experience wasn't a good plan.

Throwing patch updates and AV at the endpoints with an insane hope that it would stick wasn't much different from what they were already doing. A complete overhaul of their policy was in order. Instead of "feeling the customer's pain," their policy needed to be "please make the pain go away."

Chaos had to be replaced with order, and eventually it was. Management of the desktop and notebook endpoints was turned over to IT, and mandatory system requirements were placed on all endpoints. All endpoints were configured with a firewall, AV, and the Windows built-in patch management and update process.

One contentious point had to do with administrative access to the system and who would have that level of control. IT rightly argued that only users with verifiable administrative skills who possessed a need to modify the system should have access. After a few days of discussion and many system re-images, the new policy was not to allow any user to be administrator. I'm sure you'll understand that this bent a few jaws out of joint. But, after a few days of zero productivity, all but the real hardliners came to see the wisdom of allowing IT to do their job. Exceptions were granted on a case-by-case basis.

In the end, they had the foundation for a good closed-loop process control (CLPC) system: They had control over most of their endpoints, and they had invested in network infrastructure that would (for the most part) support a migration to network access control (NAC). Had a CLPC system been in place, noncompliant systems would not have been allowed to join the network and spread the virus.

CASE STUDY 2

A large package-shipping company

FAILURE MODE: WHAT WENT WRONG

This story starts with our customer saying, "Get in. I don't care how you do it so long as you don't break anything or hurt anyone." This wasn't a simple scan and report. This was a complex cat-and-mouse game that would test the customer's ability to detect and report what we were doing. We called them "womb to tombs" because everything from physical attacks to social engineering, and everything in between, was permitted. These were fun because we knew that it was only a matter of time before we got in. And get in we did.

What we discovered was a fairly well-run shop with a centralized IT department that controlled the configuration of the endpoints fairly well. Simple scans didn't turn up anything from the outside, so we knew that we would have to get inside. It turned out to be simple enough. We just walked in with our notebook, sat down in a conference room, and plugged in. Once connected, we had complete access to their entire network from a conference room!

HOW THE ENDPOINT WAS INVOLVED

This was a case in which the endpoint was the attacker and the network was the victim. Had the network been capable of defending itself, the attacking—well, really sniffing and snarfing—endpoint wouldn't have been able to join the network.

THE IMPACT

At this point, the impact could have been catastrophic. We had access to routers, switches, their entire server farm, and all the desktops. We did a basic scan of the internal network and discovered hundreds of potential targets of attack. If we had been bad people, we could have easily stolen data, destroyed data, disrupted processes, and generally wreaked havoc until they decided to have a meeting about it. They would have come into a conference room with two strangers in it, and I'm sure somebody would have put the pieces together rather quickly. We documented our findings and were gone in less than 30 minutes. To prove our point, we left a marker on one of the file systems that proved that we were there. We also copied some PowerPoint presentations describing the next set of services that they were planning to deploy.

Because this customer was wise enough to know that they didn't have a good idea of their security posture, the impact was generally low and distributed over a longer period of time due to careful planning.

The executive who had requested the assessment was considering retiring at the end of the year. When we were through, he commented to me that he was going to move up his retirement plans.

MISSING PROCESS CONTROL

Although they did have a good handle on the endpoint, they didn't have a good handle on the network. The support people were desktop people who had moved up through the ranks and believed the garbage that their network vendor was feeding them about simplicity and ease of use. When a new box came in, they just plugged it in and waited for the vendor's engineer to show up. In many cases, switches were patched into place to address some pressing and acute need for the day, only to be left when the situation passed. This was the case in the conference room. To accommodate a demonstration of one of the new database services that was going to be offered online, a connection had to be made to the internal server development network. The cable connecting the conference room to the Internet was replaced with a cable that connected the conference room to the internal network.

HOW IT COULD HAVE BEEN AVOIDED

This is a case where CLPC and NAC would have been a deterrent to access. The network would have noticed that we didn't have the required authorization, and we would have been shunted to a remediation network or only allowed Internet access. At a minimum, there should have been a manual process in place or a timed firewall rule that allowed access from the conference room to the internal network for the period of the test only.

CASE STUDY 3

Manufacturer of satellite-based communications equipment

FAILURE MODE: WHAT WENT WRONG

Like most situations that lead to security issues, this wasn't a cut-and-dry vulnerability discovery exercise. It really started out as an episode of "America's Dumbest System Administrators." We were called in to investigate a claim made to HR that the corporate system administrator and his assistant were storing porn on a Windows server share. As was our standard practice, we ran a scan from the outside and discovered that the Internet router, the router that connected them to the hostile world, had a default password on it!

An internal scan of the network revealed that there were several unauthorized file servers running in various stages of update. Virtually every machine had a vulnerability that would allow remote compromise or elevated privileges.

Analysis of the system administrator and the assistant system administrator systems uncovered numerous infections and back doors. One system even had BackOrifice (known as BO) installed on it. Analysis of other endpoints within the enterprise helped identify (through the similarity of infection) those who had taken advantage of the porn available.

And yes, they were running a peer-to-peer (P2P) sharing network that allowed them to collect and exchange porn between them. It was one of the few complete collections of the Pam Anderson videos that I'd ever seen.

HOW THE ENDPOINT WAS INVOLVED

In this instance, the endpoints were part of the perpetration but also the detectors. Although this started out as a case of abuse, it quickly turned into a case of poor administration and planning.

THE IMPACT

This was another case of "boy, did you guys just dodge a bullet." If attackers had managed to discover this router, they could have changed the configuration and set the password to something a tad more difficult than the default password.

In addition, there was the concern that sensitive and proprietary information had leaked out of the network. However, the firewall was configured to provide Network

Address Translation (NAT) services, and the enterprise was using a private Internet Protocol (IP) address space. Analysis further concluded that due to an installation error, BO would not have been able to communicate through the present network as it was configured.

It took approximately a week to clean up all the systems, add AV, and reconfigure the network to a more secure posture. The system administrator received a week of unpaid leave, as did the assistant system administrator. Others who were suspected of viewing the questionable material received remedial sexual harassment and acceptable-use training.

MISSING PROCESS CONTROL

Well, it didn't help starting with a brain-dead system administrator who was more interested in a "collection," but the lack of a vulnerability management (VM) process coupled with the lack of a managed AV program exacerbated an already bad situation. A VM program would have uncovered the open router and the inconsistent patch management on the endpoints. It would have also uncovered the rogue servers in the first place. The lack of oversight led to a careless decision on the part of the system administrator and his assistant.

HOW IT COULD HAVE BEEN AVOIDED

All roads lead back to the lack of adult supervision and a documented security plan. I'm not talking about a policy; they had the benefit of having some silent partners who made it clear what the policy was. However, there was no real plan or vision to implement it. Systems were built and installed as needed to execute on the start-up's business objectives. Not uncommon, but at some point the adults take over, and policy and process begin to seep into the system. In this case, the lack of any senior IT people *within the company* left a vacuum with respect to the greater objectives of the IT group. As much as I'd like to point to a CLPC failure here, this is a perfect example of a human failure. Our recommendation was for them to hire a senior IT person as soon as possible so that a one-year plan could be fleshed out.

You can have the greatest technology in the world, but if it's not implemented effectively and the people aren't part of the solution, they will be part of the failure.

CASE STUDY 4

Large software company that specializes in security software

FAILURE MODE: WHAT WENT WRONG

I almost had to laugh when I learned about this one. One day I got an email from a very angry system administrator telling me that one of our systems was attacking his Domain Name System (DNS) server. I thought, "Hmm, that can't be possible. We're a security company!" But, a complaint is a complaint, and it must be investigated. So, doing my due diligence, I began looking into the issue. After a few hours, I came to the stark realization that sure enough, we were in fact attacking his DNS server. As much as this is an issue, it's not the real problem here. More on this in the section "The Impact."

So, you might be questioning how this could happen. I did! The story goes something like this: An instructor was ramping up a class to teach DNS administration and decided to install and configure BIND prior to the class starting. The self-starting instructor picked what he thought was a fictitious name for his class company and used it to configure the DNS database. Unfortunately, there was a real DNS server out on the Internet with the exact same name. To keep a long story short, the classroom DNS server slave decided to try a zone transfer and was banging on the real DNS server. It wasn't hard to track down the source of the bogus zone transfer requests, and the owner naturally wanted them to stop, so he sent an email to our abuse and security email addresses. This is where is starts to get strange. After not getting an answer for more than two weeks, the real DNS domain owner starts to copy people he knows in our organization. I was forwarded the email because it made it to the security operations folks and they were rightfully mystified, and concerned, about what to do.

HOW THE ENDPOINT WAS INVOLVED

In this case, the endpoint was the attacker. Misconfiguration was the root cause, but the network did not attempt to stop the rogue requests. A DNS zone transfer is something that should be monitored and logged. Oh, and on occasion, the logs should be examined.

THE IMPACT

Outside of one very irked DNS administrator and an embarrassed instructor, the impact was pretty low. It took about a day to put all the pieces together, but there was no real loss of productivity or leakage of data.

MISSING PROCESS CONTROL

It was abysmally clear to me that outside of some minor procedural failures, the internal incident response process (IRP) had failed completely. It took *two weeks* for a victim of our misguided attacks to get any attention. Sadly, what did get our attention was his threat to turn over copies of the emails and logs to the press.

HOW IT COULD HAVE BEEN AVOIDED

The neat thing about CLPC is that it's an automatic function. As the temperature goes up, the thermostat kicks in, and the AC starts. Just because something is supposed to be automatic doesn't mean that it doesn't require calibration occasionally. An IRP is supposed to be started when an event makes it into the queue. To test that it's working properly, you have to, on occasion, submit an incident with a known outcome. For example, if you want to test the AV portion of your IRP, you open a ticket saying that a system has been infected with some virulent piece of malware. That should drive the IRP into action, the proper personnel should be notified, the proper collaborations should occur, the appropriate actions should be taken, and the appropriate entries should be made to the ticket. All of this and time stamps, too! Only then can you observe how fast and effective your IRP process really is and where it needs to improve.

Unfortunately, most of our processes, such as the test scenario outlined in the preceding paragraph, are still human driven—meaning that someone has to kick-start them before anything happens.

This never happened. The short answer is that this could have been avoided by a regular test of the IRP.

KEY POINTS

Clearly, there are still failures related to the fact that human-driven processes are always susceptible to failure. There were differences and similarities in these case studies, but the common thread was always process. As we begin to embrace CLPC as a philosophy, we can better understand how to build our security solutions around it.

DIFFERENCES AND SIMILARITIES

The organizations in these case studies differed with regard to their size and the maturity of their security program. However, these differences didn't seem to matter. As you can see in Table 13-1, the one common element was a process-related failure.

Table 13-1   The Common Thread in the Case Studies: Process Failures

Case Study	Process Failure	Human-Induced	Asked for Help	Implemented Fix	Happen Again
1	Yes	Yes	No	Yes	No
2	Yes	Yes	Yes	Yes	No
3	Yes	Yes	Yes	Yes	No
4	Yes	No	No	No	Yes

We had two very large, worldwide enterprises fail—one in a catastrophic way, and one in a fairly subtle way.

We had what would be considered a start-up dodge a bullet because of a system administrator-induced failure (never tell Batman how you're going to kill him), only to come away stronger from the incident because they knew to ask for help. Finally, we had a medium-size software company fail because they failed to test their processes.

Some followed best practices and failed, whereas others didn't follow them and failed. The main similarities between these case studies has to do more with how the discovery process began than what processes were missing. In all of these cases, it was an outside entity that told them that they had a severe problem. Yes, two of the case studies knew enough to understand that they had a problem, but neither of them understood the scope of the failure and how far reaching it could turn out to be.

The good news is that they were all process-oriented failures and not technology failures. Process failures have the benefit of helping you examine your solution from a philosophic perspective rather than the "tear out the old box" mentality that a technology failure induces.

People played an important role in the failure and the solution, or nonsolution in the case of the last case study. In the last case study, an active decision was made not to do anything different because they hadn't finished examining all the parameters. Well, analysis paralysis is a mode that many folks get into when the really don't understand the problem and refuse to ask for help.

CLPC PHILOSOPHY

Although this book has been about closing the trust loop with endpoints, CLPC is really a philosophy that embraces the notion that we can use our processes to self-govern our networks. CLPC says that our decisions and our actions have consequences and that we can use those consequences to help make the solution better.

Let's go back to our thermostat model so that we can compare it to our present-day networks. What we would find is that instead of a thermostat that automatically senses the temperature, we would have a person turning the heater on and off based on how he felt at the moment. The person could be sitting in a chair or roaming around the room to get a better idea of how the room "feels." But, if that person happens to be wearing a parka and it's cold outside, there's not going to be much help for those who are counting on the "heater person" to regulate the temperature in the room.

Closing the loop removes the subjective nature of much of the control process. We have set-points, and we measure to see whether we're above, below, or at the set-point. There's nothing subjective about running an IRP test to see how your organization reacts. Either it does, or it doesn't.

REMAINING WORK

A great deal of work remains to be done. With more and varied types of endpoints, we're going to find ourselves with a colossal management problem that isn't going to be solved with more and better-trained bodies. Our architectures are going to have to embrace the requirement associated with establishing a level of trust through an integrity check. This means more software, and that means better software assurance programs to ensure that the software we're using is trustworthy. It also means that at some point we're going to have to hand off the job of verifying that trust to a third party.

We can't wait on the next version of Windows, Linux, OS X, or the next wave of disruptive technology that may open our networks to serious attack. We need to analyze our networks as CLPC problems and find ways to automate the feedback loops and control points. Without automation, and CLPC, we're never going to survive the next big failure that will inevitably come.

Glossary

802.11 A set of IEEE standards that describe wireless LAN/MAN protocols.

802.1x An IEEE standard for port-based authentication.

AAA Authentication, authorization, and auditing.

ACL Access control list.

AD Active Directory. A Microsoft database of user and group information.

ADS Alternate data stream. A file construct in Microsoft Windows.

AIM America Online Instant Messenger.

AIX Advanced Interactive eXecutive. IBM's version of UNIX.

AP Access point. A device that connects wireless radio equipped endpoints with a wired network.

API Application programming interface.

ATM Asynchronous Transfer Mode. A protocol that uses fixed-length packets.

ATM Automated teller machine.

Attack surface A combination of applications and systems available to attack.

Attack vector An entry point for attack or the chosen mode used to exploit a vulnerability or flaw in an application or operating system that can be used to subvert or co-opt an endpoint or network.

Bang-bang A bimodal control that is either on or off.

BlueTooth A short-range radio transceiver system designed to connect peripherals to devices (for example, a headset to a smartphone).

BOOTP Bootstrap Protocol. RFC 951. A UDP-based protocol used by network endpoints to obtain an IP address.

Bot Web robots are automated applications that carry out repetitive tasks, such as collecting personal information or sending spam. The usage here implies malicious intent and behavior.

Botnet A group of bots controlled by a central source.

BSD Berkeley Software Distribution. A version of UNIX developed at the University of California, Berkeley.

C++ A computer programming language.

CD-ROM Compact disc read-only memory. An optical read-only method for distributing digital information.

CERT Computer Emergency Response Team.

CLPC Closed-loop process control, a method for analyzing and controlling a system (in this case, a network).

CNAC Cisco Network Admission Control. Cisco's proprietary version of NAC.

CSI Computer Security Institute.

CVE Common Vulnerabilities and Exposures. An index of standardized names for vulnerabilities.

DHCP Dynamic Host Configuration Protocol. RFC 2131. DHCP provides required IP configuration information to requesting endpoints.

DMZ Demilitarized zone. In network contexts, it is a portion of the network that the firewall provides to allow controlled Internet access to corporate network resources.

DNA In genetics, DNA is deoxyribonucleic acid, the building blocks of life. When referenced in this book, it means the basic settings of the system.

DNP Distributed Network Protocol used between remote terminal units.

DOS Disk Operating System.

DSL Digital Subscriber Line is a method of connecting a computer or site to the Internet.

DVD Digital video disc. A high-capacity optical read-only data storage medium originally designed for movies but has since been adapted to general data storage.

EAP Extensible Authentication Protocol. RFC 3748. A universal authentication framework used in point-to-point connections and wireless networks.

Embedded system Any purpose-built computing system.

EVDO Evolution-Data Optimized. A wireless radio broadband standard adopted by some CDMA cellular mobile phone providers.

FBI Federal Bureau of Investigation.

Firewall A device that separates and controls traffic from one security zone to another.

FUD Fear, uncertainty, and doubt. Scare tactics used to instill fear in potential customers.

GLBA Gramm-Leach-Bliley Financial Services Modernization Act, Pub. L. No. 106-102, 113 Stat. 1338.

GPRS General Packet Radio Service. A mobile data service available to GSM users.

GUI Graphic user interface.

HFS Hierarchical File System used in the Mac OS X operating system.

HI Host integrity. A function used to determine whether a system has complied with a stated level of policy.

HIDS Host-based intrusion detection system.

HIPAA Health Insurance Portability and Accountability Act, Pub. L. No. 104-191.

HP-UX Hewlett Packard UNIX.

HVAC Heating, ventilation, and air-conditioning system in a building or structure.

ICMP Internet Control Message Protocol. RFC 792. Used in network diagnostics and for routing.

IPM Intellectual property management or rights management.

IRIX A System V-based UNIX with BSD extensions produced by Silicon Graphics.

Kernel The section of code that provides the core functionality for an operating system.

LAN   Local area network.

LDAP   Lightweight Directory Access Protocol. LDAP systems store user authentication and authorization information similar to AD.

LEAP   Lightweight Extensible Authentication Protocol. A Cisco proprietary wireless authentication protocol.

Library   Predefined sections of code that provide services to programs and the operating systems.

Malware   Any piece of software that has malicious intent.

MAN   Metropolitan area network.

MBps   Megabytes per second.

MD5   Message Digest 5. A one-way, fixed-length output cryptographic function.

NAC   Network access control. Generally used in 802.1x authentication.

NAP   Network Access Protection. A Microsoft proprietary network access control.

NetBIOS   Network Basic Input Output System. Microsoft networking.

NIDS   Network intrusion detection system.

NMS   Network management system.

NOC   Network operations center.

OEM   Original equipment manufacturer.

OS X   Apple's operating system, version 10.

P2P   Peer-to-peer protocol or application.

PBX   Private branch exchange. System used to route phone calls in businesses.

PC   Personal computer.

PCI   Payment Card Industry, a standard to evaluate merchants and their network security.

PDA   Personal digital assistant. A handheld endpoint.

PID   Proportional, integral, derivative. The three basic control modes used in CLPC.

PLC   Programmable logic controller. A computer designed to control things such as valves, gates, motors, and switches.

PM   Patch management.

Précis   A concise summary of a book, article, or other text.

RADIUS   Remote Authentication Dial In User Service. AAA system for network access.

ROI   Rate of infection or return on investment. When used in the context of viruses, it describes the rate of infection.

Rootkit   A tool or set of tools designed to conceal unauthorized processes from detection by the operating system and other tools.

RTU   Remote terminal unit.

SANS   Sysadmin, Audit, Network, and Security Institute. Professional training and certification.

SCADA   Supervisory Control And Data Acquisition system monitor and PLC manager.

Script kiddie   A derogatory term for inexperienced hackers who use prewritten scripts.

SDLC   System development life cycle.

SEC   Securities and Exchange Commission.

Set-point   The desired value in a closed-loop process control system.

SLA   Service level agreement.

SMB   Server Message Block. An application protocol designed to share access to resources such as printers and file shares.

Snarfing   The capturing of network packets.

Sniffer   A device or software that monitors the network and captures packets based on specified criteria.

SNMP   Simple Network Management Protocol. A protocol suite used by an NMS to monitor network infrastructure devices.

Solaris   Sun Microsystems version of UNIX.

SOx   Sarbanes-Oxley Act of 2002. Pub. L. No. 107-204, 116 Stat. 745. The Public Company Accounting Reform and Investor Protection Act of 2002.

SP   Smartphone.

SQL   Structured Query Language. A standard language used to insert, extract, and manipulate data in a database management system.

SSH Secure Shell. An application that uses a secure channel to connect endpoints.

SSLF Specialized Security, Limited Functionality. A very severe Microsoft security configuration.

SUID/SGID Set user ID / Set group ID. A mode bit in UNIX and UNIX-like systems that allows programs to inherit permissions.

TCG Trusted Computing Group.

TCP Transmission Control Protocol. TCP works with the IP protocol to ensure packet delivery. Sometimes referred to as TCP/IP.

TLS Transport Layer Security. A successor to the Secure Sockets Layer protocol that provides a secure communications channel between two endpoints.

TPM Trusted Platform Module. Part of the TCG initiative, the TPM is a hardware device that securely stores critical security parameters, such as keys and certificates, in an endpoint such as a notebook computer.

Trojan horse An application that conceals its true intent or behavior by masquerading as another application.

TSA Transportation Security Administration.

TTR Time to replicate. The time it takes a virus to replicate itself in another system.

UDP User Datagram Protocol. UDP works with the IP protocol to deliver packets on a best effort (unguaranteed) basis.

UID User identification.

UNIX A computer operating system developed by Bell Labs in the 1960s and 1970s.

UPnP Universal Plug and Play. A Microsoft protocol designed to provide automatic network resource discovery.

UPS Uninterruptible Power Supply.

USB Universal Serial Bus.

US-CERT United States CERT.

VA Vulnerability assessment. Usually a process that discovers vulnerabilities in network endpoints.

VOIP Voice over IP. A technology that uses IP protocols, software, and sometimes embedded systems that provides telephone-like services to users.

Virus   A malicious piece of software that can replicate and execute itself. A virus uses other programs as carriers in the replication process.

VM   Vulnerability management. The process of ensuring that vulnerabilities are managed within the policies of the organization.

VPN   Virtual private network. A secure connection between two network endpoints.

WEP   Wired Equivalent Privacy. A weak wireless security protocol that connects a wireless endpoint with an AP.

WiFi   A brand licensed by the Wi-Fi Alliance to describe wireless networks.

Worm   A self-replicating malicious piece of code. Unlike a virus, a worm can copy itself to other endpoints.

WPA/WPA2   WiFi Protected Access. WPA is a framework designed to provide enhanced security to wireless devices.

WSUS   Windows Server Update Service.

XENIX   The predecessor to the Santa Cruz Operations version of UNIX, SCO UNIX.

Zombie   A computer that hosts one or more bots.

Index

Page numbers followed by *n* denote footnotes.

U

BOOKS ONLINE
ENABLED

THIS BOOK IS SAFARI ENABLED

INCLUDES FREE 45-DAY ACCESS TO THE ONLINE EDITION

The Safari® Enabled icon on the cover of your favorite technology book means the book is available through Safari Bookshelf. When you buy this book, you get free access to the online edition for 45 days.

Safari Bookshelf is an electronic reference library that lets you easily search thousands of technical books, find code samples, download chapters, and access technical information whenever and wherever you need it.

TO GAIN 45-DAY SAFARI ENABLED ACCESS TO THIS BOOK:

- Go to **http://www.awprofessional.com/safarienabled**
- Complete the brief registration form
- Enter the coupon code found in the front of this book on the "Copyright" page

Addison
Wesley

If you have difficulty registering on Safari Bookshelf or accessing the online edition, please e-mail customer-service@safaribooksonline.com.